T0146950

LATE MARXISM

RADICAL THINKERS }V

SET 1 ($12/£6/$14CAN)

MINIMA MORALIA
Reflections on a Damaged Life
THEODOR ADORNO
ISBN-13: 978 1 84467 051 2

FOR MARX
LOUIS ALTHUSSER
ISBN-13: 978 1 84467 052 9

THE SYSTEM OF OBJECTS
JEAN BAUDRILLARD
ISBN-13: 978 1 84467 053 6

LIBERALISM AND DEMOCRACY
NORBERTO BOBBIO
ISBN-13: 978 1 84467 062 8

THE POLITICS OF FRIENDSHIP
JACQUES DERRIDA
ISBN-13: 978 1 84467 054 3

THE FUNCTION OF CRITICISM
TERRY EAGLETON
ISBN-13: 978 1 84467 055 0

SIGNS TAKEN FOR WONDERS
On the Sociology of Literary Forms
FRANCO MORETTI
ISBN-13: 978 1 84467 056 7

THE RETURN OF THE POLITICAL
CHANTAL MOUFFE
ISBN-13: 978 1 84467 057 4

SEXUALITY IN THE FIELD OF VISION
JACQUELINE ROSE
ISBN-13: 978 1 84467 058 1

THE INFORMATION BOMB
PAUL VIRILIO
ISBN-13: 978 1 84467 059 8

CULTURE AND MATERIALISM
RAYMOND WILLIAMS
ISBN-13: 978 1 84467 060 4

THE METASTASES OF ENJOYMENT
On Women and Causality
SLAVOJ ŽIŽEK
ISBN-13: 978 1 84467 061 1

SET 2 ($12.95/£6.99/$17CAN)

AESTHETICS AND POLITICS
THEODOR ADORNO, WALTER BENJAMIN, ERNST BLOCH, BERTOLT BRECHT, GEORG LUKÁCS
ISBN-13: 978 1 84467 570 8

INFANCY AND HISTORY
On the Destruction of Experience
GIORGIO AGAMBEN
ISBN-13: 978 1 84467 571 5

POLITICS AND HISTORY
Montesquieu, Rousseau, Marx
LOUIS ALTHUSSER
ISBN-13: 978 1 84467 572 2

FRAGMENTS
JEAN BAUDRILLARD
ISBN-13: 978 1 84467 573 9

LOGICS OF DISINTEGRATION
Poststructuralist Thought and the Claims of Critical Theory
PETER DEWS
ISBN-13: 978 1 84467 574 6

LATE MARXISM
Adorno, Or, The Persistence of the Dialectic
FREDRIC JAMESON
ISBN-13: 978 1 84467 575 3

EMANCIPATION(S)
ERNESTO LACLAU
ISBN-13: 978 1 84467 576 0

THE POLITICAL DESCARTES
Reason, Ideology and the Bourgeois Project
ANTONIO NEGRI
ISBN-13: 978 1 84467 582 1

ON THE SHORES OF POLITICS
JACQUES RANCIÈRE
ISBN-13: 978 1 84467 577 7

STRATEGY OF DECEPTION
PAUL VIRILIO
ISBN-13: 978 1 84467 578 4

POLITICS OF MODERNISM
Against the New Conformists
RAYMOND WILLIAMS
ISBN-13: 978 1 84467 580 7

THE INDIVISIBLE REMAINDER
On Schelling and Related Matters
SLAVOJ ŽIŽEK
ISBN-13: 978 1 84467 581 4

First published by Verso 1990
© Fredric Jameson 1990
This edition published by Verso 2007
All rights reserved

3 5 7 9 10 8 6 4 2

Verso
UK: 6 Meard Street, London W1F 0EG
USA: 20 Jay Street, Suite 1010, Brooklyn, NY 11201
www.versobooks.com

Verso is the imprint of New Left Books

ISBN-13: 978-1-84467-575-3
ISBN-10: 1-84467-575-0

British Library Cataloguing in Publication Data
A catalogue record for this book is available from the British Library

Library of Congress Cataloging-in-Publication Data
A catalog record for this book is available from the Library of Congress

Printed in the US

For
Perry Anderson

Contents

PART II Parable of the Oarsmen

PART III Productivities of the Monad

CONCLUSIONS Adorno in the Postmodern

A Note on Editions

and Translations

I have here often retranslated quotes from Adorno's works afresh (without
specific indication). The available translations are uneven, to say the least;
E.F.N. Jephcotts's *Minima Moralia*, and more recently, Rodney
Livingstone's *In Search of Wagner*, are elegant Anglo-English; John
Cumming's *Dialectic of Enlightenment* has a stronger German accent,
which I for one must welcome since I believe, with Pannwitz, that the
translator should allow 'his language to be powerfully affected by the
foreign tongue ... [and should] expand and deepen his language by means
of the foreign language'.[1] In particular, Adorno's sentences try to recover
the intricately bound spatial freedom of Latinate declension, objects that
grandly precede subjects, and a play of gendered nouns that the mind
scans by means of the appropriately modified relative. Chiasmus here
becomes the structural echo by one part of the sentence of another,
distant in time and space; and the result of these internal operations
is the closure of the aphorism itself; definitive, yet a forthright act that
passes on, not into silence, but into other acts and gestures. Adorno
should then be the occasion of forging a powerful new Germanic sentence
structure in English; and this is why I must find altogether misguided
the strategy of Christian Lenhardt, the English translator of *Aesthetic
Theory* who breaks up sentences and paragraphs and produces a literate
and respectable British text which I can no longer even recognize (but
see on this his exchange with Bob Hulot-Kentor[2]).

Thus, unfortunately, this whole monumental undertaking will have
to be done again, something that must also be said for E.B. Ashton's
even more unfortunate version of *Negative Dialectics*, where the most
basic terms are misrendered, making whole passages (which are already
difficult enough at the best of times) altogether incomprehensible. Readers

obliged to go on using this version should make a note of the most urgent howlers: *Tauschverhältnis* is in particular not 'barter' but simply 'exchange system' (very much as in 'exchange value'): *Vermittlung* is scarcely 'transmission' but will be again recognizable as the well-known 'mediation' (and note that *mittelbar* and *unmittelbar* – normally 'mediated' and 'immediate' – are here frequently 'indirect' and 'direct' for some reason); *Anschauung* is, finally, not 'visuality' but is conventionally rendered, since the very first Kant translations, as 'intuition'. The first group of these errors (along with the significant but incomprehensible excision of the name of Karl Korsch at one point) might lead a paranoid to believe that this translation aimed precisely at producing a post- and non-Marxist Adorno 'for our time'; the third, however, could only imply a complete innocence of the philosophical tradition. Still, all the translations strike occasional sparks, and I am fortunate in having had them all to rely on.

Page references to the most frequently quoted works are given within the text, first to the German, and then to the English, versions (even where the latter has not been used), and designated by the following abbreviations:

AT   *Aesthetic Theorie*, Gesammelte Schriften, vol. 7 (Frankfurt: Suhrkamp, 1970)
       Aesthetic Theory, transl. Christian Lenhardt (London: RKP, 1984)

DA   *Dialektik der Aufklärung* (Frankfurt: Fischer, 1986, original 1944)
       Dialectic of Enlightenment, transl. John Cumming (New York: Herder & Herder, 1972)

MM   *Minima Moralia* (Frankfurt: Suhrkamp, 1986, original 1951)
       Minima Moralia, transl. E.F.N. Jephcott (London: Verso, 1974)

ND   *Negative Dialektik* (Frankfurt: Suhrkamp, 1975, original 1966)
       Negative Dialectics, transl. E.B. Ashton (New York: Continuum, 1973)

NL   *Noten zur Literatur* (Frankfurt: Suhrkamp, 1981)

PNM *Philosophie der neuen Musik* (Frankfurt: Europäische Verlagsanstalt, 1958)
       Philosophy of Modern Music, transl. Anne G. Mitchell and Wesley V. Blomster (New York: Seabury, 1973)

W   *Versuch über Wagner* (Frankfurt: Suhrkamp, 1952)
       In Search of Wagner, transl. Rodney Livingstone (London: Verso, 1981)

INTRODUCTION

Adorno in the Stream

of Time

This book offers detailed readings of three major works written wholly or in part by Adorno at various stages in his career: *Dialectic of Enlightenment*, published in 1947, the *Negative Dialectic* of 1966 and the posthumously published *Aesthetic Theory*. I have, however, drawn extensively on other books – the essays called *Noten zur Literatur*, the *Minima Moralia*, and the Wagner book, as well as other relevant materials. I have considered these writings synchronously, as parts of a single unfolding system, as though the various Adornos, in the various stages of their youth and decay (as in *2001*), were all 'sitting around a table in the British Museum' together.

In historiography – whether it is that of a form, a national population, or a single productive psyche – the decision about continuity or discontinuity is not an empirical one; as I've said elsewhere, it is taken in advance, as a kind of absolute presupposition, which then determines your subsequent reading and interpretation of the materials (sometimes called 'the facts'). We are very well placed to see that today, we who have witnessed the unfurling of a great wave of counter-revolutionary historiography designed to 'prove', for example, that the French or Russian revolutions accomplished very little save to interrupt, with their mindless bloodshed, a peaceful economic progress already on course and well under way. Such 'history' offers a true Brechtian estrangement-effect, which runs in the face of common sense (that is to say, our received ideas) and gives us something new to argue about: the argument will be most productive if it also includes some rethinking of periodization itself, which has come to be one of the central theoretical issues for an age that is at one and the same time profoundly ahistorical and avid for historical narratives and narrative reinterpretations of all kinds – an appetite, as it were, for poststructural gossip (including the newer histories) that is something like a compensation for the weightlessness of a fall out of history unlikely to last for long.

The alternative – an account of Adorno's career in various stages,[1] including as its obligatory backdrop the exciting wartime flights across Europe and North America, and the postwar return to a Germany in rubble (with the subsequent emergence of a student movement in the sixties), done in the various appropriate Hollywood and Tv-docudrama styles – has generally ignored the philosophical or aesthetic components, whose lifelong persistence it is not difficult to show,[2] and fastened on the easier matter of political opinion: in other words, when did he stop believing in Marxism? (or rather, since Horkheimer and the 'School' are the inescapable intellectual and financial context here, when did 'they' stop believing in Marxism?). I will argue against this rather shallow view of the nature of political commitment, ideological choice, and philosophical and literary production. Apostasies are real enough, and excellent dramatic material; but this is not at all what happened to Adorno during the Cold War and after the return to Restoration Germany in the Adenauer period. He went on, indeed, to write his two major works, examined in the present study: projects that establish him as one of the greatest of twentieth-century Marxist philosophers; and as my title suggests, it is to document the contributions of Adorno to contemporary Marxism that the present book was written.

It is not, indeed, people who change, but rather situations. This can also account for the alterations in my own views of Adorno, whose work has itself varied in significance for me according to the historical decade: Adorno was for me a crucial methodological discovery in the declining years of the Eisenhower era, when it seemed urgent to invent some conception of the dialectic itself in the North American context. This was then the period in which I used Adorno's musical analyses (to which I will revert very little in the present volume) as practical demonstrations of the ways in which what we used to call the 'social and historical background' – indeed, the class and ideological background – was not *extrinsic* but very precisely *intrinsic* to the business of formal analysis.

Readers of *Marxism and Form*, however, will have sensed my increasing distance, by 1971, when the book was finally published, from what I took to be Adorno's hostility towards the Soviet Union, the Third World, and (reading it overhastily from his essays on jazz, like everyone else) the Black movement in this country. But the new decade, known in retrospect as the sixties, meant (for me at least) sympathy with all those things. In the age of wars of national liberation, Adorno's sense of Apocalypse seemed very retrogressive indeed, focused as it was on the moment of Auschwitz, and obsessed with the doom and baleful enchantment of a 'total system' that few enough – in a 'pre-revolutionary' moment defined notoriously by the sense that *'tout est possible!'* – sensed impending in our own future in the middle distance.

The seventies – the age, in this country at least, of Theory and theoretical discourse, of *jouissances* that ranged from structuralism to poststructuralism, from Maoism to narrative analysis, and from libidinal investments to Ideological State Apparatuses – were essentially French; Adorno (along with Lukács and so many other Central European thinkers, with the signal exceptions of Benjamin and Brecht) seemed an encumbrance, not to say an embarrassment, during the struggles of that time, and prompting those still committed to him into elaborate translation schemes to 're-concile' Adorno with Derridean orthodoxy. While all this was going on over here, the French intelligentsia was in the meantime in the process of full de-Marxification; so that the next decade drew the curtain open on a wealthy and complacent, depoliticized Europe, whose great theoreticians were dead and whose indigenous philosophical traditions were buried. (I will say more about the fortunes of Adorno and the dialectic in the Bundesrepublik today in the conclusions to this volume.) To that Europe, learning analytic philosophy and pioneering its own forms of business management and international trade, the America of the postmodern made echo: losing its industries like fleas but leading a whole new world economic system, into which even the former Eastern bloc seemed eager to leap.

Here at length, in this decade which has just ended but is still ours, Adorno's prophecies of the 'total system' finally came true, in wholly unexpected forms. Adorno was surely not the philosopher of the thirties (who has to be identified in retrospect, I'm afraid, as Heidegger); nor the philosopher of the forties and fifties; nor even the thinker of the sixties – those are called Sartre and Marcuse, respectively; and I have said that, philosophically and theoretically, his old-fashioned dialectical discourse was incompatible with the seventies. But there is some chance that he may turn out to have been the analyst of our own period, which he did not live to see, and in which late capitalism has all but succeeded in eliminating the final loopholes of nature and the Unconscious, of subversion and the aesthetic, of individual and collective praxis alike, and, with a final fillip, in eliminating any memory trace of what thereby no longer existed in the henceforth postmodern landscape. It now seems to me possible, then, that Adorno's Marxism, which was no great help in the previous periods, may turn out to be just what we need today. I will return to the relations between Adorno and the postmodern in my conclusions.

As for Marxism, however, it would be too easy to add that anyone surprised by the characterization of Adorno as a Marxist has not read much of his admittedly difficult writing, and also that most available secondary discussions tend to leave the Marxism out, as though it were some curious set of period mannerisms which a postcontemporary discussion no longer needs to take into consideration. But to those – non-Marxists and anti-Marxists as well as the Marxists themselves – who think it is interesting to argue about the degree and authenticity of Adorno's Marxism (was he not really, after all, just as Hegelian, if not indeed rather a post-Marxist?), I will suggest that it might be productive, for one brief moment, to revive the old distinction between science and ideology which has fallen, like so much else, into disrepute today. 'To be a Marxist' necessarily includes the belief that Marxism is somehow a science: that is to say, an axiomatic, an organon, a body of distinctive knowledges and procedures (about which, were we to develop the argument, one would also want to. say that it has a distinctive status as a discourse, which is not that of philosophy or of other kinds of writing).

All science, however, projects not just ideology but a host of possible ideologies, and this is to be understood in a positive sense: ideology as the working theory of a specific practice, the latter's 'philosophy' as it were, and the ensemble of values and visions that mobilize it and lend it an ethic and a politics (and an aesthetic as well). The various Marxisms – for there are many of them, and famously incompatible with one another – are just that: the local ideologies of Marxian science in history and in concrete historical situations, which set not merely their priorities but also their limits. To say, then, that the Marxism of Lenin, or of Che, or of Althusser, or of Brecht (or indeed of Perry Anderson or of Eagleton, not to speak of myself), is *ideological* now simply means, in the critical sense of the term, that each one is situation-specific to the point of encompassing the class determinations and cultural and national horizons of its proponents (horizons which include, among other things, the development of a working class politics in the period in question).

As for Adorno's Marxism, it is obviously also determined (that is to say, limited) by all those things, which used to be called 'factors'. What is odd is only that a standpoint such as that of historical materialism – for which the primacy of the historical situation is central – should show as much perplexity in the face of this plurality of Marxist 'ideologies' as any 'bourgeois philosophy'. To acknowledge Adorno's Marxism in this spirit certainly does not mean to endorse his positions as a program (indeed, much of Adorno's philosophical work turns precisely on this question of how we are to engage a living thought that is no longer historically current). In particular, his views on political art have been a stumbling block for some, who forget that these opinions were the price he paid for keeping alive a now unseasonable conception of the deeper political vocation of modernism itself. His attitudes towards 'actually existing socialism' were clearly class-conditioned (as was his lack of sympathy or understanding for Third World revolutions); but at a time in which the socialist countries themselves are engaged in a momentous process of transformation, they need no longer detain us, except as historical testimony to the dilemmas of left intellectuals during the Cold War. But he seems to have had more sympathy for the student movement of the sixties than he was willing to express publicly[3] (a sympathy not a little tarnished by the deathless shame of having called the police into the University).

But any assessment of Adorno's political positions must not omit his academic praxis as such – his systematic intervention into the intellectual life that survived the war in what became the Federal Republic (involving any number of influential academic survivors of Hitler's universities) and in particular the responsibility he actively took for the reconstruction of sociology – a turn of destiny all the more unusual for a one-time aesthete and expert on musical questions. Adorno's vigorous and voluminous polemics and *mises au point* on the nature and function of sociology (which constitute a missing third term alongside *Negative Dialectics* and *Aesthetic Theory* and which I will discuss in the course of the first part) seem to have involved two stages or concurrent propositions. The so-called Frankfurt School returned to Germany surrounded – legitimately or illegitimately[4] – by the prestige of American empirical research: Adorno was capable of using this to pound his more metaphysical enemies in German social philosophy, while also turning on empiricism itself (and positivism) and subjecting that in turn to the critique of the dialectic (a word he used a great deal more in his sociological writings than in his philosophical ones). We have today come to a far keener sense of the significance and the objective dynamics of those 'ideological state apparatuses' which are the professions and the disciplines, something which ought to put us in a better position to appreciate what can now be called a genuine form of praxis in this area on Adorno's part.

Nor are these lessons outmoded either, even though the brief triumph of the dialectic on the West German scene seems to have given way to new and undialectical currents – that of Habermas, which of course critically descends from Adorno and Horkheimer, while modifying them beyond recognition[5] – and that of the various Anglo-American

influences, which are all decidedly hostile to dialectical thought. But –
except in anthropology, where the worldwide impact of Lévi-Strauss's
structuralism had a distantly comparable role in transforming the discipline – the other social sciences, unless I am mistaken, do not seem to
have known any comparable internal 'revolution' (save, belatedly, for
the extraordinary one-man effort of Pierre Bourdieu in sociology, whose
general impact cannot yet be assessed). The dialectic remains for
them a methodological timebomb; it can also be expected to play a significant role in the very different traditions of the social sciences in
the socialist countries, where it may spark new thoughts and new possibilities for intellectuals not primarily committed to whoring after Western
gods.

In any case, it is worth noting that the emphasis on sociology now
completes the traditional philosophical triad of the good, the true and
the beautiful as that is uniquely inflected in Adorno's work: the modulation of ethics into sociology (of a historical cast) is clearly the crucial
strategic move here, and thereby the least immediately recognizable
formal intervention. So it is that in Adorno the academic disciplines,
having missed their chance at reunification in Marxism itself, live on
in outwardly respectable but inwardly problematized forms.

But as to how Marxist this all may be, I would like, on a theoretical
level, to continue to insist on the relevance of the distinctions proposed
in *The Political Unconscious* to judgements of this kind: Adorno was
indeed not far from my mind when I suggested that the levels of the
political (immediate historical events), of the social (class and class consciousness), and of the economic (the mode of production), remain for
us in some paradoxical interdependent independence from each other
(or are relatively autonomous, if you prefer that language). This recognition was meant, if not to solve, then at least to neutralize what seemed
to me false problems and meaningless polemics in such areas as those
of the 'transition to capitalism', where proponents of an active shaping
role of working people seemed to confront those for whom the disem-
bodied forces and logic of capital were somehow at work. These however
seemed to me to offer two utterly different ways of construing or con-
structing the object of study, along with 'explanations' of utterly distinct
levels of abstraction: so that at length it becomes problematic even to
affirm that disagreement or contradictory, incompatible 'interpretations'
are involved here.

Something of the sort is also what I would wish to affirm about the
spirit of Adorno's Marxism, and in particular the notorious absence from
it of class judgement (actually, at all the crucial polemic moments, Adorno
is quite capable of making local class-ideological judgements of a particu-

larly decisive and devastating kind).[6] Adorno's contribution to the Marxist tradition is not, however, to be sought in the area of social class, on the second level of my tripartite scheme: for that one goes elsewhere (to E.P. Thompson, for example).

Where he does have an indispensable contribution to make, which we will not find elsewhere, is on my third 'level', that of analysis in terms of the economic system or mode of production. The originality, indeed, of his philosophical work (discussed here by way of a commentary on *Negative Dialectics*, in Part I) as well as in his aesthetics (Part III is a commentary on *Aesthetic Theory*, while Part II attempts to characterize Adorno's social view of art itself, partly on the basis of *Dialectic of Enlightenment*), lies in his unique emphasis on the presence of late capitalism as a totality within the very forms of our concepts or of the works of art themselves. No other Marxist theoretician has ever staged this relationship between the universal and the particular, the system and the detail, with this kind of single-minded yet wide-ranging attention (few contemporary thinkers have in any case combined this philosophical sophistication with a properly aesthetic sensibility; only Croce and Sartre come to mind, while Lukács, still in many ways a far greater historical figure, looks in this respect like something of a caricature). To be sure, in a period, the poststructuralist, in which we no longer have 'concepts' – in a period, the postmodern, in which we no longer have 'works of art' either – Adorno's offering may seem like a useless gift. At the least, it may serve to instruct the enemies of the concept of 'totality' in the meaning and function of this kind of thinking and interpretation, to which I will pay close attention in the following pages; in any case, Adorno's life work stands or falls with the concept of 'totality'.

As for the current ratings of Adorno's stock, I have been surprised by the increasing frequency of comparisons with his arch-enemy Heidegger[7] (whose philosophy, he once observed, 'is fascist to its innermost cells'[8]): the basis of these *rapprochements*, besides a kind of general neutralization of everything threatening for consumer society in both these philosophies, evidently has to do with the tendential mystique in Adorno of the so-called 'non-identical', or Nature. Meanwhile, the stress of the Frankfurt School on motifs of domination has seemed to awaken fleeting similarities with Foucault (who in any case, in a moment of abandon, suggested his own 'affinities' with these Germans he had not read until the end of his life[9]). The tortuous and hypersubtle 'undoings' of *Negative Dialectics* in its way with the Concept have also seemed to many to offer the proverbial family likeness with Derrida and deconstruction. (In my opinion, no very solid foundation for a 'dialogue' between this last and Marxism will be laid by wishing away the basic differences;

I have myself in another place suggested that Adorno's fundamental problematic is in some ways closer to de Man than to Derrida.[10])

Against all these comparisons I want to argue the following: what looks
like an approach to a more Heideggerian idea of Nature – Being here
replaced by Non-identity – is set in an altogether different perspective
if we grasp the fundamental role of natural history in Adorno. But this,
meanwhile, will also modify our stereotypes about the Frankfurt School
attitude towards science (they are normally thought to be against it)
and also in turn dispel the impression of some deeper similarity with
Foucault, since their very conception of natural history itself removes
everything that is anthropological and ideological about the latter's theme
of 'power'. As for deconstruction, I think that the impression of a family
likeness here rests on the ambiguity of the so-called 'history of Western
metaphysics', borrowed from Heidegger, and in its grandly mythical and
unhistorical lines seeming not unlike 'dialectic of enlightenment' itself.
But Error, what is called metaphysics or identity, is in Adorno the effect
of an increasingly powerful social system, while in Heidegger it is that
of an increasing distance from some original truth: even though, for
him, power, in the form of Latin and the Roman Empire, plays a part
in the distortion, sapping, and repression of that truth. Of course power
for Heidegger returns in modern technology; but it cannot be said that
he stresses the omnipresence of the social within the forms of error or
the inner constraints of metaphysical thought, as Adorno tries to do.
Meanwhile any stress on subjective error as a force of agency in its own
right is bound to slip into idealism.

I should, in the light of these attitudes towards philosophical comparison, now probably say something about my own approach to Adorno's
philosophical texts, which it may not be sufficiently clarifying to characterize in terms of narrative analysis. Indeed, if a narrative can be detected
at work in a philosophical essay – and one can easily imagine its exoteric
forms, the 'adventures' of a concept, the struggle between the protagonist-
concept and its enemies or opposite numbers, the Propp-style passage
through a series of tests and trials, philosophical synthesis as marriage,
and so forth – it seems more interesting to stage this narrative structure
in more modernist or 'reflexive' terms – that is to say, in terms of the
crisis of representation. At that point, what becomes interesting in a
philosophical text is not merely how its 'concept' manages to win
through, but how it managed to get said in the first place, and at what
price. 'Modernism' is in this sense that deeper skepticism about the possibility of representing anything – which is to say, finally, about saying
anything at all – that in the face of the palpable fact that sometimes
things do get said or represented gives way to a curious exploration of

the structures and the preconditions, the electoral fraud, cheating, rigging in advance, and tropological footwork that enabled such representation in the first place; not excluding a cool analytic assessment of what had to be abandoned *en route*, left unsaid, lied about, or misrepresented.

In modernism, however, the referent itself still survives, albeit problematically; so that the possibilities of the speaking subject (or its structural impossibilities) can also be staged in function of the structure of the object – in the present case, that turns out to be a kind of 'preestablished harmony' between Adorno's own modernism and the approach I am proposing. It is, in other words, because Adorno is himself so keenly aware of the nature of philosophical writing as a linguistic experiment, as *Darstellung* and the invention of form, that it becomes interesting and appropriate to look at his own work in the same way. But then I need to correct this formulation of the matter in turn, and to insist that although Adorno certainly does have a 'style' (like the rest of the 'modern masters', for whom this category is an objective and a historical one), and although I sometimes talk about it as such, I doubt if the reading I propose can be thought of as a literary one in the restricted or trivialized sense.

Adorno's modernism precludes assimilation to the aleatory free play of postmodern textuality, which is to say that a certain notion of truth is still at stake in these verbal or formal matters. As with aesthetic modernism itself, indeed, what you are able to construct in language has a certain truth by virtue of that very wresting of language, not merely from silence as such, but from the baleful properties of the proposition form, the perils of thematization and reification, and the inevitable (and metaphysical) illusions and distortions of the requirement to begin and end at certain points, and to appeal to this or that conventional standard of argument and of evidence. So the deeper message of my book, at the level at which Adorno himself in his particularity becomes indistinguishable from the dialectic, has to do with celebration of the dialectic as such. This may at least today have the benefit of a certain novelty.

So may my title, which simply introduces a German expression of long standing (*der Spätmarxismus*) to the English-speaking public. I find it helpful above all for a sharpening of the implication I developed above: namely, that Marxism, like other cultural phenomena, varies according to its socioeconomic context. There should be nothing scandalous about the proposition that the Marxism required by Third World countries will have different emphases from the one that speaks to already receding socialism, let alone to the 'advanced' countries of multinational capitalism. Even this last is of course profoundly 'uneven' and 'non-synchronous' and other kinds of Marxism are still vitally relevant to it. But this book argues the special relevance of Adorno's Marxism, and of its unique capacities within our own equally unique 'late' or third stage of capitalism. The word means nothing more dramatic than that: still, better late than never!

Killingworth, Connecticut
August, 1989

PART I

Baleful Enchantments

of the Concept

One

Of the two most influential misreadings of Adorno – as a post-Marxist and as a postmodernist – the second will be dealt with in our conclusions. The notion of his post-Marxism, however, rests on a misunderstanding of one of Adorno's basic leitmotivs, namely 'non-identity', from which, thematized and reified and turned into a philosophical program of some sort, all kinds of unwarranted consequences are drawn, as will be shown below.

Adorno is, however, the philosopher of Identity in a very special sense: it is with identity as such that both *Dialectic of Enlightenment* and *Negative Dialectics* begin: for this word can subsume the 'concept' and the 'system' fully as much as 'enlightenment' or 'science'. To write a philosophy of identity, however, does not mean to celebrate it or to pose as its ideologue: what has often been described as the Frankfurt School's 'critique of Reason' is in fact a systematic exploration of a standardization of the world imposed fully as much by the economic system as by 'Western science'. *Negative Dialectics* must be approached by way of this fundamental conceptual premiss, which constitutes the absolute and contradictory situation of philosophy itself, as well as of the various local polemics and skirmishes staged in the book's separate chapters. Before that, however, *Dialectic of Enlightenment* had sealed the fortunes of this concept by making it available in the form of a mediation, and above all one which included the 'existential' materials of daily life (along with those, famously, in which the identity-form is printed on mass culture). As befits a deliberately discontinuous work, we will deal with *Dialectic of Enlightenment* episodically throughout this book, returning at later moments to its conception of culture, its diagnosis of anti-Semitism, and its vision of natural history.

Here, however, at the threshold of a philosophical analysis of identity, it seems appropriate to insist on the face it wears and turns on daily life – namely repetition as such, the return of sameness over and over again, in all its psychological desolation and tedium: that is to say, neurosis. In that limited appropriation which Adorno makes of Freudian conceptuality (and which in some contexts looks crude and old-fashioned, when it does not, as in others, open up new layers and levels of the analysis), neurosis is simply this boring imprisonment of the self in itself, crippled by its terror of the new and unexpected, carrying its sameness with it wherever it goes, so that it has the protection of feeling, whatever it might stretch out its hand to touch, that it never meets anything but what it knows already. To put it that way, however, is to begin to wonder – not merely 'psychologically' – what it would take to have the strength to stand the new, to be 'open' to it; but even more: what that new might be, what it might be like, how one would go about conceptualizing and imagining what you can by definition not yet imagine or foresee; what has no equivalent in your current experience.

At that point, there slowly emerges the counter-image or -mirage of the neurotic self locked utterly into its own 'identity' – namely, the unrepresentable vision of the ceaseless flow of the absolutely new, the unrepetitive, the great stream which never comes twice and which Deleuze calls the 'flux' of perpetual change, in which neither subject nor object can yet be imagined, but only the terror and exhaustion of radical difference without markers or signposts, without moments of rest or even those spatial folds into which, like the bull into its *querencia*, we withdraw to lick our wounds and to know a few instants' peace. To shed our defenses and give ourselves over absolutely to this terrifying rush of the non-identical is of course one of the great ethical fantasy-images of the postmodern and the very delineation of the 'schizophrenic hero': why postmodern social space – the most standardized of all 'administered societies', from which the Other and otherness has been the most successfully exorcized – should be thus fantasized as the primal flux of schizophrenic difference is another and a puzzling question, which can only be answered sociologically (a word I use here for shorthand, until we can replace it with the much more complicated conception of the dialectic Adorno will spell out for us).

These two absolutizing and frightening glimpses of a closed self and a primal flux are, however, useful in grasping the *function* of the compromise formations that variously come into being throughout human history with their more familiar everyday shapes: garden-variety 'psychic identity', for example, which filters away enough of the radically new to allow what is left to be tolerable to experience, while it tirelessly reassures us that we really still do have a persistent identity over time, that my personal consciousness is still somehow 'the same' throughout all the unexpected peripeties of the biographical adventure, and that all the new dawns still reveal a world and an expanse of objects which, however they have changed their places, retain their older names and remain somehow, and however distantly, familiar. Ego is thus, in that larger sense of personal identity, a defense mechanism but also a weapon, an instrument of praxis and survival.

But Adorno only marginally includes an anthropology and a social psychology, and will open these levels, and that of the psychic subject itself, up to other forms of conceptuality, as we shall see in a moment. It is, however, worth pausing here in order to characterize the situation with which thought itself is confronted by the terms of the preceding discussions, a situation or a dilemma which then not only accounts for a certain philosophical ideal in Adorno's practice but also for the significance for him of certain peculiar aesthetic strictures as well.

If the concept is grasped as 'the same', as what makes things the same as well as inscribing a sameness – a return of recognizable entities – on the psyche, then the struggle of thought (at least at a certain moment of its history) has to undermine that logic of recurrence and of sameness in order to break through to everything sameness excludes: I put it this way in order to be able to describe this last – the 'non-identical' – both in terms of otherness and of novelty (rather than in the conventional terms of either the real or the referent, which would reconvert all this into a dualism: the concept being for Adorno just as real as anything else). But we must reach this experience of the new and of the other through conceptuality: that operation in Adorno which most closely approximates Habermas's critique of irrational philosophies turns rather on various intuitionisms (Bergson, Husserl, even Heidegger in a certain sense) which are stigmatized for their tendency to abandon conceptuality as such and to try for a more direct, immediate contact with the 'real'. Is it possible to do something to the concept, which otherwise tendentially locks us into sameness, in order to use it as a mode of access to difference and the new?

> Thought need not rest content in its logical regularity; it is capable of thinking against itself, without abolishing itself altogether; indeed, were definitions of the dialectic possible, that one might be worth proposing. (ND 144/141).

It is therefore not a matter of jettisoning the inherited categories of philosophy, which in any case continue to inform daily life in the guise of common-sense realism; no more than intuitive immediacy, the invention of new utopian concepts and neologisms offers no escape from the 'iron cage' of the concept and its identities. But how the concept can be used against itself is a complicated matter which we will try to characterize later on.

For the moment, that other feature of what the concept represses – the New – reminds us that this situation, this dilemma, is in some sense also an aesthetic one and, particularly in the area of so-called modernism, knows specifically aesthetic and artistic equivalents, which we will discuss at some length in a later context. It seems more worthwhile at this point to underscore the significance of Adorno's interest in a somewhat more traditional aesthetic and linguistic structure, namely the epic, about which it has not sufficiently been observed that he also has a theory, to be derived from several points in his work; implicitly, in the 'Odyssey' commentary in Dialectic of Enlightenment, which stages the emergence of epic language and narrative from the ever-sameness of myth; and explicitly in two crucial essays in the Noten zur Literatur, 'On Epic Naïveté' and the enormous 'Parataxis', on Hölderlin (and not exclusively given over to the obligatory onslaught on the famous Heideggerian exegesis of the poet).

Adorno does not seem to have known Erich Auerbach's influential analysis of epic in terms of this same category of parataxis (but as part of an unstable dualism between the additive time of epic – 'and ... and ... and ...' – and the more syntactical and periodic linear and causal temporality of what he calls 'hypotaxis', using the Old Testament as a strong form and Ur-counterpart to Homer).[1] Both commentators share, of course, the traditional view of the stasis of epic time – its 'serenity' as a series of isolated moments and 'centered' sentences which themselves have something of the mesmerized stillness of the tableau. But where Auerbach assumes that these epic sentences simply follow one upon another in all the regularity of the paratactic stream, it will come as no surprise to find Adorno posing the problem in terms of our preceding description: namely, as that of generating the new moment, temporal change, out of mythic repetition and sameness. The focus is on the syncategorematic and the particle, connectives that link these seemingly stable and monadic sentences, which turn on themselves like the solar system, together in a larger sequence or passage of textual time; and on the anaphoric echoes and reprises that weave the separate sentences desperately into some larger temporality.

What Adorno reads, however, is not the serene logic of such connectives – the 'and' – but rather the violence of the yoking of the sentences and the epic illogicality of the sense of these otherwise functional words:

'but', 'however', 'meanwhile', Hölderlin's *nämlich* – a sense which, by denying the continuity at the same moment that it establishes it, foregrounds the peculiarity of the epic operation itself and stages 'parataxis' as a wilful inscription of the new and the break within the stable reproduction of a sameness and a repetition often associated with epic, but in reality far more deeply characteristic of the mythic world which epic seeks to cancel and transcend. There is a way in which this peculiar classical syntax can stand as an emblem for Adorno's philosophical practice fully as much as the more obvious formal inventions and solutions of the modern. In particular, the remarkable way in which death finds itself inscribed in the tranquil imperturbability of Homeric language – the grisly execution of the maids, whose commentary concludes the '*Odyssey*' chapter in *Dialectic of Enlightenment* – suggests interesting parallels with some of the ultimate aims of *Negative Dialectics* itself.

We must now, 'however', return to the matter of the concept, and in particular to the multiple and rotating significance of the term 'identity' as Adorno deploys it. This functional polysemousness has earlier historical and philosophical parallels:

> In the history of modern philosophy, the word 'identity' has had several meanings. It designated, for example, the unity of personal consciousness: that an 'I' remains the same throughout all its experiences. This is what was meant by the Kantian 'I think, which should be able to accompany all my representations [*Vorstellungen*]'. Then again identity meant what was supposed to be regularly or nomothetically [*gesetzlich*] present in all rational beings, or in other words thought as logical universality; including the equivalence with itself of every object of thought, the simple A = A. Finally, the epistemological meaning: that subject and object, however mediated, coincide. The first two levels of meaning are by no means strictly differentiated, even in Kant. Nor is this the result of a careless use of language. Identity rather shows up as the zone of indifference between psychology and logic within idealism itself. (ND 145, note/142, note)

The sea-changes in meaning of the concept are therefore here already designated as levels – that is, as the epistemological space of emergent disciplines and specialized codes (so that it is perhaps not irresponsible to grasp the term *gesetzlich* – literally, 'lawful', and here standing for the conceptual regularities and uniformities of Reason itself – as a hint and foreshadowing of the emergence of some properly juridical or legal level as well – the identity of the *legal* subject – something rarely developed in Adorno himself but in which many of us today are keenly interested). Nor is the ultimate level – the economic – here evoked, but it will emerge at its proper time and place.

We have at any rate here moved from the psychic level of identity, the unity of the subject, to the properly logical one, at which for the first time the central space of Adorno's deployment of identity and non-identity comes into view: namely, that of the *concept* (*Begriff*, rather than *Idee*, 'idea', which has a very different meaning in Hegel, and also in the great 'Epistemo-Critical Prologue' to Walter Benjamin's *Origin of German Tragic Drama*, a text of supreme importance for Adorno, both in his first philosophical years and then again in *Negative Dialectics* itself, and one to which we will return).

In the philosophical framework, therefore, the *concept* is the strong form of identity, subsuming a great variety of different, really existing objects under the same term or thought (the objects being different by definition, since they all exist separately). The primacy of the concept therefore implies a historical moment in which universals come into being, in which abstractions are wrested from the primal flux of sheer names that would seem to characterize preconceptual thinking: when we think, however, of Lévi-Strauss's analysis of this last as perceptual or qualitative science [*pensée sauvage*], and also of Adorno's account of the dynamics of enlightenment, a process which for him has no beginning, then it would begin to seem that functionally the primacy of the concept (in Western philosophy) is not so different after all from the elaboration of magical names, since both are forms of 'enlightenment' in the sense in which they secure domination over nature, and organize the 'blooming, buzzing confusion' of the natural state into so many abstract grids.

Meanwhile, the concept – any concept – asserts and enforces the conviction that it corresponds to the thing, to its object: how that relationship is conceived surely plays across a broad variety of epistemological fantasies, from notions that it represents some inner truth of the thing all the way to the feeling that it is somehow 'like' the thing. Rare indeed are those who, like the Dickens character, celebrate the capacity of the philosopher to produce concepts utterly unlike the thing itself: 'If you was to take and show that man the buoy at the Nore ... and ask him his opinion of it, Wal'r, he'd give you an opinion that was no more like that buoy than your uncle's buttons are.' It is true that Althusser, whose epistemology is in this sense radically non-identitarian, liked tirelessly to remind us that 'the concept of sugar does not taste sweet'; but the therapeutic shock of this reminder cannot last long, and my hunch is that anyone trying to conceptualize the property of sweetness will ultimately end up persuading himself that the mind triumphant manages to incorporate sweetness within itself as part of its thought.

The failure is not simply the result of the mind's weakness, or its attachment to an outmoded philosophical ideology or epistemology: it is, on the contrary, inscribed in the concept itself, whose whole dynamic seeks to secure and perpetuate the feeling that it reunites subject and object, and reenacts their unity. Adorno, who still uses the language of ideology and false consciousness, will sometimes go so far as to suggest that this primal illusion of the identity of the concept with the thing is the strong form of ideology itself and provides its very definition:

> Ideology by no means always takes the form of explicitly idealistic philosophy. It does its secret work within the very foundational construction [*Substruktion*] of something affirmed as first or primary (no matter what the latter's content), within the implicit identity of concept and thing, which justifies the world as it is, even when a doctrine summarily teaches the dependence of consciousness on being. (ND 50/40)

We will return to the matter of firstness later on in the framework of Adorno's view of philosophical *Darstellung* or writing-form; what might be added to the remarks just quoted is only the supplementary turn of the screw that the identification of the concept with the thing also implicitly (but also often explicitly) has the result of our believing that the concept is a thing, of our living among our concepts as though they were the things of the real world. The term demanding to be pronounced at this point is clearly the word 'reification'; and that Adorno's leitmotiv of identity can be seen as his variant on the now traditional apparatus of the critiques of reification (from Marx on) seems to me demonstrable, but also paradoxical in the light of his not infrequent denunciations of vulgar or schematic Marxism in general and of reification theory in particular. Such passages seem, however, to involve two kinds of anxiety, one of form and one of content, so to speak. Adorno's materialism, which specifically makes a place for a life among objects and things, senses a kind of moralizing spiritualism in the use of the slogan of reification as a reproach – as though it were desirable to divest oneself altogether of material furnishings! In particular, the reifying impulse in modern art is affirmed as a necessity and evaluated positively. But this amounts to something a little more complicated than a reversal of Marx's reproach that Hegel confounded alienation with objectification; since Adorno's perspective historicizes the problem and includes reification as such (as an intensified effect of commodity production) within even non-alienated objectification today.

Formally, however, the problem posed by the term 'reification' is of another kind and turns, as we shall see later in more detail, on the unwanted 'thematization' of the single-shot motif or explanation, no matter how locally valid. This then becomes a substantive ideological or even anthropological 'theory' in its own right, at which point its form contradicts its content by virtue of conveying an autonomous message in the first place. In short, Adorno's objection would frequently seem to be the (pertinent) one that most often the concept of reification is itself reified, or at least easily reifiable. Characteristically, then, Adorno criticizes 'reification' in the name of the moment of truth of reification theory.

As for identity itself, however, in so far as it has been characterized functionally in terms of domination and repression, an alternate or complementary description emerges negatively, in the direction of what identity excludes. Even the classical dialectic (still organized around identity) 'must unquestionably pay the price of a bitter sacrifice in the qualitative multiplicity of experience' (ND 18/6). Hegel himself is still at one with the older identitarian philosophical tradition in his indifference 'to non-conceptuality, individuality, and particularity; to what has been since Plato written off as transitory and incapable of promotion to genuine philosophical significance [*unerheblich*], and on which Hegel himself plastered the label of "lazy existence"' (ND 20/8). The suggestion here of a certain asceticism in conceptuality, of renunciation coupled with *ressentiment* at that very renunciation, is certainly present and very consistent with Adorno's attitudes (not only towards the repressive functions of identity); elsewhere he derides the aversion to rhetoric of traditional philosophers, 'who consider the body of language as sinful' (ND 66/56).

Yet clearly enough, as such overtones of a language of desire and repression indicate, this moment – in which we approach the nature of identity by way of a characterization of 'non-identity' – discloses that zone of Adorno's thinking in closest proximity to many of the now familiar thematics of poststructuralism. We have already tactically evoked the Deleuzian flux: here the word 'heterogeneity' seems inescapably to impose itself, and to draw along behind it a whole ideological baggage tending to reassociate Adorno with postmodernism and post-Marxism, an association against which we argued in the introduction to the present volume. A rather different perspective on Adorno's conception of otherness and the non-identical will emerge later in the discussion of *Aesthetic Theory*, where a thematic of nature and natural beauty equally unexpectedly seems to turn Adorno back into a much more traditional kind of aesthetic philosopher, but one no less incompatible with dialectics and Marxism than the poststructural kind. It is certain that his emphasis on the way in which reason and the concept tendentially filter out the qualitative (the perceptual and even the bodily) is a congenial theme at the present time, while the repression of the particular by the general and of the individual by the universal seems to return us decisively to precisely those anti-'totalitarian' and anti-utopian positions from which Adorno's anti-identity theory must be sharply distinguished (that it involves a historical critique of the nominalist tendency in modern art fully as much as an acknowledgement and a foregrounding of it will be clear only later on, in our discussion of *Aesthetic Theory*).

A passing remark, early in *Negative Dialectics*, makes it clear, however, that all of these themes are first and foremost to be grasped within another tradition, namely the Marxist one. This crucial phrase identifies 'what cannot be subsumed under identity' – that is to say, everything that has been evoked above variously under the notions of difference and heterogeneity, otherness, the qualitative, the radically new, the corporeal – as 'what is called in Marxian terminology *use value*' (emphasis added; ND 22/11). This is the decisive clue, not merely to the basic philosophical argument that subtends Adorno's conception of identity and non-identity – *Capital*, volume I, Book I, Part I – but also to the ultimate identity of 'identity' itself, which we have observed to take on the forms of psychic identity and of logic and epistemology before coming to rest (at least provisionally) in the economic realm of exchange and the commodity. The weak form of the argument merely supposes a *homology* between these processes (economic abstraction is structured *like* psychic abstraction, which in its turn is structured *like* philosophical abstraction or unity); while its stronger form asserts a priority of the 'economic', in the sense that stamping goods as uniform and producing uniform goods is a more complex functional activity than the production of uniform thoughts.

Marx's classic chapter is in effect a meditation on the mysteries of identity (which we take for granted): how is it, when the consumption (or 'use') of any specific object is unique, and constitutes a unique and incomparable temporal event in our own lives as well, that we are able to think of such things as 'the same'? Sameness here is not merely the concept of the category of this particular object (several different things being steaks, cars, linen, or books) but also, and above all, the equivalence of their *value*, the possibility we have historically constructed of comparing them (one car for so many pounds of steak), when in terms of experience or consumption – in other words, of use value – they remain incomparable and speculation is incapable of weighing the experience of eating this particular steak against that of a drive in the country. Exchange value, then, the emergence of some third, abstract term between two incomparable objects (an abstraction which, by way of the historical dialectic narrated by Marx in this chapter, ultimately takes the form of money), constitutes the primordial form by which identity emerges in human history.

The 'exchange relationship' [*Tauschverhältnis*] is the other great leit-motiv that sounds throughout Adorno's work, and it is strictly 'identical' with that more philosophical leitmotiv named 'identity' which we have been tracing here. Now the philosophical and anthropological evocation of the will to domination inherent in the identical concept gives way to a more vivid sense of the constraints of the economic system (commodity production, money, labor-power) secretly inherent in all manifestations of identity itself; meanwhile, this infrastructure of the concept then also makes it clear why its effects (sometimes also called 'ideology' as we have seen above) cannot simply be thought away by the thinking of a better thought, by new forms of philosophizing and more adequate (or even more Utopian) concepts. History already thinks the thinking subject and is inscribed in the forms through which it must necessarily think.

'Society precedes the subject' (ND 132/126); thought's categories are collective and social; identity is not an option but a doom; reason and its categories are at one with the rise of civilization or capitalism, and can scarcely be transformed until the latter is transformed. But Habermas is wrong to conclude that Adorno's implacable critique of reason (*Verstand* rather than *Vernunft*) paints him into the corner of irrationalism and leaves him no implicit recourse but the now familiar poststructural one of *l'acéphale*, cutting off the intolerable, hyperintellectual head of the formerly rational being. He thinks so only because he cannot himself allow for the possibility or the reality of some new, genuinely dialectical thinking that would offer a different kind of solution in a situation in which the limits and failures – indeed the destructive effects – of non-dialectical 'Western' reason are well known.

Two

Everything therefore turns on whether we can imagine such a radically different, alternative way of thinking or philosophizing, let alone ourselves practice it. Dialectical thinking has often been described as reflexivity, self-consciousness, 'thought to the second power', the distancing of ordinary thought 'procedures [so] as to widen its own attention to include them in its awareness as well'.[2] That is a way of putting it, but its effectiveness depends very much on the freshness of this rhetoric of self-consciousness, which, at a time when 'consciousness' itself has been called back into question as a concept or a category, has apparently ceased to convey very much. Reflexivity (if you prefer) is part of the baggage of a modernist thinking no longer very authoritative in the postmodernist era.

Negative Dialectics gives us another way of characterizing the dialectical process (now purged of Hegelian idealism, at least so far as Adorno is concerned). We are now asked (but the figures are mine) to think another side, an outside, an external face of the concept which, like that of the moon, can never be directly visible or accessible to us: but we must vigilantly remember and reckon that other face into our sense of the concept while remaining within it in the old way and continuing to use and think it. If the notion of the 'Unconscious' seems occasionally to impose itself, we should resist it as some ultimate philosophical solution and see that notion also as a kind of shorthand, one figure among many others which equally sought to endow the thinking mind with a dimension of radical otherness that, at least on Lacan's and Lévi-Strauss's reading of Freud, must always structurally elude us, and remain forever out of reach. Like the astronomer (Lévi-Strauss's comparison[3]) we can reckon the presence out there of some massive invisible body or gravitational source which can never be part of our experience, even though we can use its hypothesis to rebuke and therapeutically to discredit unmediated conscious thinking.

But this way of putting it offers a misleading way of characterizing Adorno: the Frankfurt School's pioneering use of Freud applied the latter's categories as a kind cf supplementary social psychology (repression and the damaged subject as indices and results of the exchange process and the dynamics of capitalism) but never as any centrally organizing concept.[4]

In order to see how thought could be imagined to 'think against itself', we must return to the starting point of the first chapter, which set out to rewrite stereotypical (post-Marxist) versions of two fundamental concepts in Adorno, identity and totality. Of identity we have seen that it is in fact Adorno's word for the Marxian concept of exchange relationship (a term he also frequently uses): his achievement was then to have powerfully generalized, in richer detail than any other thinker of the Marxist or dialectical tradition, the resonance and implications of the doctrine of exchange value for the higher reaches of philosophy. Of totality we will now assert that Adorno is not merely not an enemy and a critic of this copiously stigmatized idea, but that it comes very precisely as the solution to the problem of thinking with and against the concept that has been posed above. The fundamental operation whereby the concept can be retained and dereified all at once (to use a different kind of shorthand) involves its reinsertion into totality or system (a term whose slippage between notions of a philosophical system and of a socioeconomic system will be significant and even crucial, as we shall see shortly). As for totality, it plays a strategic role in freeing us from the 'spell' of the concept, as the following preliminary characterization (an argument against Croce) already suggests:

> What is differentiated will appear divergent, dissonant, negative just as long as consciousness is driven by its own formation towards unity; just as long as it measures what is not identical with itself against its own claim for totality. It is this which dialectics exhibits to consciousness as a contradiction. (ND 17/5-6)

Yet there is a suggestion in this passage that the drive towards totality (Lukács's *Totalitätsintention*) may have something illicit about it, expressing the idealism and the imperialism of the concept, which seeks voraciously to draw everything into its own field of domination and security. Something of this is certainly present in Adorno, nor is it alien to other thinkers who have been stigmatized as 'totalitarian' in their insistence on the urgency and centrality of the notion of totality; the misunderstanding lies in drawing the conclusion that philosophical emphasis on the indispensability of this category amounts either to celebration of it or, in a stronger form of the anti-utopian argument, to its implicit perpetuation as a reality or a referent outside the philosophical realm. In that case no critique, satire or representational denunciation would ever be possible, since it would simply reconfirm what it claimed to be stigmatizing.

The moment of truth in this misunderstanding becomes more visible when we turn to that more purely philosophical modulation of the notion of totality which is the notion of a philosophical system, or of the ideal of systematic thinking. *Negative Dialectics* is certainly on the face of it a repudiation of the ideal and the practice of philosophical systems (even that of Hegel); as has already been observed, it seems to urge a practice of thought which at its outer limit would authorize the writing of just those provisional, fragmentary, self-consuming conceptual performances celebrated by properly postmodern philosophy.[5]

What must now be affirmed, however, is the opposite of all this: namely, that no matter how desirable this postmodern philosophical free play may be, it cannot now be practiced; however conceivable and imaginable it may have become as a philosophical aesthetic (but it would be important to ask what the historical preconditions for the very conception of this ideal and the possibility of imagining it are), anti-systematic writing today is condemned to remain within the 'system'. We may make a beginning on this paradox by returning to certain anti-utopian arguments associated with so-called post-Marxism: for it is certain that in denouncing philosophical system, in proposing some radically unsystematic dialectics, in arguing against 'system' itself, Adorno retains the concept of the system and even makes it, as target and object of critique, the very center of his own anti-systematic thinking. This is the sense in which it can – and must – be affirmed that he perpetuates the primacy of system as such: his most powerful philosophical and aesthetic interventions are all implacable monitory reminders – sometimes in well-nigh Weberian or Foucauldian tones – of our imprisonment within system, the forgetfulness or repression of which binds us all the more strongly to it, in ways reminiscent of the illusions of identity, with which it is of course in one sense virtually synonymous.

Identity is, however, something like occluded system, totality forgotten or repressed, at the same time that it continues the more effectively to perform system's work. This is the sense in which the conscious reintroduction of system or totality comes as a solution to the closure of identity; it cannot free us from the latter's illusions and mirages, since no mere thinking can do that, but it suddenly makes these last visible and affords a glimpse of the great magic 'spell' [*der Bann*] in which modern life is seized and immobilized. (This essentially romance figure has a paradoxical dynamic in contemporary thought, since it is precisely enlightenment and the *desacralization* of the world – Weber's *Entzauberung* – which can be characterized as the realm of a whole new fetishization: a term Marx explicitly borrowed from eighteenth-century anthropology).[6]

System is very precisely that outer face of the concept, that outside forever inaccessible to us, evoked above; yet to see how this might be so, we need experimentally to record the inner transformations or dialectical polysemousness of this twin notion of system/totality in much the same spirit as our account of the levels of reference in the concept of identity. What looks like the ideal of philosophical system is, then, in a second moment deconcealed as the claims of reason and the universal – indeed, of abstraction as such: whose systematizing operations within the concept it may be convenient to register by way of the dialectic of form and content. The in-forming presence of system within even the most isolated and free-standing 'concept' can be detected in its form, which remains abstract and universal, whatever its local content may happen to be. But this clarifies the figure we have proposed of another 'face' or an 'outside' of the concept, since we cannot think the form and the content of a given concept simultaneously or in the same way: attention to the form of a thought seems at once, in a kind of Gestalt perception, to discredit the thought's content – that is to say, its official meaning or reference: to bracket it, so that it falls to the level of an optional example and its inherent 'belief' evaporates or becomes fictional.

Thinking the concept in the usual fashion, however, means 'believing' it and attending to its content, in such a way that the perception of its form becomes a trivial annoyance and a distracting interruption. What needs to be invented, therefore – and what in my opinion Adorno's dialectics proposes – is a new kind of stereoscopic thinking in which the concept continues to be thought philosophically and cashed at face value, while in some other part of the mind a very different kind of intellectual climate reigns, a cruder and more sociological set of terms and categories, in which the form of that concept is noted and registered in shorthand and in which the existence of the financial and banking system thereby presupposed is somehow reckoned in.

For as we have seen in our discussion of identity, abstraction itself – very much including its most sophisticated philosophical equivalent in logic and in the form of universals – is revealed at another level to be at one with the logic of equivalence and exchange; that is to say, with the logic of capital. The exchange relationship, the abstract value form in which identity is primordially conceived, cannot exist as a punctual event, as an occasional matter or an isolated, optional or random act; it is at one with the exchange system itself, so that it is at this point that the philosophical term 'system' modulates into the essentially social or socioeconomic concept of totality (something Adorno often invokes in the sociological and even Weberian terminology of bureaucratic or 'administered' society [die verwaltete Welt], but more often and less euphemistically simply as 'late capitalism'). This ultimate deconcealment of the nature of the systematic makes it clear why we cannot simply renounce 'system' and let it go at that; even more why 'totality' remains an indispensable name for the infrastructural dimension of reason and abstract thought today – its other or family name, as it were:

> The dialectical mediation of the universal and the particular does not allow a theory that opts for the particular to treat the universal overzealously as a soap bubble. If it did that, theory would be incapable of registering the pernicious supremacy of the universal in the current state of things, nor could it project the idea of another state of things in which the universal would find itself stripped of its bad particularity insofar as individuals were restored to what rightly belonged to them [namely, Besonderheit, which is to say precisely specificity, particularity, individuality]. Nor are on the other hand conceptions of a transcendental subject acceptable, a subject without society and without those individuals whom for good or ill it integrates. (ND 199-200/199–200)

Adorno's language here will, however, be misleading to the degree to which the philosophical concepts he manipulates (universality, particularity) seem in this passage to be on the same level with each other, as though one could simply think them together in a 'synthetic judgement', with whatever inversion of the philosophical and logical hierarchy of subject and predicate seems desirable. But the burden of his critique of Hegel lay precisely in the accusation that Hegel thought the relationship between the two poles from the point of view of universality: 'the difference between the universal and the particular developed by the dialectic is the one dictated by the universal itself' (ND 18/6). This distortion is the effect of the very form of universalizing philosophical language, which, in trying desperately to designate what is other than the universal, continues to use an abstract terminology and the very form of logical opposition or dualism to convey its protest against the operations of that language and that logical form. To say 'particular' is to reinforce the 'universal', no matter what you go on to do with these words.[7] I stress the effect at this point, not merely to illustrate the preceding discussion of the lateral distortion by the philosophical and universalizing systemic form of its content, but also because Adorno's warning, in spite of itself, tends to obscure the radicality of the double standard he himself practices, which we have begun to describe here.

This is to say that purity in philosophical thinking or writing (Adorno already approaching the poststructural position that these are in fact the same), the unmixed or 'intrinsic', is as impossible as it is undesirable: something that holds for the individual concept as well and also – paradoxically for those who think of Adorno as in this area the very quintessence of the aesthete – for the work of art. What the concept cannot say must somehow, by its imperfection, be registered within it (just as the monadic work of art must somehow 'include' its outside, its referent, under pain of lapsing into decorative frivolity): otherwise the powerful force of identity will reign through it unchecked. Those for whom dialectical thought in general, and Adorno's writing in particular, are uncongenial have seen this impurity at work more vividly than the sympathizers: they evoke long, heady, supersubtle 'dialectical' disputation, followed by the inevitable lapse into vulgar-Marxist interpretation of a summary type, the 'explanation' in terms of late capitalism that solves everything.

Nor is it wrong to observe that the 'interpretant' – late capitalism, 'administered society', the fragmentation of psychic subjects in the monopoly period, etc., etc. – is never the object of the same kind of prodigious intelligence deployed in the great philosophical periods that precede it and to which it gives a kind of closure. But the double standard does not mean the establishment of a boundary between topics that are fair game for the dialectic and truths that are supposed to be left untouched (since they constitute the foundational or Archimedean point in terms of which the other kinds of operations are conducted). It means rather, within the same thought, designating the outside of that thought which can never be mastered by it on its own terms.

The summary deictic indication in passing of late capitalism, system, exchange, totality, is not a reference to other sets of thoughts or concepts (such as Grossman's or Pollock's theory of late capitalism,[8] or Weber's of bureaucracy) which can be criticized in their own terms for their coherence and validity and their ideological quotient. It rather gestures towards an outside of thinking – whether system itself in the form of rationalization, or totality as a socioeconomic mechanism of domination and exploitation – which escapes representation by the individual thinker or the individual thought. The function of the impure, extrinsic reference is less to interpret, then, than to rebuke interpretation as such and to include within the thought the reminder that it is itself inevitably the result of a system that escapes it and which it perpetuates: even there where it seeks radically to grasp and confront the element in which it bathes and which infiltrates and determines its subjective processes fully as much as the objects for which it seeks to account.

We therefore find ourselves obliged to take form into account if we want to deal seriously with content; for Adorno's 'theories' of late capitalism are inseparable from what we may call the 'totality-effect' in his writing and *Darstellung*. It is an effect that might be evoked in terms of Deleuze's great (Leibnizian) theory of the filmic modern,[9] as a continuous loop between the present of the image or shot, the world-totality behind it of which it is only an aspect, but which expresses itself only through that aspect, and the mobile sequence by which the shots succeed one another (and also convey the modifications in the totality beyond them). Adorno's sentences are, then, just such individual 'shots', edited into a larger formal movement (the constellation or model, as we shall see shortly), small- and large-scale dimensions through both of which the absent totality perpetually feeds. (Indeed, by way of Eisenstein, Deleuze characterizes one form of this modernist and 'totalizing' system as the dialectic itself.)

The philosophical objection that can be made to this form of thinking or writing is therefore essentially no different from the problem which on the level of language produced the notion of the 'hermeneutic circle': if we must pass through the individual sentences, or even through their larger locally staged argument and architectonic, where would that conception of totality, which is supposed to open up the other face of their particular meanings ever come from in the first place? How could we ever acquire a conception of the universal or the total system – if we are condemned to pass through particulars? The obvious response – that we evidently acquired the notion of the universal somewhere, since we now have it – is vitiated by a postmodern situation in which it seems possible to read particulars one by one without any transcendent universal or totality from which they derive their meaning; and in which we also harbor the deep suspicion that such universals as may still survive are in reality stereotypes that include no new information content.

A more satisfactory (although not at all satisfying) response may be afforded by turning the problem into its own solution: this very contradiction between the universal and the particular constitutes Adorno's diagnosis of the modern world, and cannot in that sense be solved but only thematized and foregrounded, taken as a symptom in its own right. In his post-Hegelian philosophical language, reconciliation [*Versöhnung*] – whether this is understood philosophically, existentially, socially, or aesthetically – is very precisely to be taken as a lifting of the tensions and contradictions between the universal and the particular: the common understanding that it involves a reconciliation of subject and object is thus erroneous, except to the degree to which object here designates the larger social order and subject the individual or particular. From this perspective, then, interpretation as such – the reading of the particular in the light of the absent universal – is dialectically transformed and 'sublated': producing a new mode of interpretation in which the particular is read, not in the light of the universal, but rather in the light of the very contradiction between universal and particular in the first place. Interpretation now means turning the text inside out and making it into a symptom of the very problem of interpretation itself.

But this philosophical solution – if it is one – scarcely removes the local discomfort of garden-variety interpretive acts and operations; nor does it effectively address the malaise readers have sometimes felt with Adorno's own interpretations. That he was keenly aware of the issue may be judged by the following remark on interpretation in a more specifically literary or aesthetic context:

> What is self-defeating [*das Fatale*] about all forms of interpretation of art, even the most philosophically responsible kinds, is the way in which they find themselves obliged to express what is shocking and unaccustomed by way of what is already familiar, in so far as they must necessarily express it by way of the Concept; they thus explain away what alone demands explanation: as passionately as works of art long for interpretation, they all equally passionately betray conformism, even against their own will.[10] (NL 101)

The consequence is that 'conformism' – in this case, conformism to the preexisting idea or stereotype – returns in the form of interpretation to defuse and domesticate what in the work – as sheer unassimilable particularity and uniqueness – struggled to resist it. This is the spirit in which, in one of the grimmer caricatures of Adorno's own 'method', a hostile critic enumerates the 'findings' of Adorno's principal essay on Proust (including page references to the complete edition of the *Noten zur Literatur*):

> The whole is the untrue (p. 203), bourgeois society as a closed system of preestablished disharmony (p. 206), non-identity of the ego (p. 206 ff.), the breakdown of experience in alienation, beauty's continuing existence as mere appearance (p. 207 ff.), impossibility of love in the function-dominated totality (p. 209 ff.), etc.[11]

This seemingly definitive etcetera does not take into account the remarkable evocations of Proust in the concluding chapter of *Negative Dialectics*: references that surely constitute a luminous 'interpretation' of a wholly novel stamp (although it may be agreed that the critical faculty flags somewhat in the essay in question, without conceding any of the implied critique of Adorno's method itself).

This operated, at its moments of greatest intensity, as a kind of Gestalt modification of the hermeneutic circle. The logical relationship of the particular to the universal is in any case never that of the traditional Aristotelian subsumption of species under genus. Still, in so far as the reader habitually sorts judgements out into the canonical major and minor premises, Adorno's propositions may be said deliberately to invert these, by way of a perceptual play on the blurred zones of our lateral perception. The attention systematically directed to the particular, to the text or phenomenon to be interpreted – and for which the interpretandum is the presupposed totality summoned to the outlying field of vision – finds that what has been said, unexpectedly, addresses that totality itself and modifies it, not the particular that was its pretext. Meanwhile, a thematization of the totality (monopoly capitalism, for instance) that drew in this or that isolated historical particular as a mere example or illustration proves itself to have been a subterfuge for the striking modification, the interpretation by way of shock and novelty, of the putative example itself. Adorno himself describes this process – which can clearly not lend itself to a 'linear' argument about anything – in connection with the elective affinity of the essay as a form with cultural matters:

> [The essay] sinks itself into cultural phenomena as into a second nature, a second immediacy, not in order to 'reduce' those, but rather to lift their illusions by its persistent immanence. It is as little deluded as 'philosophies of origin' about the difference between culture and what underlies it. But for the essay culture is not some epiphenomenon above being that must be eradicated, but rather its object of criticism, what it posits [thesei], is the underlying itself, the false society. This is why origins mean no more to the essay than superstructures. It owes its freedom in the choice of objects, its sovereignty over all priorities of subject-matter or theory, to the fact that for it in some sense all objects lie equally near the center: that is to say, to the principle that everything is bewitched. (NL 28)

Rhetorically, then, we may say that Adorno's way with interpretation, and the dimension of an outside and an absent system that he seeks to reconfer on particulars of experience, turn on the possibility of shifting the positions perpetually between particular and universal, transforming the putative universal without warning into a particular, unmasking the alleged particular as a universal in true sheep's or grandmother's clothing.

This play of positions may indeed be traced down into the very syntax of the sentences themselves, about which we have already noted an excessive fondness for the transformation of nouns in subject positions without warning into objects.

Three

It may now be useful in passing to specify at least two kinds of thinking which are not to be confused or identified with the dialectical stereoscopy or 'double standard' we have observed at work in Adorno. It may now seem, for example, increasingly urgent to return to our hesitations about the rhetoric of self-consciousness and reflexivity, and to specify more explicitly (as we shall also do when we come to Adorno's aesthetics) the ways in which 'a thoroughgoing critique of identity gropes its way towards the preponderance of the object' (ND 184/183).

It would be a great mistake to suppose that the kind of awareness of the outside of thought we have been describing here can be achieved by heightened and more alert introspection of the phenomenological type (it should be recalled that Adorno began his philosophical career with a radical critique of Husserl). The only way in which the subjective processes of the mind can be prevented from sealing us back into idealism is to seize on those fitful moments in which, they unexpectedly betray their objective nature: something the logicians have always sought to show about the forms and syntax without, however (even in Hegel's *Logic*), taking the next step towards specifying the *derivation* of those objective 'mental structures' and their relationship to that larger realm of objectivity (or reality),[12] which is of course for Adorno the social rather than the natural (even though, following the example of Marx's relationship to Darwin – human history as a part of natural history – he also develops an interesting conception of natural history, which will be examined later).

The difficulties of achieving a new dialectical objectivity are evidently asymmetrical, since owing to the inequality in the concept of mediation, the subject falls into the object in an utterly different way than the latter into the former. Object can only be thought by way of subject, yet ever perseveres as an other to this last; subject on the other hand is in its very structure and from the outset also object. The object cannot be thought away from the subject as an idea; but the subject can certainly be removed from the object in thought. (ND 184/183)

This final asymmetry reminds us, if we needed the reminder, that Adorno's celebration of the preponderance of the objective, here and throughout, has nothing to do with the positivistic (or even empiricist) excision of subject positions altogether.

Nor is the slogan of objectivity in Adorno the symptom of that rather different kind of anti-subjectivity which seeks to humiliate the subjective dimension in a spirit of ascesis, self-hatred, or *ressentiment*: on the contrary, it is meant to generate a new space for the emancipation of the subject itself; while at the same time its own realization depends on precisely that emancipation:

> In what are, at the present historical stage, most often called oversubjective judgments, what really happens is that the subject has merely automatically echoed the consensus omnium. It could restore the object to its own rights, instead of being satisfied with a bad copy, only where it resisted the least common denominator of such objectivity and freed itself qua subject. Objectivity today depends on that emancipation, rather than on the tireless repression of the subject. The oppressive power of the objectified within subjects, a power that blocks them from becoming subjects, also blocks knowledge of the objective; such is what happened to what used to be called the 'subjective factor'. Subjectivity too' v is rather mediated as objectivity, and such mediation demands analysis more urgently than the traditional kind. That objectivity to which every kind of subject, including the transcendental one, is yoked, finds its own mediatory mechanisms prolonged by the subjective ones. (ND 172-3/170-71)

But it is very precisely the emergence in Adorno of the analysis of just such hidden forms of objectification within the subjective that we have been outlining here: the concealment of identity within the very form of the concept, the perpetuation of external system by the very nature of abstraction or universalizing thought; and it seems quite correct for Adorno to see this as the most original feature of his own dialectical practice. To reveal the social dimensions of abstract thought: to put it that way is to ignore the dialectic of the explanandum and the intricacies at work within any reified conception of the social and within sociology itself. Discussing Weber, Adorno remarks that in fact, philosophical conceptuality is the most adequate area for dealing with the thing itself [*Grund der Sache*], in so far as social research at least becomes false when it limits itself to those interdependencies within its own domain that ground the object, and ignores the latter's determination by the totality itself. Without the overarching [philosophical] concept such internal interdependencies mask the realest dependency of all, namely that on society, and society cannot be adequately ranged under the individual *res* that has its concept 'under' itself. Society, however, appears only through the particular, thereby enabling the [properly philosophical] concept to be transformed on the occasion of determinate knowledge. (ND 166-7/164-5)

It is hoped that the reader will by now not be tempted by this rather tortured passage to conclude that Adorno is merely advising the sociologists to add a philosopher to their team and to let him provide the ultimate theoretical framework. On the contrary, we have tried to show that no 'philosophical concept' is adequate either: each one must be analyzed symptomatically for what it excludes or cannot say. What Adorno reproaches the sociologists with generally is that they do not get on with that work, but rather assume that the larger or more abstract 'concepts' – such as society itself, freedom, bureaucracy, domination – are the end-point of thinking and the ultimate framework for interpretation. On the contrary, those concepts demand dialectical analysis the most urgently, and it is by way of their formal pseudo-universality and 'scientific' abstraction that the ultimate shackles which the social imposes on our thinking about the social become revealed although not removed.

This is clearly the moment to say something more about Adorno's role and work as a sociologist, which can easily be misunderstood if the only work that springs to mind is the famous volume on anti-Semitism called *The Authoritarian Personality* and published in the United States virtually at the moment of the postwar return to Germany. Indeed, to put it this way is also to compound the misunderstanding and to assume that Adorno was interested in 'authoritarianism' for what it had to say about 'prejudice', rather than the other way round. Even in the chapter of *Dialectic of Enlightenment* officially consecrated to anti-Semitism, this phenomenon (not, to be sure, a matter of mere disinterested curiosity for its authors, just as one must not imagine that the funding of the *Studies in Prejudice* project was unmotivated) is not, as for liberalism, a mere aberrant empirical matter, which may be studied in isolation from 'late capitalism' generally, but is in its function, and in its significance as a psychic symptom, at one with the fabric of this last, the social totality itself, that remains the principal object of study and the dialectical framework in which alone such local inquiries can take on their meaning.

Anti-Semitism, then, which betrays the regression of the psyche under industrialization and rationalization, along with its violent mesmerization by the archaic modes of appropriation and relationships to nature its victims seem to represent, is grasped as a form of cultural envy that reveals the relationship of the subject to the social totality under modernization in a peculiarly privileged way (as we will see later on, in a different context). What is characteristic of Adorno's sociological perspective is then this attempt to cross the particular with the general and hold them together in their contradictory tension, which is lost at once when the empirical lapses back into the status of yet another mere research project.

Viewed from the other perspective, however, from that of the 'general' rather than the 'particular', Adorno's sociological propositions tend towards a lapidary concision that transforms brief essays, such as the fundamental statement simply entitled 'Society',[13] into verbal objects of great density, like shrunken dwarfs: this is to be explained by the fundamental asymmetry between subject and object, and by the consequent fact that 'society', the universal, the system itself, is as 'fictive' and non-empirical as it is real. The social totality 'cannot be grasped in any immediate fashion, nor is it susceptible of drastic verification'.[14] In practice, this means that Adorno's sociological theorization will always be metacritical, separating the necessarily imperfect use of the sociological concept out from the materials it seems in the process of interpreting, and finding the conceptual coinage of the sociologists fully as historically and socially revealing as the data they thought they were collecting. But it is not a matter of the sociology of sociologists exactly, although the emergence and function of the discipline are present to Adorno's mind, particularly in those moments when it becomes uncritical and apologetic, lapsing into an ideational reproduction of the status quo; rather, even at their most intellectually energetic, the concepts of sociology cannot but be flawed and fractured, since their very object is contradictory, faithfulness to it thereby requiring a certain transfer of the social contradiction into thought.

So it is that just this subject–object tension – the real 'individual' caught in an 'imaginary' social order, the existential fact itself produced by the universal system of identity that obliterates it, the psyche whose very solitude, anomie, and irrational spasms are somehow social and collective to their very core – reproduces or externalizes itself in the very history of the emergent sociological discipline by way of the twin antithetical figures of Weber and Durkheim, both of whom are right and wrong, true and false, simultaneously. To Weber's forms of 'comprehension' – the elaborate typologies of the ratio of means to ends – corresponds Durkheim's insistence on the alienating objectivity of the social 'fact': very precisely because 'society is both known and not known from the inside'.[15] To Weber's grasp of a certain subjectivity at the moment of its eclipse by rationalization, then, asymmetrically corresponds Durkheim's great dictum that the explanation of social phenomena in psychological terms must always be false, as well as his insistence on the primacy of the collective (which has in modern times become invisible). But the truth cannot be said to lie somewhere in between them, any more than the tension can be resolved by means of some conceptual synthesis or the invention of a 'third way', since it corresponds very precisely to social objectivity: Adorno's sociology thus poses the embarrassing question whether the comprehension or intuition of a contradiction can itself be other than contradictory, unless it involves the production of the *concept* of contradiction.

All of this is reproduced and acted out in more contemporary forms in the relations between sociology and psychology (or psychoanalysis), which cannot be 'synthesized' any more than they may be allowed to 'succumb to the temptation to project the intellectual division of labor onto the object of their study'.[16] The rift between public and private, social and psychological, is a dramatic externalization (although not the only one or even the only type) of the epistemological contradictions of 'a society whose unity resides in its not being unified'.[17] It seems clear that Adorno sometimes felt his sociological mission better served by forcing his readers to confront such paralogisms than by the other intellectual practice available: to work one's way through them in dialectical steps, which involves the construction of mediations. That these exist is virtually given in advance by the dilemma and the contradiction, which causes the seemingly psychological to convert without warning into a social datum, while social 'facts' dissolve ceaselessly back into ideologemes.

So it is that Weber squares this circle by way of the intuition of a 'rationality of self-preservation',[18] which links the existential to the social order and keeps them at arm's length from each other at one and the same time: Adorno's formulation, indeed, suggests a greater relevance of Weber for the construction of *Dialectic of Enlightenment* than might have been deduced from its Freudo-Marxian-Nietzschean trappings. Psychology meanwhile becomes 'sociological' not merely in the origins of its drives ('scars inflicted by society',[19] 'the dimension of split-off irrationality that complements the prevailing rationality'[20]), but also in their social possibilities of expression and gratification

which have today become wholly a function of profit interests.... Even the man whose calculating rationality yields all the advantages it promises cannot attain to real happiness through them but must, like all the other customers, knuckle under once again and take what those who control production offer.[21]

But it could be argued that even these 'mediations' are little more than reenactments of the fundamental contradiction, which essentially allows for no more satisfactory methodological resolution than the sheer alteration of the two perspectives:

> The separation of sociology and psychology is both correct and false. False because it encourages the specialists to relinquish the attempt to know the totality which even the separation of the two demands; and correct in so far as it registers more intransigently the split that has actually taken place in reality than does the premature unification at the level of theory. Sociology in the strict sense, despite constant tendencies to subjectivize it (also on the part of Max Weber), never loses sight of the objective moment of the social process. But the more rigidly it disregards the subject and his spontaneous impulses, the more exclusively it comes to be dealing with a reified, quasi-scientific *caput mortuum*. Hence the tendency to imitate scientific ideals and approaches, which are, however, forever incapable of accounting for specifically social phenomena. While priding themselves on their strict objectivity, they have to settle for the already mediated end-products of the scientific procedure, with sectors and factors, as if they were the real, unmediated object. The upshot is sociology minus society, the replica of a situation in which people have lost contact with themselves.[22]

The objection can now be entertained that Adorno's is essentially a philosopher's sociology – that is to say, a critique of the sociological tradition from a somewhat different conceptual and disciplinary level: that he calls for such a thing, indeed, we have already seen, just as he will call for an analogous primacy of philosophy over art criticism at the end of *Aesthetic Theory*. But surely the very force of the arguments just summarized goes a long way towards discrediting the distinction, implicit in this kind of reproach, between sociological practice and theory, production and mere criticism, between doing sociological field-work and sitting at home to rethink the basic categories and concepts. For the premiss is not merely the obvious one: that our conceptualization of society has real and practical consequences for its objective existence; but above all, the inverse of this proposition – that repression of the concept of society and the social system has a vital part to play in perpetuating its domination. This is the sense of the warning, even more timely today than when it was issued in the sixties: 'Not only theory, but also its absence, becomes a material force when it seizes the masses.'[23]

The critique of sociology thereby becomes a form of praxis in its own right, as exemplified by Adorno's polemic struggles within a postwar but not altogether reformed German sociology: these struggles, as has already been observed and according to the structure of the social contradiction itself, were necessarily battles on two fronts at once, and aimed as much at promoting a certain kind of empirical research within an otherwise relatively metaphysical and speculative tradition as at criticizing the unreflexive and merely operational use of contradictory categories as though they were classificatory concepts. It has often been pointed out, however (most notoriously by Althusser), that metaphysics and empiricism are two dialectical sides of the same ideological coin: so that the so-called positivism debate,[24] the implacable war on positivism that became the way in which Adorno conceived of his sociological vocation, ended up resuming both strands of the critique. I will return at the end of this book to the relevance of such a mission in the contemporary intellectual situation.

Of no less practical relevance than this 'critique of the subject', however, is the 'critique of the object' that is at one with it, and can be formulated in terms of a denunciation of the market of no less unexpected actuality:

> The first objective abstraction takes place, not so much in scientific thought, as in the universal development of the exchange system itself; which happens independently of the qualitative attitudes of producer and consumer, of the mode of production, even of need, which the social mechanism tends to satisfy as a kind of secondary by-product. Profit comes first. A humanity fashioned into a vast network of consumers, the human beings who actually have the needs, have been socially pre-formed beyond anything one might naively imagine, and this not only by the level of industrial development but also by the economic relationships themselves into which they enter, even though this is far more difficult to observe empirically. Above and beyond all specific forms of social differentiation, the abstraction implicit in the market system represents the domination of the general over the particular, of society over its captive membership.[25]

This passage, then, reconfirms the primacy of exchange in Adorno's philosophical diagnoses of identity and abstraction, which can now be summarized by way of the following themes.

Abstraction is first of all collective and not individual; objectivity is present within the subject in the form of collective linguistic or conceptual forms which are themselves produced by society, and thereby presuppose it. This has very much to do with the division of labor, and in particular with the primal separation of manual from intellectual labor which is the precondition of abstract thought itself. But we shall also see – particularly when we come to deal with some of the extraordinary formulations of *Aesthetic Theory* – that it also has very much to do with that classical Marxian notion which is the development of productive forces: these too, as a social and historical phenomenon, are inscribed in the 'concept' and lend it their force, capitalism in that sense being the achievement of ultimate abstraction by way of machinery. Finally, this social language should not displace the in-forming presence of history itself within the concept and its form: not merely the history of philosophy as this lies concealed and encapsulated within the most apparently free-standing and unattributable neologism, but also the history at one with the raw material – language – on which philosophical abstraction essentially works,[26] and which continues to mark it at the very moment in which such raw material is transformed, beyond recognition, into the Idea:

> Whenever philosophy became equal to itself, it seized on the non-conceptual as its object along with the historically existent: and this, not merely beginning with Schelling and Hegel but already *à contrecœur* in Plato, who baptized the existent as the non-existent and yet wrote a doctrine of the state in which the eternal Ideas have a family likeness and an intimate relationship with empirical determinations such as exchange value and the division of labor. (ND 141/137)

Four

This insistence on the social, the collective, exchange, the division of labor, the dynamics of history, however – in other words on the 'preponderance of the objective' within abstract thinking – now demands a complementary warning and caution on the other side of the matter; and to do justice to the complexity of Adorno's position obliges us to differentiate it sharply from another methodological alternative with which it may sometimes seem to have no little in common – namely, the sociology of knowledge. For Adorno equally tirelessly insists that his dialectic is not to be confused with that, which he denounces equally implacably, and whose master thinkers – Mannheim, but also Veblen and Spengler – are the object of some of the most brilliant critiques in that volume of Adorno's most centrally consecrated to sociology – above all to the sociology of ideas and of culture – namely, *Prisms*.

The external classification schemes of the 'sociology of knowledge' were an abomination to him, but symptomatic of something else. Mannheim is dispatched in this way: 'the sociology of knowledge sets up indoctrination camps for the homeless intelligentsia where it can learn to forget itself',[27] a vision that already has something in it of that 'end of ideology' which Cacciari and Tafuri learned specifically from the Frankfurt School: namely, the interest technocracy has in 'Enlightenment'-type critiques and 'demystification' of belief and committed ideology, in order to clear the ground for unobstructed planning and 'development'.[28] What stands in the way, like the unique accidents of a terrain that must be levelled, is the content of the past – organic and inherited forms, superstition, collective habits, the resistance of a specific cultural history or social psychology: rooted beliefs that for Enlightenment are an impediment to Reason in its universalizing and identitarian vocation, and which block the perfect fungibility of subject and object alike, in a postmodernism which from this perspective stands revealed as the triumph of bureaucratic technocracy over the remnants and survivals, the lags and residual content, against which it struggled for so long during the modern period.

To put it this way, however, is to grasp a deep affiliation between the sociology of knowledge and the 'sociology of culture' which is homologous with it and in which the deeper aporia of both is, if anything, even more dramatically revealed. For Adorno's critique of the sociology of culture begins with what endows this last at its most powerful with the very motive power of its perception: very precisely the loathing for culture as such, *ressentiment* for the aesthetic 'supplement' in all its forms, a jaundiced eye alert to all those moments in which the pretense of culture to its own autonomy and rightful function shows its shabby edge: the first of such moments being the very use of the reified word 'culture' itself, which separates and trivializes its objects in advance so that lengthy demonstrations of its distance from 'life' or 'reality' become unnecessary (a dialectic worked out on the philosophical level by Marcuse's great essay 'On the Affirmative Character of Culture'). Thus, not only Spengler and Huxley, in their fashion, but above all Veblen are driven by an anti-cultural, anti-aesthetic impulse which constitutes their object of study (by separating it out) in such a way that its very sham and impotent autonomy serves to condemn itself.[29] Yet this power of the great *Kulturkritik* is not the result of personal idiosyncrasy, but has its own historical specificity:

> With respect to aesthetics, the conclusions Veblen derives from his critique of consumption as mere ostentation are very close to those of functionalism [*die neue Sachlichkeit*], which Adolf Loos formulated at about the same time. Where the practical is concerned they resemble those of technocracy.[30]

The violence with which Loos repudiates 'ornament' and the 'ornamental', identified by him on the one hand with crime as such and on the other with 'perversion', is a strategic move in the high modernist purge of academic and 'fine-arts' canons of 'beauty' at the same time that it prepares the hygienicist ethos of Le Corbusier: but to condemn it solely for its puritanism is to preempt the most interesting part of the analysis in the name of psychological diagnosis. What must be noted is, first, that Adorno marks the philosophical prolongation of this attitude in pragmatism, contemporary with Veblen, whose dislike of 'transcendent' ideas and abstractions (today sometimes stigmatized as 'theory' itself) is thus assimilated to this revulsion against ornament, against what supplements sheer immanence and stands as a form of philosophical luxury or indulgence (abstract or 'continental' philosophy and system here coming to play the role of decorative 'culture' on the other level).

Yet these contemporary identifications and family likenesses (*Kulturkritik*, pragmatism, functionalism) also make it plain that we encounter in them a historical impulse which cannot simply be rebuked by choosing a different philosophical option. But the deeper reason why this anti-aesthetic impulse cannot simply be 'disproved' lies in the fact that it is at work within the works of art themselves and at the very heart of the production of modernism, whose motif of the guilt of art (Thomas Mann's *Doktor Faustus*) and nominalistic impatience with the 'lie' of art and the complacencies of old-fashioned aesthetic appearance [*Schein*] are among the most crucial features for any understanding of the modern, as we shall see in the next chapter. We cannot, therefore, simply refuse the critique of culture and go on celebrating this last under the guise of some disengaged aestheticism: we must somehow go all the way through it and come out the other side (Adorno's 'solution' here will therefore be the very paradigm of that 'impure' mode of thought we have been trying to characterize on the philosophical level).

The dilemma of the cultural has in fact very significant consequences – as Adorno demonstrates in one of the most brilliant 'fragments' of *Minima Moralia*, entitled 'Baby with the Bath Water' (47–50/43–5) – for what has often been thought of as one of the essential working principles of the Marxist tradition: the distinction between base and superstructure: it being understood that very serious qualms and reservations about this, ranging all the way to the most drastic proposals for its total removal, are also a recurrent part of the Marxist tradition, virtually from Engels himself onward. Raymond Williams's extensive and influential critique of the doctrine is thus only one of the most recent of many suggestions that we give it, as Perry Anderson once put it about another staple of the Marxist tradition, a decent burial; the post-Marxists did not bother to wait for the family's permission. It is one thing, however, to drop the matter altogether; but quite another to find a better and more satisfactory *substitute* for it, as Williams tries to do by proposing the Gramscian notion of hegemony. What happens is that in so far as the new idea proves to be an adequate substitute, and performs the functions of the old one in a suitable way, all of the arguments against the old concept return in force against the new one; whereas if it turns out to be relatively unassailable, what gradually dawns on us is that it is not a substitute at all, but a wholly new and different idea. (Much the same can be observed about proposals to substitute for the old and shopworn concept of ideology any number of new terms and ideas, such as discourse, practice, episteme, and the like.) My own position has always been that everything changes when you grasp base-and-superstructure not as a full-fledged theory in its own right, but rather as the name for a problem, whose solution is always a unique, ad hoc invention.

But we must initially separate the figuration of the terms base and superstructure – only the initial shape of the problem – from the type of efficacity or causal law it is supposed to imply. *Überbau* and *Basis*, for example, which so often suggest to people a house and its foundations, seem in fact to have been railroad terminology and to have designated the rolling stock and the rails respectively, something which suddenly jolts us into a rather different picture of ideology and its effects. Engels's notion of 'reciprocal interaction', meanwhile, sounds like the positivistic science textbooks of his day; while Gramsci's military and strategic conceptions of 'hegemony' seem far enough removed from the placid landscape of those older Second International dwellings and foundations. Benjamin suggested, in the *Passagenwerk*, that the superstructure might be thought to *express* the base – thus giving us a kind of linguistic model (albeit a prestructuralist one). It would not be doing violence to Sartre's thought, meanwhile, to suggest that for him the *situation* (in the multidimensional class and psychoanalytic senses he gave to that term) stood as the infrastructure to which the act of 'free' choice brought a superstructural response and solution. But if we stress the limiting force of the situation and minimize the creative features of the freedom inventing itself within it, we then have something closer to Marx's own remarks on the relationship between ideologues and class-fractions in *The Eighteenth Brumaire*, from which the elaborate Lukácsean system of ideological epistemology in *History and Class Consciousness* subsequently derives.

Meanwhile, we have here essentially been concerned to argue that Adorno's stereoscopic conception of the coexistence of the universal and the particular constitutes his particular version of the base/superstructure opposition, since the universal (concept, system, totality, exchange system itself) is the immediately unknowable infrastructure, while the particular stands as the act or event of consciousness or culture that seems to be our only individual reality, at the same time that equivalence controls it like a force field.

But none of these figures (and others are surely conceivable) fatally suggests the operation of any inevitable causal or deterministic law. What is distinctive about the Marxist problematic lies in the centrality of this problem and this question, conceived to be the most urgent and fundamental one – namely, the relationship to be established between 'culture' (or consciousness, or 'existence') and its socioeconomic context, or 'base'. Once the problem is acknowledged, the local solutions may range from the most lawful of all – the most vulgar and demystifying registration of ideological reflex and collective bad faith – to the local hypothesis of a mysterious autonomy of the cultural under certain circumstances, not excluding situations where culture runs on ahead and seems itself for a brief time 'determinant'. It is when one has decided in advance that the relationship to be thus established is no longer an interesting or an important question that we may speak, using Adorno's formula, of throwing the baby out with the bath water.

To be sure, Adorno also means it the other way round, in the spirit of his analysis of Veblen: to see culture as a 'superstructure' is also already to have thrown the baby out with the bath water, for it implies that culture must always be grasped as something like a functional lie, creating 'the illusion of a society worthy of man which does not exist', so that it would be preferable, on such a view, to do away with those illusions and to 'demand that relationships be entirely reduced to their material origin, ruthlessly and openly formed according to the interests of the participants'. Thus a (perfectly proper) denunciation of illusion turns into a new kind of illusion in its own right: 'this notion, like all expostulation about lies, has a suspicious tendency to become itself ideology'. A Marxian materialism, then, tends under its own momentum towards an anti-aesthetic anti-culturalism in which it oddly meets the *ressentiment* of its fascist opponents:

> Emphasis on the material element, as against the spirit as a lie, gives rise to a kind of dubious affinity with that political economy which is subjected to an immanent criticism, comparable with the complicity between police and underworld. (MM 49/44)

As can be imagined, this is very precisely the kind of paradigmatic situation and contradictory dilemma for which 'negative dialectics' has been devised in the first place:

> If material reality is called the world of exchange value, and any culture whatever refuses to accept the domination of that world, then it is true that such refusal is illusory as long as the existent exists ... [yet] in the face of the lie of the commodity world, even the lie that denounces it becomes a corrective. That culture so far has failed is no justification for furthering its failure. (MM 49/44)

The methodological conclusion, then – a conclusion which holds not merely for *Kulturkritik* but for thinking on all its other levels – is that we must denounce culture (as an idea but also as a phenomenon) all the time we continue to perpetuate it, and perpetuate it while continuing tirelessly to denounce it. It is with culture as with philosophy, which famously 'lived on because the moment to realize it was missed' (ND 15/3); there is, as we shall see, a utopian power in keeping alive the impossible idea of philosophizing (as of producing culture) even while ruthlessly exposing the necessary failure to go on doing it today. (In the same way, according to my own proposal, the stigmatizing term of superstructure needs to be retained in order to remind us of a gap that has to be overcome in some more adequate way than forgetting about it.) For like philosophy, culture is itself marked by the original sin of the division between manual and mental labor:

> Cultural criticism is, however, only able to reproach culture so penetratingly for prostituting itself, for violating in its decline the pure autonomy of the mind, because culture originates in the radical separation of mental and physical work. It is from this separation, the original sin as it were, that culture draws its strength. When culture simply denies the separation and feigns harmonious union, it falls back behind its own notion.[31]

The point of this digression on cultural theory in Adorno has been to emphasize the presence at work within its dilemmas of the same contradictions we have underscored in philosophical thought, in the analysis of the 'concept', which can neither be taken at face value as an autonomous instrument for grasping some Real distinct from it, nor debunked in the fashion of the sociology of knowledge or vulgar *Ideologiekritik* for that dimension of the lie and the illusion which is, in our society, inherent in it. What is not yet clear is what it might mean, in concrete situations, to think by means of a concept which is itself somehow 'false' in its very form. As for the peculiar contradictions in which the sociology of knowledge and sociological critique of culture thereby find themselves imprisoned, these are rather to be grounded in some deeper philosophical notion of the *heteronomy* of critique itself – the paradox of the possible distance of a part, the mind, from the whole of which it is a part – which will be examined later.

Five

'It is an innate peculiarity of philosophical writing', Walter Benjamin once said, in a statement which will be of the greatest significance for us in the present context, 'to confront anew, with every radical turn in thought, the question of *Darstellung*.'[32] This question – that of philosophical *presentation* or *representation*, of the very form of the laying out of philosophical conceptuality in the time of the text, as well as of the traditional genres of that form (Benjamin mentions the Spinozan pseudo-Euclidean 'demonstration', the great nineteenth-century system, the esoteric essay by which mystical doctrine is transmitted, and the scholastic tractatus) – will now return again in Adorno as the clue and the key to the ways by which the philosophical concept, with all its truths and untruths, can be 'set in motion' (to quote Marx's own oblique reference to his *Darstellung*).

The matter of *Darstellung* will also afford some final insight into the status of 'totality', of which we have said both that the concept, in some sense its body serf, reproduces its untruth and its form of domination, and that it is itself somehow unthinkable and unrepresentable, very specifically in our present sense of the word. Yet the isolated thought about anything (what has here and throughout pompously been termed the 'concept') – however accurate and pertinent it may otherwise be – carries its untruth invisibly, within its very form (identity and exchange): talking about it means talking about its content, and adjustments in that remain within a Newtonian world from which the other one lies hidden virtually by definition. It is therefore tempting to suppose that the formal untruth of every individual concept might be driven into visibility by the process of revealing their links and interrelationships with one another. Yet the system that might thereby emerge – something like Hegel's 'objective spirit': the great absolute web of all the error and delusion and passionate conviction held together and believed and spoken at any moment in human history – would that not also (if we begin by denying it validity as an after-image of objective totality) be something like a representation, at best the object of a structural sociology of the epistemes of our period?

Either project – the system of our concepts or the system of the things to which these concepts try to correspond – fatally reintroduces the mirage of system itself, not to speak of the old antithesis between subjective and objective of which we now know at least that, although it cannot be eluded, it cannot be dealt with head on in that immediate form, but must be only provisionally outsmarted by some ruse (to which Adorno's dialectics seemed to provide us with a handbook and an operating manual).

It is as though, in *Negative Dialectics*, these totalizing dilemmas of a systematizing philosophy (it being understood that, owing to its object, genuine philosophy is always somehow driven by that impulse) were to be disarmed by the acting out (or the mimesis) of a kind of pseudo-totality (the shamanistic overtones of this formulation are authorized by the Frazerian tribal speculations included in *Dialectic of Enlightenment*). Pseudo-totality: the illusion of the total system is aroused and encouraged by the systematic links and cross-references established between a range of concepts, while the baleful spell of system itself is then abruptly exorcized by the realization that the order of presentation is non-binding, that it might have been arranged in an utterly different fashion, so that, as in a divinatory cast, all the elements are present but the form of their juxtapositions, the shape of their falling out, is merely occasional. This kind of *Darstellung*, which seeks specifically to undermine its own provisional architectonic, Benjamin called configuration or constellation, terms to which Adorno added the apparently more awkward 'model', offering three formal demonstrations of it in the second half of *Negative Dialectics*.

An initial qualification needs to be set in place, however, before we try to characterize this peculiar structure, and that has to do with the notion of the fragment, so often loosely evoked in connection with Benjamin as much as with Adorno, and sometimes vaguely assimilated to the Nietzschean aphorism when not to Schlegel's aesthetics itself.[33] That this impressionistic notion does not take us very far is indeed already apparent from these comparisons, since there does not on the face of it seem to be much that is fragmentary about a 'simple form' like the aphorism, so powerfully dominated by an aesthetic of closure. That modern thought or experience is somehow 'fragmentary' might be an instructive feature of yet another *Kulturkritik* of modern times, but only if fragmentation is seen as the situation and the dilemma to which modern thought responds, not as one of its general qualities or properties: where in any case the very universality of the phenomenon makes it less than useful as a way of specifying what is distinctive about Adorno or Benjamin. Nor is a short piece like 'Baby with the Bath Water', referred to above, in any meaningful sense fragmentary: it is a complete statement, whose closure is not the least stunning thing about it; while many of the alleged fragments from Benjamin are just that: notes and jottings recovered post-humously, which this writer was accustomed to transform into essays that, however idiosyncratically, obeyed the formal logic of the discursive genre.

Some clarification is surely to be gained by differentiating between the fragmentary and the discontinuous: for this last is a basic fact of life in both Adorno and Benjamin, sometimes foregrounded by the blanks and gaps between the paragraphs, sometimes exacerbated by their very absence and by the wilful elimination (particularly in Adorno) of virtually any paragraph breaks at all, in the towering wall of water of a text that carries us forward across bewildering shifts and changes in its topics and raw material. The distinction imposes itself not least because the notion of the fragmentary seems to designate the object, while that of discontinuity stresses the distance between those objects: the stars that make up a constellation are not normally thought to be 'fragmentary' without a good deal of preliminary metaphorical footwork. That the notion of the configuration, the constellation, or the model demands a correspondingly micro-category seems clear: a way of dealing with the elements or building-blocks fully as dramatically as a snapshot of those heavens from over a great distance does for their relationships. We will return shortly to the way in which the individual 'concept' is positioned in this momentary and provisional 'total system'. Later on, however, the account of the overall formal *Darstellung* of such constellations will be augmented by attention to the 'mimetic' sentences that make it up.

As is well known, Benjamin staged two major demonstrations of this form – one of which, owing to his untimely death, remained 'fragmentary' in the literal sense of that word. These are *The Origin of German Tragic Drama* and the legendary Arcades project or *Passagenwerk* ('Paris – Capital of the Nineteenth Century'), some nine hundred pages of which were finally assembled in book form a few years ago. It is customary to distinguish these two efforts in terms of their philosophical outlook: thus the book on tragic drama, particularly on the strength of that obscure and enigmatic 'Prologue' from which we have already quoted above, is generally described as idealistic, when not somehow mystical in some more thoroughgoing sense; while the Arcades project, on the basis of its raw materials as well as of our biographical knowledge about the

author during this period, is said to be Marxist and materialist and
accounted a 'contribution' to the development of historical materialism,
particularly in the area of cultural historiography. This is all surely right
on some level of generality, although it seems to me to presuppose propositions about belief, intellectual development, and ideological commitment
which are very crude indeed and probably demand rethinking.

   Another such proposition – closely related to those and comparable
for the persistence in it of a very traditional conception of the individual
subject – has to do with 'influence'. That Benjamin had a decisive influence
on Adorno the path-breaking work of Susan Buck-Morss has established
beyond any doubt.[34] But is influence to be understood simply as the
transfer of some new thought from one person's head to another's? In
that case, it might be preferable to talk about the awakening of new
interests (not to say a whole new problematic) in the mind of the individual on the receiving end of the 'influence' in question. Perhaps, however,
Adorno's omnipresent theme of 'mimesis' offers a new way to use this
notion of influence, which designates something that really happens just
as surely as it misinterprets it. 'Influence' in this new sense would then
describe the ways in which the pedagogical figure, by his own praxis,
shows the disciple what else you can think and how much further you
can go with the thoughts you already have; or – to put it another way,
which for us is the same – what else you can *write* and the possibility
of forms of writing and *Darstellung* that unexpectedly free you from
the taboos and constraints of forms learnt by rote and assumed to be
inscribed in the nature of things. This, at any rate, is the way in which
I want to grasp Benjamin's 'influence' on Adorno, as just such a liberation
by mimesis and as the practical demonstration of the possibility of another
kind of writing – which is eventually to say: another kind of thinking.
At that point, then, the putative idealistic content of the book on tragic
drama, as that is contrasted with the 'materialist' content of the Arcades
project, becomes less significant than the conception of philosophical
form they both share, which Benjamin seems to have been able to awaken
in Adorno's mind as a philosophical aesthetic and ambition.

   We must therefore begin again with the notorious 'Epistemo-Critical
Prologue' [*Erkenntniskritische Vorrede*] to *The Origin of German Tragic
Drama*, in order to capture the terms in which, at that time, Benjamin
thought his own writing praxis. The 'Prologue' begins with a fundamental
distinction between truth and knowledge which, although something
like it is everywhere at work in modern thought, has not yet found
its philosophical historian (it is, for example, an inaugural distinction
in many existentialisms, but also at work in oppositions between science
and ideology in the Marxist tradition, and finally finds its echo in Adorno's

differentiation of 'truth-content' from that ideological false consciousness which can be present simultaneously with it, in certain kinds of works; see the example of Wagner below).

This opposition will then gradually be rearticulated along the lines of a form–content distinction between Idea [*Idee*] and Concept [*Begriff*], a distinction which does not return in Adorno although its effects can be strongly felt in him, as I will show. His avoidance of the word *Idea* – we have seen that the notion of the *Concept* is everywhere in his work – easily translates into our own contemporary discomfort with the conceptuality of the transcendent or the metaphysical: something I now propose to express by way of the suggestion that (although Plato is explicitly evoked here) we postpone the facile solution of describing Benjamin's position as 'Platonic', a characterization which at once consigns it to a realm of past thinking virtually by definition inaccessible to us, as does the related category of 'mysticism'. The distinction between Idea and Concept is of course crucial to Kant, and also very much present in Hegel, however dialectically transformed, but it cannot be said to be the most vital and usable part of their heritage. It seems best, therefore, to leave all such traditional connotations aside from the outset, and try to deduce a fresh meaning from Benjamin's own argument.

Concepts stand on the side of things and knowledge of things, Ideas on the side of 'truth'. Concepts are therefore instruments of analysis of phenomena, and also mediations, whereby the empirical realities – otherwise mired in immediate experience and in the here-and-now – somehow gain transmission and access to the realm of truth: so far Kant! Concepts are therefore by their nature somehow always multiple:

> Phenomena do not ... enter into the realm of ideas whole, in their crude empirical state, adulterated by appearances, but only in their basic elements, redeemed. They are divested of their false unity, so that, thus divided, they might partake of the genuine entity of truth. In this their division, phenomena are subordinate to concepts, for it is the latter which effect the resolution of objects into their constitutive elements. (OGT 213-14/33)

It is therefore as though the fundamental mission of the concept were to destroy the apparent unity of ordinary realities, analyzing and disjoining these last into a swarm of concepts which can then be reassembled in some new and unaccustomed way. The individual concepts remain fixed and trained on the multiple aspects of the reality in question; but it seems to be the very fact of their multiplicity (no single one 'equals' the object or can claim 'identity' with it) that lends them their mediatory function, which Benjamin oddly describes in a dual fashion:

Through their mediating role concepts enable phenomena to participate in the existence of ideas. It is this same mediating role which fits them for the other equally basic task of philosophy, the representation [*Darstellung*] of ideas. (OGT 214/34)

If mysticism there be here, it would surely lie in this suggestion that the 'contemplation' of the ideas ('truth') can somehow be disjoined from their presentation or representation in the philosophical text: even if one insisted on distinguishing between thinking on the one hand and writing or language on the other, it would not take much ingenuity or effort to imagine 'thinking' as pre-sketch and trial run (the Heideggerian *Vor-wurf*) of writing, *Darstellung* or expression. In any case Benjamin will shortly take pains to exclude all overtones and suggestions of the contemplative and of that static, intuitive-perceptive *Anschauung* systematically repudiated by Adorno as well in a variety of contexts: meanwhile the tireless emphasis on representation or *Darstellung* which marks the stunning originality of this text would also seem, in advance, to undermine the possibility of some experience of truth that might be separated from its laying out in time and in language:

Knowledge is possession. . . . For the thing possessed, representation is secondary; it does not have prior existence as something representing itself. But the opposite holds good of truth. For knowledge, method is a way of acquiring its object – even by creating it in consciousness, for truth method is self-representation and is therefore immanent in it as a form. (OGT 209/29–30)

With these qualifications, then, we reach the heart of the matter, which is the relationship between *Darstellung* or representation and the Idea. Now suddenly, in a flash of light, the grand formulations are possible and stand revealed:

Ideas are to objects as constellations to stars. This means, in the first place, that they are neither their concepts nor their laws. (OGT 214/34)

The Idea is therefore simply the 'system' of concepts, the relationship between a group of concepts: as such it has no content in its own right, is not a quasi-object (as the concept is) nor the representation of one: 'ideas are not present in the world of phenomena' (OGT 215/35), any more than constellations 'really exist' in the sky. Meanwhile, it becomes clear that philosophical writing or *Darstellung* will consist in tracing the constellation, in somehow drawing the lines between the empirical concepts thus 'configured' together. But the concepts represent *aspects* of empirical reality, while the Idea (and its philosophical notation) represents the *relationships* between them. We must also stress the way in which Benjamin's characteristic language here seems to ward off and to evade the temptation of the subjective, to forestall in advance (without in any way resolving them satisfactorily) rhetorical questions that might reposition such an 'Idea' within the human mind (does not the constellation exist only as a projection of the human viewer? And is not the relationship between phenomena or between the concepts of phenomena, essentially an achievement, or at least an operation, of the mind itself?). The pseudo-Platonic language, then, might be seen as a way of going around behind the great Kantian 'solution' and somehow preempting it.

But now a doubt still remains and we need to get some handle on the content of these mysterious Ideas, whose form now seems clear enough. Despite the warning – and in the absence of any examples or illustrations – the slippage back into Plato still seems fatally to impose itself, and we continue to wonder whether such Ideas are not finally to be grasped 'merely' as the old Platonic abstractions: of the Good or the Beautiful, or of Justice (or Kant's freedom, God and immortality of the soul). But this is not at all the kind of philosophizing Benjamin has in mind, although he takes a peculiar detour to outflank it. For the next topic in the 'Prologue' then again raises the mirage of Benjaminian mysticism with a vengeance, as it restages the archetypal motif of magical language: the act of naming, in which, not unexpectedly, Adam reappears to displace Plato:

> The structure of truth ... demands a mode of being which in its lack of intentionality resembles the simple existence of things, but which is superior in its permanence. Truth is not an intent which takes its determinations and characteristics from empirical reality; rather truth consists in the power that stamps its essence on that empirical reality in the first place. The state of being, beyond all phenomenality, to which alone this power belongs, is that of the name. This determines the manner in which ideas are given [or are revealed as data, *Gegebenheit*]. But they are not so much given in a primordial language as in a primordial form of perception, in which words possess the nobility of their naming function, unimpaired by the operations of knowledge as such. (OGT 216/36)

> Ideas are displayed, without intention, in the act of naming, and they have to be renewed in philosophical contemplation. (OGT 217/37)

Now we can move more quickly; as the context of the 'Prologue' suggests, and as Benjamin will tell us in another page or so, 'tragedy' is just such a 'name' and an 'Idea', and will here become the object of a properly philosophical *Darstellung*, the tracing of an enormous constellation out of 'empirical' concepts. In hindsight, we also know that a similar name, a similar idea, is somehow inherent in the notion of the 'arcade' in the later project. Suddenly, the traditional Platonic repertoire of abstractions – whatever their social and historical content may have been in Plato's day – is radically transformed into a flood of modern 'ideas' of a far more concrete and historical type, such as *capital* itself, or bureaucracy, or dictatorship, or even Nature or History, in their modern senses, or finally 'Paris – Capital of the Nineteenth Century'!

These new 'ideas' are not to be seen as some 'fall' of the Platonic problematic into the secular dynamics of modern times. Rather, these new abstractions – like Adorno's system or totality, they are at one and the same time utterly non-empirical (not given as knowledge or immediately) and the realest matters to us in the world, the matters which constrain us the most absolutely – pose new 'epistemological' problems to which Benjamin's deliberately archaic solution provides a fresh answer that is retained in *Negative Dialectics*. The discursive context of the Benjamin 'Prologue', therefore, would be more adequately grasped by juxtaposing it with efforts like Weber's cumbersome attempt to theorize the sociological 'ideal types' than with the Platonic or even Hegelian predecessors in the older philosophical tradition.

Before documenting Adorno's own faithfulness to this notion of the constellation or configuration, a few final features of Benjamin's conception need to be set in place. First, owing very precisely to his sense of the originality and the non-traditional nature of his proposal, Benjamin will seek sharply to differentiate it from traditional conceptions of abstraction – such as the general and the particular, or the typical – which would draw his whole argument about the Idea and the concepts back into familiar logical categories. The individual concepts, for example, which register various aspects of the empirical reality and whose configuration makes up its Idea, far from being somehow representative, characteristic, typical or average, must register its extremes; only in its ultimate, convulsive manifestations can the real be grasped, not in its least common denominators (OGT 215/35). This perverse emphasis on the atypical and on the dissonance between 'species' and 'genus' would be enough to distance Benjamin decisively from both Plato and Weber; its spirit can be most immediately grasped in the literary problematic of the book on tragic drama, where it makes more sense to approach a genre from its most uncharacteristic and extreme productions than in its low-level routine reproductions. But it will also be appropriate to translate this methodological insistence of Benjamin into Adorno's very different language, thereby stressing the way in which conceptuality in our time necessarily approaches the nominalistic, and fastens under its own momentum on the unique cases and events – rather than, as before, to their pallid abstractions, which have for us become empty words.

Words indeed pose the second question on which we must dwell for a moment; for it does not seem to me overingenious but indispensable, and still very much in Benjamin's own spirit, to augment his account with a further remark on the way in which the language of the Idea necessarily overlaps that of the concepts. What is absolutely undesirable is to be misled by the terms of the discussion back into the effort of isolating a group of Idea-words which are distinct from those used in conceptuality: such a sacred list would return us, in all kinds of ways, to the Platonic system. For it is obvious, when we begin to think about it concretely, that the same words will have to change places frequently. The study of a certain kind of existential metaphysic, for example, may well involve the posing, as Idea, of the objective existence of the 'tragic' (as in Unamuno's *Tragic Sense of Life* or Raymond Williams's *Modern Tragedy*). But 'tragic' here in Benjamin simply designates a feature of the reality of the form, perhaps an extreme one, which is reformulated into one of the group of concepts that will at length be organized into the 'name' of the overall phenomenon – that is to say, the Idea. Thus, although the book on tragic drama itself certifies the existence of an Idea of 'tragedy', the concept of the 'tragic' in our contrasting example has nothing to do with that 'Idea' and operates on a different level altogether.

In the same way, it might be found useful to come at some general idea of the market by way of a concept of the 'free' (as in free trade, freedom of contract, and the like): such a concept would take its place in a whole constellation, but would have little enough to do with that very different thing, the Idea of freedom (as we will in fact shortly observe Adorno to map it out). We can in fact appeal to Benjamin's own text for authority to add this new methodological complication to his account: for in a passage already quoted above, he has specified the word for an Idea to be very precisely a *name*, and now we can better understand why the matter of naming is a crucial step in his argument and in his differentiation between ideas and concepts. In the Idea, as we recall, 'words possess the nobility of their naming function, unimpaired by the operations of knowledge as such'. This is to say that 'freedom' is a word now used as the name of an Idea; whereas the attribute 'free' does not involve such naming, but stands as a non-naming word that has a function in the process of knowledge and of knowing the object.

Finally, it will be necessary to complete this account with Benjamin's idiosyncratic description of the relationships between Ideas as such. This remains an astronomical figure, very precisely to distinguish it from the relationship between concepts to each other which was described as a constellation. Here, however, among the Ideas, autonomy reigns along with harmony:

> These latter can stand up on their own in perfect isolation, as mere words
> never can. And so ideas subscribe to the law which states: all essences exist
> in complete and immaculate independence, not only from phenomena, but
> especially from each other. Just as the harmony of the spheres depends on
> the orbits of stars which do not come into contact with each other, so the
> existence of the *mundus intelligibilis* depends on the unbridgeable distance
> between pure essences. Every idea is a sun and is related to other ideas just
> as suns are related to each other. (OGT 217–18/37)

They are related to each other in so far as each one is also a star; yet
a star that hangs like a sun in any particular heaven becomes thereby
incomparable, the horizon of a whole world and the only true reality
or referent, as Derrida once put it. Within that hegemony, only the
one unique sun is conceivable and cannot be thought together in the
same breath as the glittering swarm knowledge vainly identifies as other
suns. Concepts are those distant stars whose juxtaposition can be grasped
in the figure of the constellation; Ideas, meanwhile, although multiple
and equally discontinuous, offer no analogous standpoint beyond them
from which to grasp their star-like coexistence: which is to say, returning
to the question from which we began, that they cannot be yoked together
in the form of philosophical system, and that the philosophical exposure
to any single Idea blots the others out with its light. The discontinuities
of *Negative Dialectics* are therefore already implicit in this Benjaminian
figure – which, however, returns in a somewhat more explicit form in
the realm of Adorno's aesthetics, as we shall see later on.

Six

Adorno has other, alternate figures for the constellation as the form of philosophical *Darstellung* – even though this last is centrally positioned in *Negative Dialectics* (163–8/161–6), where it is more loosely celebrated as a method that unpacks the historical content of the *concept* (as has been observed, Adorno abandons the vocabulary of Idea and returns to a more general Hegelian usage):

> Cognition of the object in its constellation is cognition of the process stored in the object. As a constellation theoretical thought circles the concept it would like to unseal, hoping that it will fly open like the lock of a well-guarded safe-deposit box: in response, not to a single key or a single number, but to a combination of numbers. (ND 166/163)

That the contents of this box will not look like the findings of a 'history of ideas' any more than those of a 'sociology of knowledge' we have already assured ourselves. Meanwhile, since Benjamin's modern readers have always been perplexed by his insistence on the 'timelessness' – about the Ideas, of which we have tried to argue that they are in fact social and historical in nature – it is worth observing the way in which Adorno here uses the spatiality of the figure of the constellation to argue explicitly against 'linear causality', but in the name of history itself (he is evoking Weber as an unconscious practitioner of the constellation method):

> But the capitalist system's increasingly integrative trend, the fact that its elements entwine into a more total context of functions, makes the old question about *cause* – as opposed to *constellation* – more and more precarious. (ND 168/166)

Meanwhile, the sciences themselves 'probably operate not so much with causal chains as with causal networks' (ND 263/266). This however, is a rather different kind of timelessness than the eternal Platonic one; and it seems perfectly proper to associate it with the name it has received in another compartment of contemporary thought – to wit, that of the *synchronic*, which does not imply any stasis of time or history, but rather a thinking which does not involve the temporal as such: timeless in its suspension of the category of time and temporality, rather than in its otherworldly invariance. Having gone that far, we might as well identify this account of causal networks and constellations with Althusserian structural causality: an intersection whose significance is reinforced by Althusser's interest in the problem of *Darstellung* in Marx; without, however, having the same kind of formal results for his own philosophical practice as those we shall observe in Adorno.

There are, however, other, non-astronomical figures for that practice which are no less instructive. They need to be prefaced by a proposal: I think it would be helpful for those of us who write on Adorno to eschew with all rigor and self-discipline, and for an indefinite period, those inevitable musical analogies that have become virtually a convention of Adorno criticism, save in instances where they are absolutely unavoidable. Such is unexpectedly the case right now: *Negative Dialectics* in fact offers three full-dress demonstrations of what we have been calling the constellation method; these are the three concluding monograph-length studies of freedom, history, and 'metaphysics'. These chapters are however explicitly designated as 'models', a term that has always seemed to me aesthetically and philosophically inappropriate in this otherwise linguistically very self-conscious writer, whose relationship to the reified inertia of sheer terminology is normally subtle and alert, gun-shy and ever on the point of dialectically stampeding. 'Model', however, strikes one as just such an inert term, and one borrowed from the most reified forms of scientific and social-scientific discourse at that: the discipline of sociology is of course always present in Adorno's mind, even during his most formal philosophizing, but what is present of it is more often its constitutive limits and the mark left on it by history in the form of specialization, rather than its right to supersede philosophy, particularly in matters of terms and names.

At best, it might seem as though the awkwardness of this word reflected a malaise in Adorno's practice which he himself generally displaced onto other people (most notably Kant and Sartre, in the 'Freedom' chapter, ND 222-5/223-6) – namely, the dilemma of the philosophical *example*, whose optionality immediately disqualifies the authority of the concept it was supposed to illustrate. But it is difficult to read these three 'model' chapters as anything but 'examples' of the new method, thereby at once transforming it into that 'methodology' which it sought above all to avoid becoming. A star can no doubt serve as the example of 'starness' generally; but the sun cannot be an example of anything. The term 'model' might then, unconsciously, acknowledge that kind of failure, by the very way in which it draws attention to itself.

Everything changes, however, when we discover that the word 'model' has in fact for Adorno a specifically *musical* provenance, and was appropriated by Schoenberg from a loose and common-sense acceptation as 'exercises' (one of his books is called *Models for Beginners*) for an increasingly specialized and articulated meaning, which will be instructive for us here. Model, in later Schoenberg, designates the raw material of a specific composition or its thematic point of departure: which is to say, for twelve-tone music, the specific row itself, the particular order and configuration of the twelve notes of the scale which, chosen and arranged in advance, *becomes* the composition, in so far as this last is 'nothing more' than an elaborate series of variations and permutations – both vertical and horizontal – of that starting point. What in classical music was separated – the initial 'themes' and their later 'development' – is here reunited. Speaking of the moment of Beethoven in *Philosophy of Modern Music*, Adorno has the following to say:

> Now, in association with development, variation serves in the establishment of universal, concretely unschematic relationships. Variation becomes dynamic. It is true that it still strongly maintains the identity of its initial thematic material – what Schoenberg calls its 'model'. Everything remains 'the same'. But the meaning of this identity reveals itself as non-identity. The initial thematic material is so arranged that preserving it is tantamount to transforming it. There is in fact a way in which it no longer exists 'in itself', but only with a view towards the possibility of the whole composition. (PNM 57/55–6)

If the philosophical analogy we have attributed to Adorno on the strength of this new meaning of the word 'model' is accurate, then a certain earlier or classical philosophy might also be described in much the same way, as the ostensible separation of an 'initial thematic material' – the philosophical idea or problem – and its ulterior development – philosophical argumentation and judgement. This separation means that the concept in question precedes the philosophical text, which then 'thinks' about it, criticizes and modifies it, solves or refutes the problem: such a text presumably has a narrative time not unlike that of sonata form, where something climactic and decisive finally happens – the climax in the philosophical argument is reached – after which a coda shuts down the process by drawing the conclusions. (In the passage just quoted, of course, Adorno characteristically raises the valences of this account, since he also wants to argue that something like Schoenberg's solution is already secretly at work in Beethoven as well: just as one might also want to argue that certain crucial texts of classical philosophy are already 'negative dialectics' without being aware of it.)

What we must retain, however, is the implication that 'twelve-tone' philosophy will do its work differently from the classical text: the concept or problem will not be independent of the *Darstellung* but already at one with it; there will be no conceptual events, no 'arguments' of the traditional kind that lead to truth climaxes; the text will become one infinite variation in which everything is recapitulated at every moment; closure, finally, will be achieved only when all the possible variations have been exhausted. It does not seem superfluous to add, in the light of the numerological obsessions of artists Adorno admired, like Thomas Mann or Schoenberg himself, that – most uncharacteristically for this author – the third and final 'model' of *Negative Dialectics*, on metaphysics, is divided into 'chapters' and printed in the form of twelve numbered sections.

Seven

All of this, however, still defines the larger movement of Adorno's way with concepts, the way in which a twelve-tone philosophy plays out the configurations and the constellations it finds in its path and invents all at once. The texture of this philosophy is, however, not yet reached by such description, which might also, as we have said, obtain in some measure for the Benjaminian projects that preceded it. Yet what strikes one as radically original in Adorno, and as a practice and a philosophical micro-politics that has finally very little in common with Benjamin any longer, is his deployment of the dialectical sentence itself, to which even the energy of Marx's great chiasmatic syntactical acts offers but a distant family likeness. The truest precursor here would seem to be not Benjamin, and certainly not Nietzsche, but the extraordinary Austrian rhetorician Karl Kraus, not so much untranslatable as shamelessly ignored in English, perhaps because the greatest of his self-producing utterances – which rise from the journalistic immediacy of the week-by-week Vienna of his day and of his private journal, *Die Fackel* – tend to rend their contexts and to blast apart the essay framework that offered the pretext for their production, so that Kraus's writings cannot really be read, but only his isolated rhetorical periods:

> In these great times which I knew when they were this small; which will become small again, provided they have time left for it; and which, because in the realm of organic growth no such transformation is possible, we had better call fat times and, truly, hard times as well; in these times in which things are happening that could not be imagined and in which what can no longer be imagined must happen, for if one could imagine it, it would not happen; in these serious times which have died laughing at the thought

that they might become serious; which, surprised by their own tragedy, are
reaching for diversion and, catching themselves redhanded, are groping for
words; in these loud times which boom with the horrible symphony of actions
which produce reports and of reports which cause actions; in these times
you should not expect any words of my own from me – none but these
words which barely manage to prevent silence from being misinterpreted.[35]

What Adorno found here, I want to suggest, is the very paradigm of
an expressive syntax, in which the actual machinery of sentence structure
is itself pressed into service, in all its endless variety, and mobilized to
convey meaning far beyond its immediate content as mere communication and denotation. To Kraus, far more than to Adorno himself, might
well apply Benjamin's idea that 'speech communicates itself',[36] and perhaps also his idiosyncratic notion of language as 'non-representational
mimesis'.

It is not clear to what degree Adorno discovered the possibilities of
the notion of mimesis in Benjamin's infrequent use of it: what is certain
is that he went on to make it mean much more than Benjamin did
– perhaps too much more (involving at length a whole anthropology
in *Dialectic of Enlightenment*) and at the same time something just slightly
distinct, just slightly different. If anything, comparability is afforded by
a different Benjaminian word and notion: for nothing in the older writer
offers quite so many purely formal analogies to the peculiar status of
mimesis in Adorno – a foundational concept never defined nor argued
but always alluded to, by name, as though it had preexisted all the texts
– as Benjamin's notion of *aura*, which otherwise has nothing to do with
it.[37] It is as though, in both these writers, a kind of repressed foundational
longing found its way back into their writing by way of these magical
terms, which are evoked to explain everything without ever themselves
being explained, until at length we become persuaded that they could
never themselves be explained or grounded, and mark the root of some
archaic private obsession, as in the Ur-sounds and names of the great
modern poets. 'Aura' and 'mimesis' are therefore the hostages given to
the unique and the particular which free an extraordinary universalizing
thought and language to go about its business.

Yet there is one sense of the otherwise protean term 'mimesis' which
Negative Dialectics allows us to specify and to use: the price for this
new applicability lying, to be sure, in a reduction and a specialization
that radically cut it off from Adorno's other deployments of the charged
word. At the local climax of his discussion of causality, in a remarkable
passage that would merit the closest commentary, Adorno complexly
rehearses the dialectic of subject and object at work in that very 'dialectic

of enlightenment' that produced the concept of causality in the first place, as a handle on the objective relations, hierarchies, interactions, dominations and subordinations at work in the world of things. Projection (a later and degraded psychic phenomenon, developed at the greatest length in the 'Anti-Semitism' chapter of *Dialectic of Enlightenment*) is not at all what Adorno has in mind when he evokes a certain necessary 'affinity' between the subject and things that is presupposed by any form of knowledge: enlightenment builds on this just as surely as it wishes to exterminate it:

> Consciousness knows only so much about its other as the latter resembles it, but not by extirpating itself along with that resemblance. ... The less it tolerates any affinity to things, to that degree its drive towards identity increases ruthlessly. (ND 267/270)

All these considerations would be at work in a genuine critique of the concept of causality, about which he also says that it is a privileged place to observe the operation of identity on the non-identical. And then he says this about the concept itself:

> In it thinking fulfills its mimicry of the spell it had itself cast on things; it does so on the very threshold of a sympathy before which that spell would vanish altogether. Between the subjective component of the concept of causality and its objects there exists an 'elective affinity' that is in fact a premonition of what happened to those objects at the hands of that subject. (ND 267/270)

This notion of a mimicry – a strong form of mimesis – at work within the very technical concepts of science and philosophy themselves, a mimetic impulse that embarrasses them and which they seek to deny (in the strong Freudian sense), if not to repress altogether, seems to me to offer useful clues to Adorno's own philosophical practice, which would then in this sense constitute a virtually psychoanalytic acting out or talking cure, *abreaction*, of precisely that repressed mimetic impulse, allowing us once again to grasp some older relationship of the mimicking subject to its other or nature: a relationship we cannot reinstate or reinvent as such in 'modern times', any more than the Freudian therapy invites us really to become children again, yet whose recovery by way of memory – indeed, whose anamnesis – is therapeutic in its own right.

Whether philosophy can actually do that, whether the most powerful or formally ingenious or evocative philosophical sentence structure can intervene with effects of this kind in the reader's mind, is open to some doubt; nor is that doubt reduced or even usefully articulated by the way in which Adorno, following Benjamin's strong lead, systematically excludes issues of reception from his aesthetics and therefore, implicitly, from his account of the power of the texts of 'critical theory' as well. Or rather, he disposes of a powerful account of the refusal to receive – that is to say, of resistance – in the Nietzschean doctrine of *ressentiment* (see Part II, below); as for reception, however, or the possibility in our time for a subject to take a critical stance in the first place, this is inscribed as a description of the uncharacteristic trajectory of the individual subject, and generally evoked as the anachronistic survival of an older individual-ism and an older set of class attitudes into the new world of the total system and the 'administered' or bureaucratic society (ND 50–51/40–41) – that is to say that the possibility of reception is generally explained as the accident of class privileges that isolate the critical subject from the tendential movement of social and systemic *Gleichschaltung*.

None the less, and leaving its possible effects aside, it would seem plaus-ible to examine Adorno's sentences in terms of their mimetic component: something often meant anyway when philosophical practice is loosely described in terms of aesthetics:

> To represent the mimesis it supplanted, the concept has no other way than to adopt something mimetic in its own conduct, without abandoning itself to it utterly. (ND 26/14)

The force of this will not adequately be felt, however, unless we under-score the qualifier and remind ourselves of Adorno's absolute hostility to the assimilation of philosophy to aesthetic writing, to play, to art, to *belles-lettres* generally; this absolute differentiation of philosophical thought from artistic production – most unseasonable in the present intellectual climate – is the price to be paid for the detection of those features of the philosophical argument which do have something in com-mon with artistic practice:

> The freedom in a thought can be found there where it transcends that object of its thinking to which it has bound itself in resistance. It is a freedom that follows the expressive drive of the subject. The need to lend suffering a voice is the precondition of all truth. For suffering is the objectivity that weighs the subject down; what it experiences as its most subjective capacity, expression, is objectively mediated. (ND 29/17–18)

It will be seen that here already, in the philosophic defense of a mimetic moment in philosophy, the mimetic has begun to act itself out in Adorno's language. This is something that can be clarified by substituting a more recent terminology for that of mimesis, a terminology which was not available in its contemporary forms to Adorno and which, like all transcoding, imposes a certain interpretive violence on his thought: namely, the language of *narrative*. For on the face of it, and beyond the Cratylism of this or that isolated word or name (as, for example, in poetic diction), it is not obvious how sentences could be said to be mimetic in the first place, without making a laborious detour through the language system by which they are produced, a detour that ultimately involves a comparative view of the various possible structures of human language. Such a detour, which causes the work of a Humboldt or a Whorf to rise up like an immense monument or mountain range, then permits the analyst to grasp the unique syntactical spirit of a given language or system of languages as one form of the mimesis of the relationship of those speakers to being and to the world in general (the tense system, presence or absence of subjects and objects, nomination, etc.). Without that global perspective (which might be implicit in some attempt to grasp the relationship of the dialectic to the structure of the German language, say) the mimetic possibilities of the individual sentence can be grasped only as the way in which they tend to form themselves into micro-narratives, and as it were to act out the content of what is in them abstractly grasped as philosophical thinking or argument.

This tendency is, however, surely very strong in Adorno himself, who supplements the content of his philosophical conceptions with a well-nigh gestural picture of the interaction of their components. The conception of enlightenment – that is to say, Reason generally and the inner drive of all abstract thinking in particular – as a form of domination obviously yields in advance a rich narrative schema, with *actants* and motives and violent and dramatic events: something that will be closest to the surface when we evoke the inaugural moments of Western reason itself, as in the following remark:

> Whenever something that is to be conceived flees from identity with the concept, this last will be forced to take extreme steps to prevent any doubts as to the seamlessness, closure and accuracy of the thought-product from arising. (ND 33/22)

As if this were not already ominous enough, the micro-narrative now takes on even more precise detail, and the mists of the homology lift to disclose the jungle itself:

> This system [rationalism], in which the sovereign mind imagined itself to have been transfigured and transformed, has its Ur-history in the pre-mental, in the animal life of the species. Predators are voracious; the tiger-leap on their prey is difficult and often dangerous. Additional impulses may be necess-

ary for the beast to dare it. These fuse with hunger's unpleasure into a rage at the victim, expression of which then usefully terrifies and cripples this last. In the progress towards humanity this process is rationalized by way of projection. (ND 33/22)

This is a picture whose philosophical argument may be thought to presuppose a certain anthropology (we have already expressed a certain discomfort with these features of Adorno's thought) or on the other hand, those anthropological components might well be seen, in Russian Formalist fashion, as the content Adorno had to talk himself into in order to write vivid sentences of this kind. In that case, the more interesting prolongation of this dimension of this work – not 'anthropology' as a preconception about human nature, but the entire, truly philosophical meditation on the relationship between human history and natural history – would be something like what the Formalists called a 'motivation of the device', a belief that justifies your own aesthetic after the fact. It is at any rate in the 'model' on natural history that we find the final twist in the micro-narrative outlined above, a reappropriation of the narrative for conceptual and philosophical uses, above all in the sentence that caps the discussion of the relationship of the 'instinct' of self-preservation (for Adorno the primal curse of our own fallen world) to the structures of consciousness and, indeed, to 'false consciousness' itself: 'if the lion had a consciousness, his rage at the antelope he wants to eat would be ideology' (348/342).

It is therefore the mimetic component of the individual philosophical sentence – its tendency to narrativize the conceptual – that finally springs the isolated abstract concept out of its bad identity and allows it, as it were, to be thought from the inside and from the outside all at once: an ideational content transformed mimetically into a quasi-narrative representation. This micro-work of the sentence on the isolated concept is, then, what undermines its apparent rational autonomy and pre-forms it (to hark back to the musical analogy) for its multiple positions in the larger movement of the constellation or the 'model'. The mimetic or the narrative may be thought to be a kind of homeopathic strategy in which, by revealing the primal movement of domination hidden away within abstract thought, the venom of abstraction is neutralized, allowing some potential or utopian truth-content to come into its own.

Is it necessary to add that this significance in Adorno of a mimetic mode of philosophizing by no means marks him as a mere 'littérateur'; it in no way implies the substitution of aesthetics for philosophy, since the mimetic impulse is common to both, but takes distinct forms in each. In any case, in *Negative Dialectics* Adorno argued at some length against the supersession of philosophy by literature ('no matter how hard we try for a linguistic articulation of the historicity of our topics, the words we have to use remain concepts' (ND 62/52–3).

Yet the form of the sentences must now also be seen as a form of philosophizing in its own right:[38] we shall see later, for example, the unexpected significance of that animal imagery which expressed the imperialism of the concept in the illustration just given (it sounds, indeed, the theme of the whole dimension of natural history as that is part and parcel of Adorno's philosophical 'system'). The same must now be said about the economic images and figures that lend such closure to sentences thereby transformed into veritable aphorisms. The comparison, which stages the particular with metaphoric vividness, also includes a whole economics, and this turns largely, throughout Adorno, on the relationship between individual subjects and the tendential laws of late or monopoly capital. We have already noted one proto-economic area of philosophical significance in the notion of the concept and identity, which correspond to Marx's account of value in simple commodity exchange. A whole second dimension of economic logic, however, turns on the more complex and dialectical relationship between universal and particular, which it may be convenient to separate into two general groups, the first having to do with the division of labor within the individual subject, while the second dramatizes the precarious position of individuation itself under monopoly conditions.

Thus, to take this second group first, the traditional image of the rebel is not merely objectively precarious but perhaps even subjectively illusory. Of the Hollywood rebel, for example – they seem to have had Orson Welles in mind – Adorno and Horkheimer observe that even his dissidence can be accommodated as a style or an eccentricity: 'Once his particular brand of deviation from the norm has been registered and classified by the culture industry, he belongs to it as the land reformer belongs to capitalism' (DA, 118/132). Outflanked, 'coopted', the most revolutionary peasant demands now reintegrated into a larger market strategy that seeks very precisely to break up the great estates in order to create private property and to foster a henceforth landless proletariat – the heroic simile includes this whole epic process, which constitutes a capsule textbook on agrarian reform as seen by Marxist analysis; but it also includes a preview of a whole newer film history for which stylistic innovation of the Welles type is considered a form of marketing try-out that allows Hollywood to modify and modernize its technique, while drawing innovation itself back inside the stereotypical product.[39] On the other hand, all of this can be rewritten in terms of the first mode of analysis mentioned above, the internal division of labor: 'No wrestling match is without a referee: the whole brawl has been staged by society internalized in the individual, which both supervises the struggle and takes part in it' (MM 175/134).

The more standard case, however, is that of the individual subject as anachronism: the comparison is with small business in the age of the great trusts and monopolies, and just as 'the possibility of becoming a subject in the economy, an entrepreneur or a proprietor, has been completely liquidated' (DA 137/153), so also the psychic subject, the producer of autonomous art or independent action or thought, is also eliminated; or becomes, where it survives, a precarious holdover, a sport of nature:

> When the big industrial interests incessantly eliminate the economic basis for moral decision, partly by eliminating the independent economic subject, partly by taking over the self-employed tradesmen, partly by transforming workers into cogs in the labor unions, the possibility of reflection must also die out. (DA 177–8/198)

But this economic homology – now a full-dress theory of the psyche under monopoly capitalism (see esp. DA 181–2/202–3) – opens up a number of directions. It can, for example, be pressed into service for an account of the nature and quality of the residual individual potentiality under monopoly:

> The Utopia of the qualitative – the things which through their difference and uniqueness cannot be absorbed into the prevalent exchange relationships – takes refuge under capitalism in the traits of fetishism. (MM 155/120)

In the same way, but more succinctly, the more familiar theme of reification is thus laid down: 'The more reification there is, all the more subjectivism will there be' (W92/74). (The maxim, Adorno adds, 'holds good for orchestration just as much as for epistemology'.)

But the homology can also be interrogated for its own conditions of possibility, at which point the relationship between the individual psyche, private property and time itself slowly comes into view: 'historically, the notion of time is itself formed on the basis of the order of ownership' (MM 98/79; see also ND 362/369). In this form, however, the sentence remains a kind of abstract affirmation, a mere philosophical proposition of a relatively static kind. It does not become a mimetic figure until the 'subject' enters the force field of late capitalism where the association between personal identity and private property threatens to come apart: at that point a tendency becomes visible, whose story can be told:

The individual has been, as it were, merely invested with property by the class, and those in control are ready to take it back as soon as universalization of property seems likely to endanger its principle, which is precisely that of withholding. (MM 77/64)

The figure can finally produce its own global theory out of itself, and as a figure for its own existence: this is what happens when, in one of the most stunning of the *Minima Moralia*, the figures of the tendential restriction of the individual subject, and its increasing penetration by the social division of labor, rejoin the language of *Capital* itself, and Adorno can speak of an 'organic composition of capital' within the psychic subject: that is to say, an increasingly higher percentage of mental machinery and instrumental operations as opposed to living human labor, to the free subjectivity whose role is ever more diminished. Now human creativity shrinks to machine-minding and reason to a fitful organic impulse: 'the will to live finds itself dependent on the denial of the will to live: self-preservation annuls all life in subjectivity' (MM 308/229).

But this particular figure explicitly corrects its own misreading: this is not, Adorno specifies, the thesis about 'the 'mechanization' of man', which 'thinks of him as something static which, through an "influence" from outside, an adaptation to conditions of production external to him, suffers certain deformations'. Rather, the figure is itself dialectical and includes Marx's analysis of the organic composition of capital as such.

These 'dialectical tropes', then, mobilize on the level of the individual sentence the relations between the universal, or the totality, and the particular, that have been described in an earlier chapter. They confirm what was argued there: that the term corresponding to the totality or social system is not merely presupposed in the form of inert knowledge or preexistent belief: rather it is itself specified by what happens to its opposite number, the individual subject. These figures therefore yield information about a specific moment of the operation of the social totality in its monopoly period: the adherence, indeed, to the 'state capitalist' model of the economy,[40] a model overtaken by the development of multinational capitalism today and no longer current, permits a kind of measurement of the 'damaged subject' we no longer dispose of, a measurement whose 'registering apparatus' includes images of the constriction of space, of tendential exclusion, of the obliteration of possibility and creative novelty by intensified repetition and sameness. This process could be registered in narrative or mimetic form by Adorno (and Horkheimer) because they lived through the transitional period in which smaller business and entrepreneurship were once visible, so that their absence at a later stage remains a dramatic symptom, still perceptible to the observer.

This is of course an advantage over our own period, in which social homogenization is far more complete, the past has been more definitively disposed of, and this kind of temporal or modernist dialectic seems inoperative.

Eight

In fact, far from being an 'open' or aleatory composition, *Negative Dialectics* imitates – as over a great distance, with radically different building materials, and in that 'prodigious erosion of contours' of which Gide, following Nietzsche, liked to speak – the plan of Kant's *Critique of Pure Reason.* (I am tempted to say that it *wraps* it as a postmodern reconstruction – glass shell, arches – wraps an older monument; except that Adorno is not postmodern and the more fitting analogy would be what Thomas Mann does to Goethe's *Faust.*) The uses and abuses of what we call dialectic, what one can and cannot properly think with it, and in particular the relationship to the logical forms of identity and non-identity – all this stands in for Kant's central concern with Reason itself and its legitimate and illegitimate functions.

The illegitimacy of transcendental speculation, then; the dogmatic or theological wandering among entities we cannot know (in Kant's for us now antiquated usage, the transcendental *dialectic*) – in the secular world of the mid twentieth century this place of error, temptation and confusion is clearly that of Heidegger, to whom once again a substantial section will be devoted (which we will not particularly examine here, even though a hostile critic has suggested that Adorno's principled antagonism to Heidegger, from the earliest years onward, was 'the one fixed point' in his philosophizing[41]). Kant's other asymmetrically positioned adversary, empiricism – whose overcoming was famously so important and so full of content for him – can in Adorno's period only be that far more dehumanized thing he calls positivism, something that plays a significant role in his arguments rather as a historical situation (sometimes also called nominalism) than as a significant set of philosophical positions (like Hume's) with which he has to come to terms.

Meanwhile, the structure of the 'dialectic of enlightenment' itself, as a deduction both derived and derivational, and the enigmatic concept of 'mimesis', constitute allusions at least as omnipresent, and often as inexplicable, as Kant's categories and schemata; while finally the three great transcendental ideas, whose essential unthinkability is as exhaustively demonstrated as their indispensability is affirmed – Immortality, Freedom and God – can be shown to have their counterpart in the three 'models' with which *Negative Dialectics* concludes its work. Immortality, of course, returns as such in the final section on the possibility or the impossibility of metaphysics, a most unKantian reinvention of Kant's central problematic for our own time: in Kant, this particular 'idea', or necessary but indefensible transcendental value, returns to dawn over the failure of the paralogisms of pure reason, which were unable to ground the substantial existence of the soul (which stands in for the subject's unity, the famous 'transcendental unity of apperception').

Freedom, however, corresponds to the problem of the antinomies of pure reason – that is to say, the impossibility of establishing the causalities of the universe, and whether it has a beginning or an end, is infinite or bounded, and so forth: the relevance of what we might today think of as a subjective or a psychological matter (freedom) is clarified with the antinomies of causality itself, and whether the same string of events could be read in two distinct and incommensurable ways, as a causal series (determined, as we might say today, by the social as well as the psychoanalytic) and as a concatenation of free choices and responses. The point is that for Kant this problem is not a subjective but an objective one, and here Adorno's bias towards the objective, his systematic defamiliarization of the subjective in terms of the 'preponderance of the object', is very consonant and indeed overshoots the Kantian mark by encompassing at this point ethics and those ethical paradoxes that Kant reserved for another panel of his triptych (whence the absence of a properly Adornian 'critique of practical reason', since that is already implicit here).

The idea of God, finally – that 'ideal of pure reason' that completes the contingency of the empirical world by its necessity, just as it grounds the nature and existence of the particulars of that world – becomes, in Adorno's post-Kantian and post-Hegelian intellectual context, the problematic of the Hegelian world spirit, a question about the nature of universals and the universal as such (the traditional function of the older idea of God), but also one which deploys the concept of History itself, in Adorno, as we shall see, dialectically reproblematized in terms of the 'identity' and 'non-identity' between human and natural histories. And there are other points of contact between the two texts: 'a complete enumeration of which would be a useful and not unpleasant, but in this place a perfectly dispensable, occupation'.[42]

This ambitious operation does not, then, elaborate the conditions of possibility for the validity of Marxism itself, as Kant's *Critique* did for the natural science of his own period; it is not in that sense exactly a philosophy of Marxism or a working out of its philosophical scaffolding and underpinnings (something which Lukács's *History and Class Consciousness* can be said to have done in a far more idiosyncratic and less traditional way). Its philosophical conclusions – which can be formulated as the threefold emergence of new conceptions (if not transcendental *ideas*) of mortality and materialism, of the essential impurity or heteronomy of ethics and action, and of the deep substratum of natural history at work in human history – are if anything philosophical complements to a Marxian view of history itself; as vast as is the purview of this last, which expands to include virtually all human activity and to rivalize with the philosophical bases of the various disciplines in its claim to ground them all, these three zones then fall beyond or outside even that enlarged one. Adorno's 'critical' or 'negative-dialectical' philosophy – taken now no longer as a method of some kind, but as a set of substantial philosophical results and concepts – can in that sense be said to correspond to what Sartre (not altogether happily) called an 'ideology', that is a corrective to Marxism as the 'only untranscendable philosophy of our time',[43] an unfreezing of what had dogmatically hardened in this last, and a reminder of those issues – so often called the 'subjective factor', consciousness or culture – that lie beyond its official boundaries.

On the other hand, the Kant parallel also suggests that Adorno's later preoccupation with 'non-identity', and in particular the role that nature and natural beauty come to take on in *Aesthetic Theory*, can itself be seen as a (very Kantian) slippage beyond the bounds assigned to such 'transcendental ideas', and a lapse encouraged by the very block itself (which in Adorno is what separates identity from non-identity): the atheistic and skeptical Kant, indeed, would have renounced ideas of this kind, which the deistic Kant welcomes back.

Finally, if the formative subterranean – I would prefer to say subtextual rather than intertextual – role of the *Critique* described here is plausible, then it becomes equally clear why we can rarely take the Adorno of the essay manifesto (and the open work, the fragmentary probe) at his word. These 'models' now scarcely seem chosen at random, but to have a deeper and more systematic logical relationship and to 'participate' at least in the internal coherence of Kant's own text as a fundamental historical symptom and geological upthrust of thought in the early bourgeois period.

Indeed, if the wonderful formula of the essay is to be taken at face value, that to conceptualize 'essayistically'

> is comparable only to the conduct of someone obliged in a foreign country to use the foreign language practically, rather than to cobble its elements together in schoolroom fashion (NL 21)

then it must be observed about these 'essays' of *Negative Dialectics* that what they try to speak is at least an Indo-European language related to the writer's native one.

Nine

But freedom – in the sense of free will, determinism, responsibility and choice, all things we last glimpsed in Sartre's existentialism, now so long ago – is today a rather old-fashioned problem, or rather, better still, springs as a term and a local problem from a whole seemingly antiquated problematic, redolent of a time before psychoanalysis and behaviorism, when not also smacking lightly of the dustiest academic philosophy contained in long-unopened tomes on ethics somewhere. It is therefore appropriate for Adorno to invite us to reflect on the significance of the old-fashioned and the no longer actual, in philosophy and in culture as well, if only by way of grasping more vividly the way in which this 'problem' also was implicit in the great opening move of the work, in the spectacle of philosophy somehow 'living on' and surviving itself. Elsewhere, in a remarkable meditation on Ibsen and feminism in *Minima Moralia* (No. 57), in which what looks old-fashioned about *A Doll's House* is not the 'social issue' it raises, which is no longer current, but rather the fact that it *is* precisely old-fashioned – in other words, that it has not been solved, is still with us, but in ways we no longer wish to be conscious of. Outdatedness would then be the mark of repression – 'the shame that overcomes the descendant in face of an earlier possibility that he has neglected to bring to fruition'(MM 116/93). So also with ethical philosophy, and in particular with Kant: it stands as a token and a reminder of a moment in the past in which it seemed more plausible and more 'realistic' to speculate about the freedom of the subject and of its acts than it does today.

The historicality of the concept was, however, already previewed in an earlier chapter of *Negative Dialectics*:

> Emphatically conceived, the judgement that a man is free refers to the concept of freedom; yet the concept itself turns out to be more than what is predicated of the man, just as the man turns out in his other determinations to be more than the concept of his freedom. Its concept not only asserts that it is applicable to all individual men defined as free. It is nourished by the idea of a condition in which individuals would have qualities attributable to no one under current circumstances. To praise someone as free has its specificity in the *sous-entendu* that something impossible has been ascribed to him, simply because it has manifested itself in him; it is this secret thing that strikes the eye which animates every judgement of identification that is worth making. The concept of freedom lags behind itself as soon as it is empirically applied. (ND 153-4/150-51)

The temporality of the concept lies not merely in its past history, therefore, but also in its future, as a 'broken promise' and a utopian thought that overshoots the mark, mistakenly imagining itself to have become universal.

The formal question raised most insistently by this 'model' (as by the others) then involves the *Darstellung* of such a peculiar entity in time, let alone the problem of its own antinomies and inner contradictions. Kant had already argued that freedom was what is today called a 'pseudo-problem'; but was far from wanting us to forget about the matter altogether, as positivism seems to have done, despite the fact that the word continues to be used in the juridical and penal processes as well as in what few 'ethical' dilemmas still come up from time to time. *Negative Dialectics* will not want to 'solve' this old problem exactly, nor to produce some new and more non-contradictory 'philosophy' of freedom than is to be found in the earlier efforts of the tradition:

> the topics to be discussed must be reflected on, not in the sense in which one makes a judgement as to the existence or non-existence [of the problems to which they correspond], but rather by reckoning into their determination the impossibility of nailing them down as well as the necessity of continuing to think them. (ND 211-12/212)

In the case of Kant's version of freedom – in which that account of action is inconsistent, or at least incommensurable, with the causality of the phenomenal world (where I may well freely will to do something, but it gets done by my body, under the laws of gravity, etc.); so that the Prussian philosopher will consign the language and conceptuality of freedom to the realm of things-in-themselves, while retaining it in this other one as a 'regulative idea' – Adorno can still benefit from Horkheimer's old lessons in ideological analysis:

> Since the seventeenth century great philosophy had marked out freedom as
> its own specific property interest; under a tacit mandate from the bourgeoisie
> to ground it apodictically. Yet that interest is structurally contradictory. It
> opposes the old oppression of feudalism and promotes a new one, that dwells
> within the rational principle itself. What is required is a common formula
> for freedom and oppression: the former is ceded to rationality, which then
> limits it, and is thereby distanced from an empirical world in which one
> does not wish to see it realized at all. (ND 214/214)

Yet the matter is not thereby disposed of once and for all: for, as the
aesthetic writings codify the distinction more clearly and more crudely,
ideological function must here still be differentiated from 'truth-content'
(*Wahrheitsgehalt*); while even in the realm of ideology, Kant's ingenious
satisfaction of the twin contradictory ideological requirements proves
to be little more than a provisional resting place on a road that could
only go downhill after his own time, where in particular psychology
– as an empirical science of cause and effect – was only at the beginnings
of its colonization of subjectivity, in our time so thoroughgoing as to
make one wonder where 'freedom' might be lodged somehow, let alone
what it was in the first place. Ironically, however, even reflections on
'determinism sound archaic, as though dating from the early period of
the revolutionary bourgeoisie' (ND 215/215): 'Indifference to freedom,
to the concept as well as to the thing itself, is actualized by the integration
into society, that happens to subjects like an irresistible force' (ND 215/
216). Yet this must also be described as an ideology and a choice, fully
as much as a historical process; Adorno therefore significantly adds this
second sentence: 'Their interest in being provided for has paralyzed the
interest in a freedom they fear would leave them unprotected.'

The rest of this first section seeks, however, to show how within a
range of conceptions of unfreedom, some concept of freedom none the
less remains presupposed. The argument, here and throughout, that the
two opposites dialectically entail each other, will later on become the
practical recommendation for a deliberate heteronomy in ethical thinking. Here, however, the unity of opposites is expressed genealogically:

> The identity of the self and its alienation accompany each other from the
> very beginning; whence the bad romanticism of the concept of alienation
> in the first place. A precondition of freedom, identity is at one and the same
> time also and immediately the principle of determinism itself. (ND 216/216–17)

But society, the principle of identity and integration and of the repressive
disarticulation of the psyche, also requires and posits freedom as its own
precondition; while the psychic ego is also nourished by and grounded

on that anamnesis of the archaic infantile instincts which it is its function to control and domesticate. Even Kant's *Darstellung* – his reluctant marshalling of 'examples' in the form of primary ethical 'texts' and cruxes – dramatizes the unstable yet inevitable mediation between some pure notion of freedom and its contingent circumstances, which in the long run forbid generalization or universalization.

Yet the opposite of this is also true: so at the end of this section Adorno comes to the astonishing proposition that even the seemingly inadequate Kantian conception of the 'will' (conceived as 'a faculty to make oneself act according to the idea of certain laws' [Kant, quoted in ND 226–7/227]) displays, when it is visible, a kind of bizarre supplement or additional charge (Adorno's expression is *das Hinzutretende*) in which freedom does seem to be vividly added on to normal acts and conscious or chosen behavior. But what this is might just as easily be described, in modern terms, as coming from below fully as easily as coming from above:

> The impulse, intramental and somatic all at once, transcends the sphere of consciousness to which in another sense it still belongs. With such an impulse freedom now reaches into the world of experience; this animates its concept as that of a state that could as little be blind nature as it could nature's repression. The fantasy picture of such a state, which reason will not let any proof of causal interdependency talk itself out of, is that of a reconciliation of nature and spirit. Nor is it as alien to reason as it appears in Kant's own identification of reason with will; it doesn't fall from heaven. It only strikes philosophical reason as something radically other, because will assigned to pure practical reason is a mere abstraction. The supplementary charge [*das Hinzutretende*] is precisely the name for everything that has been burnt out of that abstraction; free will could not possibly achieve reality without it. It is a flash of light between the poles of something long past and grown almost unrecognizable and what might someday come to be. (ND 228/228–9)

This rectification and recuperation of the old doctrine of will – definitively dissolved, one would have thought, by Sartre, who demonstrates that what we take to be the exercise of 'conscious' will-power is only a game we play with ourselves within a more general non-reflexive free choice deployed in order to allow us to reap the prestige of its exercise (and also, most often, to fail) – seems to stress something closer to an ontological leap of being, rather than the application of redoubled effort.

However that may be, the next section of the model swings around into the reversal of this argument and seeks rather to renumerate the ways in which all concepts of freedom also include their own unfreedom. Kant himself, on the personal and social level, seems to dramatize this in a particularly regrettable (if perhaps now comic) fashion: 'Like the idealists who followed him, Kant cannot bear freedom without compulsion' (ND 231/232). On the other hand, even if the pure formalism of duty and universal law can often (particularly in its German manifestations) look ruthless and oppressive in Kant himself and in the Enlightenment, 'there still survives in it, despite and even because of its very abstractness, real content, namely the egalitarian idea' (ND 235/236). Yet this same abstract universality requires contingent material in order to exist at all: freedom is in this Kantian sense still dialectically the same as chance:

> Freedom needs what Kant calls the heteronomous. Without what according to the criteria of reason itself is called the accidental or the contingent, freedom could as little exist as could reason's own logical judgements. The absolute separation between freedom and chance is as arbitrary as the equally absolute one between freedom and rationality. For an undialectical standard of legality something about freedom will always seem contingent: the case demands reflection, which then lifts itself above the categories of both law and chance alike. (ND 236/237)

It is, incidentally, clear from Adorno's infrequent yet mesmerized returns to the question of chance throughout his work as a whole that such reflections are very much stimulated and inspired by the speculative developments on chance and contingency in Lukács's *History and Class Consciousness*.[44]

But in order to ground his own dialectical and heteronomous conception of freedom, Adorno must first undo Kant's Third Antinomy, which purports to demonstrate the impossibility of both the concept of phenomenal freedom and of its opposite (causality without freedom) alike, and therefore sets a gap between the two too great to be bridged by any dialectic. In doing this in the next section, however, Adorno takes the opportunity to repudiate what he takes to be Marx's equally intolerable solution, the collapsing of theory and practice together in such a way that the former disappears: as can be expected, this is the occasion for a characteristically Frankfurt School plea for the contemplative in and for itself.

The sequel, however, is of the greatest interest in so far as Adorno now focuses in turn on the other column of the antinomy, in order now to rescue, not freedom, but causality. Kant's (and the Germans') ideological and class biases are again foregrounded in his identification of causality with the law: whatever 'follows in line with a rule' (quoted, ND 245/247). Substantively, what can be said about this rather compulsive notion of causality is that it is in this respect identical with Kant's definition of freedom ('following the rules') and ought then rather to apply to 'what is distinguished from compulsion' (ND 247/249). Yet the failure of Kant's operation and the palpable derivation of the transcendental description of freedom from the phenomenal rather than from the noumenal realm (ND 252/255) now open the basic structures of Kant's ethics, and above all that of the Categorical Imperative itself, to a more properly social derivation: in particular the logical argumentation by way of distinction between means and ends clearly draws on a historically original social experience:

> the distinction between subjects as the commodity of labor power, from which value is to be extracted, and those people who, while still themselves commodified, are also those subjects for whom the whole apparatus is set in motion, an apparatus that forgets and only incidentally also satisfies them. (ND 254/257).

The utopian moment in the great Kantian imperative seems to have been tarnished for Adorno, not merely because its chance to be realized (in the political universalism of the bourgeois revolution) was missed, but also because of the stubbornly repressive character of the doctrine, which wants to have nothing whatsoever to do with happiness, let alone pleasure, in its pursuit of a universal moral law as abstract as the law of non-contradiction itself. Finally, however, this seems to be attributable, fully as much as to Kant himself, the Enlightenment and the eighteenth-century German bourgeoisie or Prussian state, to the deeper operation of the principle of identity; and this will of course be Adorno's ultimate refutation of the Third Antinomy:

> The subject need only pose the inescapable alternative between free will and its lack of freedom to be lost in advance. Each drastic thesis is false. At their core the theses of freedom and determinism coincide. Both proclaim identity. (ND 261/264)

Yet at the same time both theses are also true:

> The antinomy between the determination of the individual and the social responsibility that contradicts such determination is not due to a misuse of concepts, but is real, and the moral form taken by the non-reconciliation between the universal and the particular. (ND 261/264)

Yet this new antinomy – Adorno's rather than Kant's – now drives his thought forward into its ultimate formulation, and the most elaborated statement of his conception of heteronomy:

> Freedom is, however, so entangled with unfreedom that unfreedom is not merely its impediment but also a premise of freedom's concept. No more

than any other one can this one be separated off as an absolute. Without the unity and the domination of reason, nothing like freedom would ever have been thought of in the first place, let alone brought into being: to that the history of philosophy itself can testify. There is no available model of freedom but this one: that just as consciousness intervenes in the total constitution of society, so also it intervenes, through that very intervention, in the complexion of the individual. The reason this notion is not itself chimerical is that consciousness as a form of diverted libidinal energy is itself a drive, and therefore a moment of what it actively intervenes in. Without that affinity that Kant so violently denies [between the universal and the empirical, between freedom and the phenomenal world], that very idea of freedom, in whose name he refuses the expression of such affinities, would not exist in the first place. (ND 262/265)

It is a doctrine of the mixed or the impure – or, in another language, of the identity between identity and non-identity – which we will find returning in the aesthetics, whose artistic works or monads are both closed intrinsic forms and objects saturated by the social to which they ceaselessly refer in the strong semantic sense. Yet it also draws its force, as we shall see shortly, from Adorno's philosophically original deployment of the notion of natural history (into which, in the above passage, 'consciousness' is reinserted in so far as it is also 'a form of diverted libidinal energy').

With this climax, then, as in a local coda, Adorno's reflection then proceeds down the other slope of the heteronomous concept, as though 'what happened to the idea of freedom also seems to be happening to its counterpart, the concept of causality' (ND 262/265): he has in mind essentially the sea-change from the linear causality still central for Kant to an essentially synchronic conception, 'operating not so much with causal chains as with causal networks' (ND 263/266).

Causality has similarly withdrawn into totality ... each state of things is horizontally and vertically connected to all the others, illuminates all of them [*tingiert*] just as it is illuminated by all in turn. The last doctrine in which Enlightenment used causality as a decisive political weapon, the Marxist doctrine of infrastructure and superstructure, now lags innocently behind a condition in which not only the machineries of production, distribution and domination, but also economic and social relationships along with ideologies are inextricably interwoven, and in which living people have themselves become bits of ideology. Where ideology is no longer added on to things as their justification or their mystification or glamorization, but has been transformed into the appearance of the inevitability and therefore the legitimacy of the status quo, a critique that operates with the unequivocal causal relationships of base and superstructure misses the mark. In the total society all things are equidistant from the center; such a society is fully as transparent, and its apologia as threadbare, as those people grow extinct who once saw through it. (ND 264-5/267-8)

It is then with such a causality – the 'magic spell' of late capitalism, as we shall see later on – that the subject and freedom have – *pace* Kant – a certain affinity; with such an objective dimension that the truth of the subject can alone be revealed. 'Affinity' is in this sense 'determinate negation' – that is to say, 'critical theory', 'negative dialectics'; it is also, in some hitherto undisplayed sense, mimesis:

> In it [affinity as critique] thought completes its mimicry of that spell on things which it has itself laid around them, on the threshold of a sympathy before which the spell itself would disappear. The subjective principle within causality has its elective affinity with objects in the form of a dim, unformulated realization of what happened to them at the subject's hand. (ND 267/270)

Mimesis can thus now be seen to offer a peculiar reversal or corrective of the Viconian principle of *verum factum*, in so far as it does not merely yield insight into the deeper nature of what human beings and their social order have done to the world but also grants some distant, simultaneous sense of how that might be repaired. The thought thus oddly echoes the great Brechtian principle of estrangement, which sought, by demonstrating that what we took to be natural was in reality social and the result of human praxis, to reawaken the awareness that human praxis was equally capable of turning it into something else.

   Two final sections, as it were alternative endings, review the contemporary alternatives (psychoanalysis, personalism, existentialism) to Kantian ethics, or to ethics altogether; and also the doctrine of the intelligible world and the intelligible character, which Kant consigns to the world of the noumena or things-in-themselves. In the first of these concluding discussions, the heteronomy of ethics is again decisively staged in the debate on the execution of the Nazi war criminals:

> acquittal would be a barefaced injustice, but a just atonement would be infected by that very principle of brute force, in the resisting of which alone humanity consists. Benjamin anticipated this dialectic by his remark that the carrying out of the death penalty might be moral, but never its legitimation . (ND 282/286)

In the second, along with a systematic repudiation of the 'heroism' of moral or ethical beings as such, the Utopian motif is once again sounded:

> If we dared to confer its true content on the Kantian X of the intelligible character (as that asserts itself against the total indeterminacy of the aporetic concept), that content would probably turn out to be the most historically advanced, ephemerally flaring and just as quickly extinguished consciousness in which the impulse to do right dwells. This is the concrete yet intermittent anticipation of sheer possibility, neither alien to human beings nor identical with them. (ND 292/297)

In the absence of this itself no more than intermittent anticipation of the future, Adorno notes, no ethics are really feasible in and of themselves: we either try to change the system altogether or 'try to live in such a way that we can believe ourselves to have been good animals' (294/299).

This conclusion to the freedom model, however, in fact brings us back to the *Minima Moralia* of the immediate postwar years, one of whose central programs consisted in the (well-nigh Kantian) disproof of the feasibility of ethics by way of their antinomies. A series of very small-scale 'models' rehearse, with remarkable economy and equally remarkable dialectical tact, the internal 'impossibility', in our time, of marriage (No. 10), convention (No. 16), a proper life with things (No. 18), and love (No. 110). Marriage, for example, is corrupted by its institutional association with interest, but in such a way that even if interest is absent, owing to the accident of the parties' personal worth, the institution ensures its own logic; even for those without interest, the rich and privileged, who 'are precisely those in whom the pursuit of interests has become second nature – they would not otherwise uphold privilege' (MM 29/31).

As for convention – that is, a certain prearranged artificial distance between social actors – it is in all domains (from art to ethics) a transitional phenomenon, since it must be freely chosen and thus distinct from traditional, externally imposed constraints and norms, while the impulse to liberate ourselves from those constraints necessarily ends up destroying convention itself. As for our relationship to possessions and the object world, it has been problematized by new monopoly forms of property and by an excess of consumer goods, and offers no conceivable mean:

> a loveless disregard for things ... necessarily turns against people too; and the antithesis, no sooner uttered, is an ideology for those wishing with a bad conscience to keep what they have. (MM 42/39) -

Love, meanwhile, tries to negotiate its way between the requirement of asocial spontaneity and the fact that it is bourgeois society that itself defines it as what is not social:

'the love ... which, in the guise of unreflecting spontaneity and proud of its alleged integrity, relies exclusively on what it takes to be the voice of the heart, and runs away as soon as it no longer thinks it can hear that voice, is in this supreme independence precisely the tool of society. (MM 227/172)

What each of these fables gives us to contemplate is not merely the contradictory nature of the phenomenon, nor only the impossibility of establishing a non-contradictory ethics to govern such an area, but above all the explanatory link to a historical stage of the social order, whose peculiarities alone account for these impasses, just as, more proximately, that history also illuminates the origin of the value we seek but no longer find realizable within them. They are thus all designed to show that one cannot 'get out' of ethics by means of ethics; that ethical dilemmas are socially and politically, as a series of lapidary conclusions suggest: 'wrong life cannot be lived rightly' (MM 42/39); 'no emancipation without that of society' (MM 228/173).

Yet the articulation between the ethical dilemma and the social contradiction is in all these cases expressed in terms of what we have called the crisis of nominalism, that is to say, the tension in modern society between the realm of the general and the realities of the particular. 'The universal is revealed in divorce as the particular's mark of shame, because the particular, marriage, is in this society unable to realize the true universal' (MM 31/32). Meanwhile, liberated convention, 'emancipated tact ... meets with the difficulties that confront nominalism in all contexts' (MM 37/36).

A remarkable and extended paragraph, then (No. 16, 'Just hear, how bad he was'), draws the larger conclusion by mediating on the ever more gaping distance between events in the abstract, and in particular large-scale collective catastrophes, and the micro-logical happenings of importance to ourselves, in which alone forms of sympathy are capable of making a spontaneous appearance. 'Wherever immediateness posits and entrenches itself, the bad mediacy of society is insidiously inserted' (MM 240/182) – something, Adorno adds, which is 'not without relevance to the doctrine of reason of state, the severance of morality from politics' (MM 237/180). But as he goes on to show, it is also not without relevance to questions of aesthetic representation (and indeed is further developed in the central sections on cultural representation and in particular on the problem of historical and political representation in our time: No. 94, 'All the world's not a stage'). Yet this diagnosis – which has its most immediate affinities with Benjamin's analyses of the breakdown of traditional forms of experience – is here prolonged beyond aesthetic contradictions and the crisis of representation on into the more social and philosophical issue of the various zones of autonomy and semi-autonomy in modern life.

What the paragraphs already cited demonstrate with respect to ethics – that even though to all appearances it is autonomous and demands its own specific thinking and intellectual solutions, the antinomies at work in those disprove the initial premiss of the autonomy of the ethical itself – now proves to be a lesson one can learn over a wider variety of areas, from culture (No. 22, 'Baby with the Bath Water') to folk art (No. 131, 'Wolf as Grandmother') and from politics to philosophy. Modernity, as we have since been taught by Luhmann,[45] consists in increasing differentiation, in the relative autonomization of a whole range of social levels and activities from one another: the 'liberation' of culture from the sacred, for example, or the 'liberation' of politics from ethics. Yet from another perspective it is precisely all these things together, in a coexistence and an internal overlap or identification, which make up secular society as such, that does not, however, exist empirically as an autonomous object and is not available for independent inspection. The semi-autonomy of its spheres and levels is therefore as false as it is true; the vocation of the dialectic lies in the attempt to coordinate and to respect this validity along with this sham ideological appearance. This it does, as these small-scale 'models' in *Minima Moralia* testify, by acknowledging the autonomy of a secular sphere such as ethics whose practical dependence on the social totality it then infers by way of the contradictions that result from the attempt to endow it with an autonomous theory. The heteronomy of the concept of freedom is thus merely a special case of this more general critique of the autonomy of social spheres and zones (and of philosophical subdisciplines).

Ten

It is in the Hegel 'model' of *Negative Dialectics* that Adorno's most sustained 'defense' of the Marxian view of history as such will now be staged. The characterization must, however, immediately be qualified in two ways, for as we have already made clear Adorno does not in that sense ever argue in any systematic or 'sustained' fashion. This chapter will therefore not yield his basic positions 'about' history; it will not in particular shed much light on his conception of late capitalism as an economic system; rather, essentially, it comments on the *concept* of history and on the *concept* of late capitalism (as these already exist in Hegel and in Marx and elsewhere), rotating these ideas into a variety of cross-lights, measuring their variable ideological implications, demonstrating the local paradoxes of their use (which involves both paralogisms and antinomies), and finally formulating a proposition as to the mode in which the impossible yet indispensable concept is to be handled.

This seemingly aleatory yet comprehensive treatment – it might be called something like a constellative critique – involves a systematic positioning of Hegel (his bias against the individual and the particular is tracked implacably, yet freshly, without any of the hoary remarks about the Prussian state which are normally obligatory), as of Marx, whose bias for necessity is rebuked, not least in the light of our own situation ('what corresponds to the impending catastrophe today would rather seem to be the hypothesis of some irrational catastrophe at the very beginnings of time' ND 317/323). Yet the chapter has an underlying momentum and, as it were, a thematic *telos* quite different from that of the other two models (had we not forbidden musical analogies, it would be tempting to evoke the formal differences between the various movements of a sonata): what is argued in effect is the ultimate objectivity of that absent and invisible totality which is history; this means in effect that we steer a variable but steady course for the conception of natural history that has already been promised.

The second feature of the chapter which will disorient those seeking outright statements on Adorno's 'theory' of history has to do with its terminology or, if you prefer, the philosophical thematics of the discussion, in which the obvious problems of those two contemporary *bêtes noires*, the concept of totality and so-called 'linear history' (both associated with Hegel in the popular mind), form by no means its central focus; nor are these themes or terms exactly enlisted in the argument, which turns centrally on that other great issue of the universal and the particular. It will, then, be in the light of this very different problem that totality and historical and narrative causality will be thought and rewritten.

Meanwhile, it will come as no surprise to find that, within such a theoretical framework, virtually the central issue raised by the relationship between the universal and the particular – namely, the mechanisms that block their coordination and turn their opposition into a generalized crisis (existential, social, aesthetic, philosophical, all at once) – is what Adorno will call positivism (along with its accompanying value, 'nominalism'). It seems to me desirable to understand this term in as generalized a cultural and intellectual fashion as possible: in particular it scarcely any longer, even in Adorno's period, designates positivistic philosophers as such, but rather the more general positivistic tradition in the social sciences. Meanwhile, our own situation, with respect both to philosophy and to sociology, has been significantly modified in the twenty-some years since the publication of *Negative Dialectics*, in at least its personnel and its fashions, if not its deeper tendencies: we will miss the usefulness of Adorno's diagnosis of positivism for us if we do not recognize that the tendencies he designated under that name have if anything intensified since his own death and are now, in the virtual eclipse of his own philosophy as well as of dialectical thinking generally, virtually hegemonic and unchallenged – which means that they look somewhat different.

'Positivism' is, then, in general to be taken to mean a commitment to empirical facts and worldly phenomena in which the abstract – interpretation fully as much as general ideas, larger synchronic collective units fully as much as diachronic narratives or genealogies – is increasingly constricted, when not systematically pursued and extirpated as a relic and a survival of older traditional, 'metaphysical', or simply old-fashioned and antiquated thoughts and categories. But this diagnosis – which can be extended over a wide variety of contemporary social phenomena, as has already been suggested – must be sharply distinguished from the (undoubtedly affiliated) conservative or reactionary laments about the disappearance of values, moral and otherwise, the obsolescence of the Platonic (or even the Kantian) Ideas, the breakdown of collective identities (for them, the Nation, or 'Western civilization', are the relevant entities) or the decay of conventional forms, whether in culture or in manners.[46]

These complaints about modern times and its degenerescence are as closely related to those of Adorno – who can sometimes sound like this, to be sure, in some of the more querulous notations of *Minima Moralia* – as the first aristocratic and reactionary critiques of capitalism to the left and radical analyses of the new social order that appeared a few decades later. The basic structural difference lies in the status of the 'universal' in each: for the conservatives, that term exists already and has content (of the traditional type) – the crisis of what Adorno calls positivism can then simply be resolved by reinvigorating the older collective institutions and, as part of the same process, by tracking down the forces that weakened those values in the first place, by weeding out the agents and propagators of a bad 'nominalism' and antinomianism.

Adorno's conception of the relationship between universals and particulars is, however, not of this hierarchical or Aristotelian type, where the ones become subsumed beneath the others in the classical form of Order. For one thing, the universals are as affected as the particulars by the crisis; these are now 'bad' or baleful universals, and were perhaps always that: the point of the vocation of philosophy to reidentify their operations and to make them once again visible is not in order to celebrate them, but rather to do away with them altogether. Nor is the figure of subsumption – a sign and trace of violence and domination – the way in which to imagine even an ideal *Versöhnung* or 'reconciliation' between the universal and the particular. But the argument aims at anything but producing a concept of such subsumption or logical 'reconciliation'; rather, in the name of intensifying the tensions between universal and particular, of bringing everything that is incommensurable between them to consciousness as a historical contradiction and a form of suffering for the mind, it seeks to stigmatize the repression of that fundamental tension – as in the positivistic dismissal of universals as sheer metaphysical survivals, or Heidegger's mystique of the universal as such – as a form of violence, the domination of the universal over the particular, which, however, takes the placid form of the unproblematical appearance of everyday reality.

The 'excursus' thus begins very properly with the dissatisfaction of the particular – that is to say, in this initial context, the individual, the personal subject – with whatever too insistently wants to remind him or her of the invisible shaping power of history, which everywhere exceeds the existent or the isolated fact, just as it betrays its omnipresence in all the contents of my consciousness, from the social to my very language, none of which belongs to me. The birth of history is just that acknowledgement of the totality that it has become inescapable to notice within the inexplicable swerve of the individual objects and subjects towards some unknown end. This, which Hegel called the *Weltgeist* (notoriously, he glimpsed it once incarnated on horseback during the extraordinary opening of the brief Napoleonic era), is, however, endowed with this strange invisible power

> because society's law of motion has for thousands of years been abstracting from its individual subjects, degrading them to mere executors, mere partners in social wealth and social struggle, even though it is no less true, and equally real, that none of this would exist without them and their individual spontane-ities. (ND 299/304)

This 'stored labor' of abstraction is the capital that endows History or Society with its real power, like Feuerbach's God or Durkheim's collectivity: the god of this world which, however, unlike Hegel, we must not worship. The individual waxes and wanes according to the vicissitudes of World Spirit: 'one is tempted to associate periods of ontological partici-pation in world spirit, and some more substantial luck and happiness than the merely individual, with the unleashing of productive forces' (ND 301/306), while on the other hand Adorno is intent on inscribing the unruly stupidities of the human collective, as in committee meetings ('a reminder, in its invariance, of how little the power of the universal changes throughout history, of how much of it still remains prehistoric' [ND 303/308]). All this now suddenly hardens into the Law and the antinomies of the juridical and its institutions: universals, about which it is amusing to find Hegel assure us that 'conscience will consider [them] with good reason most hostile to itself' (ND 304/310) – something Kant seems to have felt to be an advantage. But law is only the obvious and visible of all the abstractions in which individuality is straitjacketed, a lesson which nevertheless, as was pointed out at the beginning of this chapter, no one wants to hear: 'to look the supreme power of the universal in the eye does all but unbearable psychological damage to the narcissism of all individuals and of a democratically organized society' (ND 306/312).

The next section briefly recalls the fundamental principle of Adorno's thought (as of Hegel and also Durkheim) – 'the positing of an equivalence between logical categories and those of society and history' (ND 311/317); while the one that follows returns to the historiographic question itself (is a universal history possible?), which it rightly associates with the problem of necessity. Yet the category of Necessity in our time awakens the incompatible historiographic commitment to discontinuity, as the form nominalism takes in the realm of individual and collective storytelling: death, or the generations, along with demography, break up what would otherwise have the logic of a seamless web of acts and consequences. To this all but universal contemporary visceral objection to so-called Hegelian 'master narratives' (if they are not called 'linear history' instead), Adorno assents, while characteristically also dissenting in his fashion, since the worst is always certain: 'No universal history leads from the wild animal to the genuinely human being, but one indubitably leads from the slingshot to the megaton bomb' (ND 314/320). The question he wishes to raise with Marx, however, is whether it would not be better (politically better? more efficacious?) to think of history in terms of contingence rather than necessity; to attribute the fall into violence, state power, and capital to a catastrophe that need never have taken place (this was Lévi-Strauss's position on the emergence of 'civilization') rather than to see even this first invention of antagonism as 'inevitable'.

A number of painful quotations from Hegel follow, which abundantly document the latter's enthusiastic commitment to the party of the universal but are also used to argue the peculiar detemporalization which this partisanship brings to his conception of time, and finally the premature suspension of his own dialectic to which it forces him. A new section, however, shows us that of one offense, at least, Hegel is innocent: there are no Hegelian master narratives! The story of *Geist* – impressive enough as a superstructural dialectic – was unable to take on genuine historiographic content without a significant mediation, which doesn't work, although it has its own dynamic and semi-autonomy – namely the *Volksgeist*, or what we might now call the *national* principle fully as much as that of this or that *people*. But acknowledgement of this contingent fact which is the multiplicity of nations and peoples, and still seems to be equal to itself two centuries later under late capitalism, introduces a structural ambiguity into the plan for universal history: for if nations are universals as far as those existential individuals who are their subjects are concerned, they are themselves individuals with respect to some putative overall historical *telos*. They have too much individuality to be reduced to stages or moments of anything; and not the least feature of Adorno's analysis is the way he links, to this breakdown, the dysfunctionality of the great Hegelian concept of the 'ruse of reason' (also known as the 'ruse of history'):

Hegel saw through the fiction of individuality's historic being-for-itself as through that of every other unmediated immediacy, and by means of the theory of the ruse of reason (which dated back to Kant's philosophy of history), he classified the individual as an agent of the universal, a role in which it had served so well over the centuries. In doing so, and in keeping with a habitual thought structure that both schematizes and repeals his conception of the dialectic simultaneously, he conceived of the relationship between the world spirit and the individual, including their mediation, as an invariant: thereby even he, Hegel, lies in thrall to his own class, that has to eternalize its most dynamic categories in order to prevent itself from becoming conscious of the ultimate limits of its continuing existence as a class. Guiding Hegel is the picture of the individual in individualist society. This is an adequate one, since the principle of exchange society can realize itself only by way of the individuation of the contracting parties; and also because the *principium individuationis* is literally its very principle, that is to say its universal. It is inadequate because in the totality of functional relationships that requires the form of individuation as such, individuals have been relegated [by Hegel's theory] to mere executive organs of the universal. (ND 336/342)

In such a passage, the shadow of Marx falls across Hegel's nation states and a new principle of world history emerges, distinct from that of language or national culture, which is that universal 'spell' cast by exchange value over all individuality and across the frozen landscape of isolated particulars. As can be imagined, the vision of this magical spell inspires Adorno, in the scant pages to come, to his most eloquent formulations.

A short penultimate section returns to the subjectivity of the historical individual, tendentially reduced by modern psychology and psychoanalysis, which reflect the structural diminution of the contemporary psychic subject as so many symptoms but do not name the essential, or in other words happiness itself, about which we can only think negatively. This massive tendential movement, in which universal and particular alike have in the preceding pages both been equally, albeit asymmetrically, revealed as somehow objective in their truth and their reality, now at length flows into the long-awaited conclusion: on natural history itself.

Eleven

For the various background narratives in Adorno must all be completed by a more 'fundamental' but also a more enigmatic one. It has often been noticed[47] that the writer's early academic lecture on 'The Actuality of Philosophy' (1931) could in many ways be seen as a sketch for the whole program written up over thirty years later in *Negative Dialectics*; the other significant text from that same period – called 'The Idea of Natural History' – has received less attention and remains something of an enigma. One cannot say of it that it is finally worked out and given embodiment in the mature works; the last few pages of the 'Hegel' chapter in *Negative Dialectics*, to be sure, return explicitly to the theme of natural history, but merely repeat the motif, reawakening the suspicion, so often muttered by Adorno's critics and enemies, that he was constitutionally unable to transform the local flash and the local insight into the sustained duration of full-blown philosophical argument. But perhaps he was able to do something else with it.

Indeed, 'The Idea of Natural History' seems to me to offer a methodological proposal, rather than a set of theses on the matter. We are better placed today, after the extraordinary reinvigoration of evolutionary thought and the powerful rereading of Darwin himself by Stephen Jay Gould and others, to grasp what might be at stake in the strategic but unclearly motivated act of repositioning this problem at the heart of the Frankfurt School project of that period. Marx's own relationship to Darwin is well known; the abortive dedication of *Capital* Volume I (1867) to the author of *The Origin of Species* (1857) was a little more than a salute from one initiator of a Copernican revolution to another. It was meant to affirm the subsumption of human history – for the first time scientifically disengaged by historical materialism – under natural history – something henceforth indissociable from Darwin's own work and theorization. Marx's own position, he tells us in the Preface to *Capital*, 'grasps the development of the economic formation of society as a process of natural history'. Yet it was an ambiguous project; and the very concept of class struggle itself, in the somber atmosphere of Social Darwinism and the ideological leitmotiv of the survival of the fittest, is later on susceptible to all the lurid half-lights and tones of protofascism.

As for us today, looking back from the prosperous shelter of some postmodern far future, disquisitions on the prehistory of the planet and its flora and fauna surely have a strange and irrelevant unreality about them: only the old distinction between science and truth can perhaps account for a situation in which we bring assent and belief to the correctness of the facts of the matter – what our handbooks tell us about the Pleistocene, along with George Washington – without any real conviction. We remember the archeological as a sequence in Disney's *Fantasia*; and if the ancients 'believed' firmly in a host of legends and superstitions they must have also known to be preposterous, we 'disbelieve' equally in these facts and hypotheses, embodied in whole scientific disciplines which we know, *grosso modo* to be correct.[48] This is because our historical metabolism has undergone a serious mutation; the organs with which we register time can handle only smaller and smaller, and more and more immediate, empirical segments; the schematism of our transcendental historical imagination encompasses less and less material, and can process only stories short enough to be verifiable via television. The larger, more abstract thoughts – what is more totalizing than natural history, after all? – fall outside the apparatus; they may be true but are no longer representable – it is worse than old-fashioned to evoke them, rather a kind of social blunder is involved. Nor is this astonishing triumph of some ultimate positivism – which has in a few years conquered the whole earth, like Islam or Christianity – itself necessarily altogether positive for the ideological interests of the power structure; it would have been desirable to tap a few myths still, and Daniel Bell and others find themselves wishing that a little religion were still available. But it doesn't work any more; and even the new diseases cannot be made illicitly vivid to the imagination by the evocation of epic medieval or classical plagues. Still, the plague is, if anywhere, the place where human history and natural history most dramatically intersect, before the naked eye.

For there is a nightmare of natural history that is even grislier than that of the human one; and it is this that the postmodern mind has been able to repress fairly successfully (save for biological death itself) for reasons that are scarcely mysterious: what better way to avoid being reminded of the nightmare of nature than to abolish nature altogether? Yet a glimpse into the interstices that not merely open to view the pecking order of all living species, a hideous eternity of domination and hierarchy designed at least to leave its subjects alive, but also and finally the violence of nature itself, organisms obliged to eat their whole waking life long, and to eat each other (in Adorno's most frequent characterization of it) – this dizzying perspective brings with it a nausea more fundamental than the sight of the malice with which humans attempt to culturalize their own internecine slaughter. Animals, which still live here and there among us, sometimes give us some of this to see; and it has not often been noticed that, if virtually alone among the Western Marxists the Frankfurt School had a meditation on the domination of Nature and can be counted among the philosophical ancestors of the ecology movement, it also made its contribution to animal rights. The long note on 'Man and Animal' appended to *Dialectic of Enlightenment*, and perhaps attributable to Horkheimer, is surely one of central 'constellations' of that work (although Adorno included other noteworthy reflections on animals in *Minima Moralia*:

> every animal suggests some crushing misfortune that took place in primeval times ...: The masses, having been forced to toe the same line, are becoming so oblivious of the transformation they are undergoing ... that they no longer need to have it symbolically displayed. Now and again, if we scan the trivial news-items on the second and third pages of a newspaper – the front page is crammed with men's frightful deeds of glory – we may come across a few lines about a circus fire or poisoned elephants. ... Goethe's aversion to apes also indicated the limits of his humanitarianism. ... Nature herself is neither good, as the ancients believed, nor noble as the latter-day Romantics would have it. As a model and goal it implies the spirit of opposition, deceit, and bestiality. (DA 221/247, 224/251, 225/253, 227/254)

Unsurprisingly, this set piece also modulates through the 'woman question' and is also a rare but characteristic specimen of Frankfurt School proto-feminism, suggesting that gender also and preeminently marks the spot where human and natural histories bewilderingly intersect, and reminding us of the high stakes in their disentanglement.

In this form, however, natural history remains a 'vision' of nature, or in other words a *Weltanschauung* – which is to say an ideology and an anthropology – that ranges itself somewhere in between Hobbes and Robert Ardrey or sociobiology; the competing 'vision' – that of Rousseau, say – is no less aesthetic than its alternative; nor does it matter very much that the Frankfurt School can in some respects be said to combine both, in their call for a return to nature without domination at the end of what Marx called 'prehistory'. But we have learned to distinguish the very status and structure of such 'visions of the world' – in whose representations as it were, the imagining subject is personally involved – from that rarer and very different thing associated with science, which seems to give us a discourse without a subject and a way of thinking phenomena such as historical succession or diachronic change which does not involve representation as such. This is indeed, I take it, what the debate staged by the Althusserians around Marx's early writings aimed to bring out: to stigmatize these last as 'humanist' was in effect to characterize them as ideological and to underscore the way in which the vision of human nature and its potentialities, as well as of the possibilities of *alienation*, remained an anthropological one. This did not mean, I also take it, that such an ideological vision of human nature was necessarily wrong (let alone unattractive); merely that as discourse it functioned on the same level as the competing 'visions' (Stirner's existentialism, the pessimism of Schopenhauer, with those of Hobbes and Rousseau still vividly alive in the background). *Capital*, which was not a representation as such and made no place for the subject – the intoxicated spectator, witness and solipsistic but contemplative victim of the grand metaphysical spectacle – constituted, then, a kind of discourse as different from this one of the early Marx as Darwin himself from Social Darwinism.

Yet is not any return to natural history, any attempt to recover the 'natural' basis of and perspective on human history, threatened with just such a regression into this or that primal 'vision of the world'? If we wish to eschew such pictures, would it not be preferable, with Vico, to separate human history from natural history, to confine ourselves to the human arena, the space of human praxis, and let Nature 'be in its being'? But this alternative is what the Frankfurt School seems to have felt to be profoundly idealistic, in its omission of biology and death, of the brute *fact* of the generations (history has no trouble accounting for their *content*), and finally of what Sartre called the contingent metaphysical fact of scarcity itself, the struggle for life against Nature (as the Ur-datum on which that profoundly historical thing which is production and the modes of production is founded). But would this supplement of nature and biology do any more for us than add some additional volumes on the history of protein and calorie intake, on the archaic susceptibility to microbes, or the comparative erg-power of the male and female musculatures throughout the ages?

The originality of Adorno's proposal is, then, to have cut across these alternatives in an unexpected way, implying that we will not succeed in repressing the metaphysical impulse, but that it would be undesirable to achieve complete success in doing so anyhow, since that would clearly spell the triumph of positivism and empiricism as such (something to which the last chapter of *Negative Dialectics* returns). The unstable coexistence of metaphysics and its dissolution in Kant is an admirable, but unusable analogy. Meanwhile, we will not stop doing either social or natural history (that is, the 'human sciences' and the natural sciences) but, no matter what our acknowledgement of the call to unify them, will continue to alternate them only. Under these circumstances, commitment to the idea of natural history suggests this provisional solution:

> If the question of the relationship of nature and history is to be seriously posed, it can hold out the prospect of an answer only if we succeed in grasping historical being in its most extreme historical determination, that is to say, there where it is most historical, as a form of natural being, or if we succeed in grasping Nature where it persists most deeply within itself as nature, as on the contrary a form of historical being.[49] (ND 353/359)

The dualism, in other words, cannot be undone by the taking of a thought or by frontal assault – such dualisms are in any case themselves the mark and scar of profound historical developments and contradictions – but its poles may be allowed dialectically to short-circuit one another. Thus the Marxian conception of modes of production acquires the uncanny half-light of a different dimension altogether when we inspect its findings, not merely through the telescope of Lévi-Strauss's astronomer-anthropologist, but above all through the disincarnated eyes of Olaf Stapledon's space traveller in *Star Maker*, moving from galaxy to galaxy and from civilization to civilization of beings increasingly different from us biologically: from hominoids to 'nautiloids', symbiotic partner existences, crab-like beings and sentient vegetal life. But when the view from the epicycle of Mercury begins to strengthen fatalism, as in some increased conviction about the limitations placed on social life and development by biological contingencies, then one must roll this whole mental operation over and turn even this naturalization of history inside out by the defamiliarization of Nature itself as a kind of social being.

At that point Darwinian reality, unmodified, shrinks to the intellectual acts of Darwin himself and the social preconditions of his 'discoveries' in the English capitalism of the early nineteenth century: what is 'historical' about Nature now is then suddenly our own capacity to discover or to represent it as social beings, and to project it out beyond the human social world. (That this kind of transformation of nature [or scientific discovery] into a social fact is not 'relativistic', exactly, that social determinations can somehow be thought together in the mind with scientific 'truth', is one of the crucial paradoxes rehearsed by the contemporary history, sociology and philosophy of science.)

What is involved here is a reciprocal defamiliarization of the two incommensurable poles of the dualism of Nature and History, but clearly enough – and on Adorno's own formulation – this must be a perpetual process in which neither term ever comes to rest, any more than any ultimate synthesis emerges. The scanty references to Lukács's early notion of society as a 'second nature' (in *The Theory of the Novel*) do not, however, tell us very much about what such a process might look like; until it ultimately dawns on us that *Dialectic of Enlightenment* is itself its representation and its working out, an insight that would seem considerably to clarify that peculiar and idiosyncratic text. Indeed, many of us have worried at great length over what now looks like a false problem: namely the question of whether the book is to be thought of as espousing 'essentially' Nietzschean positions, or Marxian ones, or in fact Weberian ideas and principles. Perhaps, we sometimes speculated, it may be a synthesis of all of those (just as Lukács earlier performed, in the concept of reification, the supreme synthesis between a certain Marx and a certain Weber); but such a hypothesis then raised the embarrassing supplementary theoretical question of how you would go about verifying the 'success' of the new chemical combination, or on the contrary its failure to cohere.

For the book begins with fear and vulnerability[50] in the face of what is yet not even nature: but the temporality of this beginning – which ought to be mythic in the grand sense (as in Hobbes or Rousseau) and would then reconfirm the frequent and frequently bewildered characterization of *Dialectic of Enlightenment* as the staging of a kind of myth in its own right – is at once rectified and booby-trapped by a dialectical operation now most commonly associated with poststructural synchronics (especially since Althusser seems to have coined the most apt expression for it – the 'always-already'). Adorno and Horkheimer specify, indeed, that it is rather the process by which fear and vulnerability are mastered that brings temporal succession into being in first place, along with historical *telos*.

In this sense, the present – the most up-to-date form of the dialectic of enlightenment – produces the past, and more specifically that immediate past of its own present which is now stigmatized as archaic, old-fashioned, mythic, superstitious, obsolete or simply 'natural'; but this is true as far back into the past as we can see or imagine, and indeed the temporal dialectic proposed here might better be analogized in terms of optics, where with every shift in visual attention a new lateral field establishes itself, forever out of reach. Whether this is inconsistent with the Marxian vision of modes of production, and in particular with that of tribal society or primitive communism – indeed, whether the Marxian conception itself implies nostalgia for some golden age (on the order of the tradition of Rousseau, as for example in Sahlins's extraordinary 'First Affluent Society'[51]) – remains to be seen.

In any case, it should be noted that the peculiar originality of Adorno's and Horkheimer's conception of a 'dialectic of enlightenment' is that it excludes any beginning or first term, and specifically describes 'enlightenment' as an 'always-already' process whose structure lies very precisely in its generation of the illusion that what preceded it (which was also a form of enlightenment) was that 'original' moment of myth, the archaic union with nature, which it is the vocation of enlightenment 'proper' to annul. If it is a matter of telling a historical story, therefore, we must read Adorno and Horkheimer as positing a narrative without a beginning in which the 'fall', or dissociation, is always there already; if, however, we decide to reread their book as a diagnosis of the peculiarities and the structural limits and pathologies of historical vision or narrative itself, then we may conclude, in a somewhat different fashion, that the strange after-image of 'primal unity' always seems to be projected after the fact onto whatever present the historical eye fixes, as its 'inevitable' past, which vanishes without a trace when frontal vision is in turn displaced onto it.

The most dramatic paradox by way of which this 'dialectic' is rehearsed is, however, appropriately enough the discussion of myth itself, along with the anthropological paraphernalia of ritual and shamanistic techniques (which Adorno and Horkheimer probably found in Frazer). For these are also 'enlightenment': the shaman's aim and function – like that of philosophers and scientists in later history – remains that of controlling nature (encouraging fertility, bringing rain, propitiating the gods), and the techniques of the sacred must also be supposed to have a history that corresponds to the more general dialectic of enlightenment, in so far as the more efficient religions cancel out the more primitive and archaic ones, and the very coming into being of rites and ceremonies – let alone their codification and refinement – is itself enlightenment 'progress'. This serves as a piquant twist on traditional enlightenment narratives (the eighteenth century imagined itself to be the scourge of residual traces of the sacred and of superstition in general); but the rationale for subsuming witchdoctors under Western science and reason is given in the very structure of the rituals themselves, as we shall see shortly.

As for the description of this perpetual present of control and domination – of self-protection and self-preservation – it is of course immediately identified as Reason (but as what Hegel would call *Verstand* rather than *Vernunft*, and what Sartre would call analytic rather than dialectical reason) and can clearly be identified in its later and more contemporary stages as what will more generally and culturally be stigmatized as positivism (among other things, as a program and a set of mental operations, it must radically eschew self-consciousness [DA 8/4]). But in order to surprise and observe the operation of this single, totalizing, tendentially unified process at work in a variety of social materials and historical developments (each of which can then stand, succinctly and narratively formulated, as its allegory) it is the identity of the process throughout all its forms, rather than its identification with any one of them, that Adorno and Horkheimer wish to stress in their basic presentation ('The Concept of Enlightenment'): a number of the more properly philosophical versions of these same themes then recur in *Negative Dialectics*, but the contexts are more varied here, so that the two texts complete each other: the former by its articulation of the argument, the latter by its demonstration of a more existential, social and historical relevance. Both begin, however, with the matter of identity and equivalence (at which point ritual is itself unmasked as a process of mimetic substitution homologous to what will happen at later stages of scientific thought); and this first account of what Adorno will later call the magic spell [*der Bann*] logically enough leads on into its effects in necessity and time, and above all in *repetition* as a tendential structure of human life and thought (and of Benjaminian experience) under achieved Enlightenment and its domination of nature.

That this is to be grasped subjectively as well as objectively the authors stress again and again, not least by way of the image of Odysseus, whose 'resourcefulness' presupposes his equally extraordinary self-control. For the domination of the self is simultaneous with the domination of external nature; even the most modest control over threatening forces in the outside world presupposes all the initial forms of psychic repression (whose inextricable relationship to 'civilization' Freud posited in *Civilization and its Discontents*): these are then also to be numbered among the forms and achievements of Enlightenment, and can be observed, recapitulated, in children's discipline and pedagogy (or in that of the national cultures themselves, as in Norbert Elias's histories). But it will be most appropriate to grasp this repression, this domination of inner nature (which may also, with Lacan, be called the construction of the subject) in a somewhat different way as the transformation of the subject into an instrument and a weapon, a means. What remains of it as an end in itself (it would be better to think of this as the great Utopia of aimless floating and gazing at the sky – as in MM, 'Sur l'eau', 155 – rather than the already highly repressed and disciplined Kantian imperative) is then little more than its continuing existence, or in other words self-preservation – always, in Adorno, the mark of violence, whose absence, if it were possible or even conceivable, would at once constitute Utopia (the world 'almost unchanged', as he liked to say, following Benjamin on the Talmudic conception of the world transfigured by Messiah).[52]

Speculation on the consequences of just such a general removal of the need for a survival instinct leads us well beyond the bounds of Adorno's social life-world and class style (or our own), and into a Utopia of misfits and oddballs, in which the constraints for uniformization and conformity have been removed, and human beings grow wild like plants in a state of nature: not the beings of Thomas More, in whom sociality has been implanted by way of the miracle of the utopian text, but rather those of the opening of Altman's *Popeye*, who, no longer fettered by the constraints of a now oppressive sociality, blossom into the neurotics, compulsives, obsessives, paranoids, and schizophrenics whom our society considers sick but who, in a world of true freedom, may make up the flora and the fauna of 'human nature' itself.

Now three great dimensions of 'civilization' are rewritten in terms of the dialectic of Enlightenment, as tendential histories: language, thinking and philosophy, and society and the division of labor. The 'history' of language (which includes art within itself) runs a paradigmatic course between the sacred name and nominalism, the ultimate desacralization of language under positivism, which ends up in the literal and the scientific. The process is registered at an overlapping, but somewhat later stage when we rewrite it in terms of the the history of abstract thinking, which finds its ultimate forms in positivism and mathematics. With the division of labor, however, and the culmination in capitalism of the processes at work in the various modes of production, society becomes itself that totality and that Fate which was once attributed to its opposite number, Nature; and at this point the paradoxicality of the authors' formulations recapitulate the most bewildering chiasmatic pronouncements of Rousseau's Second Discourse: 'the enforced power of the system over men grows with every step that takes it out of the power of nature' (DA 38/38).

Even Rousseau, however, proposed not some impossible return to a state of nature (which Horkheimer and Adorno could posit even less), but rather the far more imperfect Social Contract: here, the breaking of the magic spell of enlightenment is still envisioned in the celebration of the dialectic ('determinate negation'/ DA 23/24); the evocation of that more profoundly Marcusean retrieval called anamnesis (DA 39/40); and finally, the forthright call for 'true revolutionary praxis' (DA 40/41), beyond which some Utopia of the non-repressive and the non-coercive might lie.

What must also be said about the multiple paths and trends of this dense chapter is that, taking as its theme equivalence, it reduces everything to equivalence; identifying the achievements of enlightenment as so many forms of repetition, it subjects its varied raw materials to a single implacable logic that makes all human history into repetition as such. The dominant form taken here by the descriptions of this repetitive process does not yet deploy the code of identity we have found at work in *Negative Dialectics*; rather, it would seem plausible to identify it as the great Weberian movement of the effacement of ends by means, which he called rationalization and the present authors instrumental reason. To be sure, Weber's selected historiographic exhibits of this process (from the sociology of religion to the history of the legal system)[13] afford nothing quite so grandiose as the '*Odyssey*' commentary here, where Odysseus's adventures become allegories of the stages of 'civilization' as they encounter and repress monsters and marvels that are reminders of so many more archaic modes of production as well as markers for deeper, more instinctive layers of the psyche that Reason must thrust further down as it emerges from it.

That the social consequences of such repression in rage, *ressentiment*, and cultural envy should then be laid in place in the 'Anti-Semitism' chapter is altogether logical; while the Enlightenment reduction of ethics itself to an instrumental and sometimes inhuman remnant (described in the 'Kant/Sade' chapter) is perhaps less inconsistent with Weber's own program, although it would certainly have surprised him (the impossible contradiction in contemporary ethics is then rehearsed in a different way, as we have seen, in *Minima Moralia*). Still, these chapters also confirm the feeling of an essentially Weberian thesis, characterized by the implacably repetitive character of the tendential enlargement of enlightenment itself, as well as by the essentially political terms – of domination, violence, and power – in which the tendency is described. This sense of the Weberian elective affinity can only intensify the question about its compatibility with a Marxian view of history.

Before that question is addressed, however, two features of the 'vision of history' outlined in *Dialectic of Enlightenment* must be addressed, which seem to complicate the picture we have given of a simple essentially Weberian mechanism replicating itself over and over again (at higher levels of sophistication) throughout the historical record. These are the intervention of the concept of 'mimesis', whose relationship to 'enlightenment' is not initially obvious; and the notorious analysis of the so-called Culture Industry, whose function here is not so clear, even though its bleakness and pessimism are consonant with the rest. (As for the addenda, they tend to confirm the repetitive structure of the analysis, which can thus be stopped anywhere, or go on forever; *Minima Moralia* can then in that sense be taken as the sequel, and the sign of the feeling that even so, not everything has been said.)

What is most enigmatic about 'mimesis' is not the content but rather the status of this concept, about which – alluded to everywhere in *Dialectic of Enlightenment* (as though we already knew what it was) – we are then in later works referred back to this volume as to its full-dress official philosophical presentation. The philosophical traditions of antiquity are mainly useful to mark conceptual differences: Platonic or Aristotelian imitation, in particular, is conceived as a handicraft potentially resulting in a product,[54] something quite distinct from the sheer activity of mimesis for Adorno, which is bounded on the one side by sheer mimicry and on the other by Frazer's concept of 'sympathetic magic' (and in particular the imitative variety, based on metaphor, as opposed to the metonymic forms of homeopathic or 'contagious' magic, to which Adorno seems relatively more indifferent). Although the (in this form relatively more recent) concept of narrative plays no formal part in Adorno's thinking, we have already seen that a deep affinity can be established between what we call narrative and what he reserves the word mimesis for. 'Mimesis' thus displaces metaphor as a fundamental category of Adorno's thought, and can be said often to function as a more adequate substitute for the primal relationship of subject and object (so often reified in post-Hegelian usage): 'mimesis' forestalls dualistic thinking by naming the dualism as such and as an operation (just as the notion of 'instrumentaliz-ation' seemed to do for the Weberian means/ends dialectic).

What it seems to superimpose, however, by way of an excess of impli-cation, is in general the anthropological – namely, the sense everywhere of mimesis as an archaic activity, and one that at least implicitly risks being attributed to some conception of human nature (implications never present in the concept of metaphor as such, or in the abstract subject–object relationship). This opens up depth and perspective when the con-cept is deployed, a historical space demanding the proto-narrative of a genesis or a genealogy; but it also strengthens the 'always-already' appear-ance of this peculiar word, which behaves as though we knew it already, and as though it had come from some other place in which its credentials were already firmly established (it would be ironic if Adorno's lifelong principled hostility to definitions – a cause in which he rightly enlists the authority of Kant and Hegel – were mainly motivated by the will to evade this particular definition in advance).

But the role of mimesis in *Dialectic of Enlightenment* is a structurally peculiar one, since this is above all the point on which the issue of the continuity or discontinuity of the history of so-called Western reason is played out. The notorious account of Odysseus as the 'prototype of the bourgeois individual' (DA 42/43) is a mere impertinence which raises only the vaguest forebodings about some slippage between class and economic materials and interpretations in Frankfurt School thought in general; the postclassical reappropriation of Odysseus as a culture hero would be enough to justify it. But most modern historiographic traditions (from idealist histories of ideas to Marxist ones) have insisted with sufficient determination on the structural specificity of Western science – which is to say, of capitalism – for the larger impertinence of *Dialectic of Enlightenment* – the genealogy of enlightenment in prehistorical times, the assimilation of scientists to shamans and animists – to require some further justification.

Is human history, in other words, to be seen as one enormous continuity – in which case what would seem to hold it together is essentially the omnipresence of power, in the form of violence and domination: that is, essentially, the *political* – or does it know some fundamental break or leap or mutation with the emergence of a purely *economic* and desacralized system in that 'minor promontory of Asia' that is Europe, a break also characterized by the emergence of science as the first henceforth purely secular form of human thought? The second alternative, however, which can scarcely posit an absolute break, demands the invention of a dialectic, in which the same term remains but is modified, as it secures the modulation from the first moment to the second (indeed, in my opinion, the modern dialectic arose from the problem of conceptualizing this social and historical double standard in the eighteenth and early nineteenth centuries).

In this case, it is very precisely the concept of mimesis which will afford this dialectical possibility: the turn of so-called Western science will now be seen as a result of the anti-mimetic taboo and of anti-mimetic regression – that is to say, the passage from a perceptual 'science' based on the senses and on quality to notations and analysis based on geometry and on mathematics. But this description, which then displaces the specificity of 'science' onto its representation and its languages, thereby allows the continuity between science and ritual – as forms of domination – to remain intact. It is in any case probably more owing to psychoanalysis than to Hegel or Marx that we are today so willing to grant dialectical continuity to the same impulse and what represses it, and to see the mimetic impulse and the anti-mimetic taboo as a single phenomenon (with contrary effects); while the psychoanalytic construction can then authorize Adorno to develop the principle further (in the Anti-Semitism chapter) and to evoke a 'return of the repressed' of this same repressed mimetic impulse. Finally, we may observe an unusual 'antithetical sense of primal words' at work in his own ambivalence about the taboo, which in the spirit of any number of post-Weberian critiques of rationality, is clearly hostile, when it designates science, but becomes strangely posit-ive and mystical when it alters just slightly to admit the 'taboo on graven images' that justifies our reluctance to describe Utopia, or even to mention happiness itself.

The second apparent hitch in the continuous history of domination afforded by *Dialectic of Enlightenment* presents itself on the occasion of the 'Culture Industry'; that chapter seems more relevant from the Ameri-can-notebooks perspective than it does from that of a general critique of Western science (or of positivism). The American perspective is, how-ever, also that of the theory of 'monopoly' of 'state' capitalism (developed by Pollock and Grossman), for it is essentially that which secures their convergence theory of the similarities between the United States of the New Deal and Hollywood, and Nazi Germany. Such comparisons, which are frequent throughout the chapter, will arouse less pious indignation if it is understood that what is meant – besides the similarities between American repressive conformism and the rapid stifling of opposition under Hitler – is what most authorities acknowledge anyhow: namely, the originality of the nascent media technology throughout this period, as it is pioneered above all in the USA and Germany and has significant impact on their respective public spheres.[55]

Minima Moralia is then what this critique of the USA looks like when the 'convergence' hypothesis is removed, and a more conventional Euro-pean background perspective is restored: it now stages a unique counter-point, as it were, between Proust and Hollywood, between social and cultural observations nourished by the twenties and by the persistence of an older aristocratic European tradition, and those that complain about the raw and brash materialism of American life (particularly as seen through the eyes of the *émigrés*). That contrast also turns on economics, but of a rather less theoretical type: 'in Europe the pre-bourgeois past survives in the shame felt at being paid for personal services or favours' (MM 259/195). This says it all, from immediate reactions to the Americans and their culture as a 'people without dignity' all the way to the horror of wage labor (particularly for intellectuals) and at length to the well-nigh metaphysical theme of self-preservation itself, as a doom laid upon the human race. In this context the occasional evaluation of the anti-capitalism of Marxists like Adorno as a set of mandarin rather than working-class attitudes takes on some plausibility.

But that is not particularly the perspective of the 'Culture Industry' chapter, which rarely stresses the economic as such, and in which working class people do appear as gullible victims ('the slow-witted, who are the ones who suffer for everything anyhow' [DA 125/139]). This chapter can be clarified, I feel, and some of the more aimless polemics about it dispersed, by the realization that it does not involve a theory of culture at all, in any sense this word has come to have for us at least since Raymond Williams. But even in the anthropologists, and in Benjamin as well, culture is a realm of protection and adaptation in which the infrastructural asperities of nature or of the economic system are mediated, rationalized, palliated and sometimes transfigured in utopian or anticipatory fashion: culture, in Benjamin, wards off the kaleidoscopic shocks of the nineteenth-century urban environment; it is evidently enough a breeding ground for false consciousness, but also for demands in which embellishment and luxury symbolically express the will to achieve some freedom beyond sheer necessity.

It is important to see that 'culture' means none of these things in Adorno; the 'Culture Industry' chapter has to do with individual works or signatures – from Toscanini to Victor Mature and Betty Grable; it also has very much to do with individual subjectivity and its tendential reduction and subsumption; but it does not include a concept of culture as a specific zone or structure of the social. This is why it is a mistake to suppose that Adorno's 'elitist' critiques of the 'Culture Industry' in any way define his attitude or position towards 'mass culture', grasped now not as a group of commercial products but as a realm of social life: irrespective of the enormous changes and mutations undergone by 'mass culture' since wartime Hollywood and on into postmodernism, Adorno does not conceive of culture as a realm of social life in the first place; and it is rather this, indeed, which needs to be objected to in his theory (unless – the other way round – the contemporary concept of culture is itself to be grasped as a reflex of the tremendous expansion of the cultural sphere and the acculturation of daily life since the 1960s).

But if the false problem of Adorno's 'theory' of culture is removed, then it becomes clear how the chapter fits into the plan of *Dialectic of Enlightenment* as a whole: it pursues the implacable expansion and penetration of 'enlightenment' (or of 'positivism', if you prefer another version) into the mind itself, into individual subjectivity, in modern times. The irony and impertinence of the Kant reference (the Culture Industry has developed a streamlined form of Kantian schematism for its products [DA 112/124]) draws its density from the privileged position of aesthetics in the period of classical German idealism, and at the beginnings of capitalism: a position based not on some canon of masterpieces but rather on the space it still offered for the exercise of a non-alienated subjectivity that was neither business nor science, neither morality nor pure reason. This enclave is what the Culture Industry now begins to colonize, a kind of last frontier and final unexplored territory for the dialectic of Enlightenment. Degraded individual works of 'art' are therefore not here evaluated for purely aesthetic reasons, from some rigid 'standard' of high art (we will see in our examination of *Aesthetic Theory* that that 'standard' excludes the products of the Culture Industry altogether); rather, they have become so many symptoms of the degradation of subjectivity.

Apart from that, the Culture Industry, as Adorno and Horkheimer see it, is not art or culture but rather business as such, and indeed a place in which the tendential convergence between monopoly and instrumentalization can be observed more clearly than in other kinds of commodity exchange. Theoretically, indeed, this chapter has the additional significance and interest of an experimental combination of two kinds of analysis often confused with each other but less compatible than is ordinarily supposed: commodification and instrumentalization. The final pages, dealing with radio, raise the paradoxical problem of what to do with a commodity which is free: are these offerings (but by extension television images as well) thereby less commodities or more (and are there degrees in commodity structure)? The same pages, however, also stage the climax of the narrative of language and its dissolution, begun in the first, enlightenment chapter: for the first magical name does not come to rest in the reifications of scientific language, but rather here, with Hitler and the American radio industry, in the final form of a language become sheer brand name.

We must now try to close this enormous parenthesis, which enumerated the peculiarities of *Dialectic of Enlightenment* in order to reposition this influential text within Adorno's work as a whole. All the features described above become clarified if we now grasp this book in terms of Adorno's thesis on the alternation of social and natural history, where it clearly becomes the natural-history variant of a more Marxian social history. The two alternatives are now to be thought of as immense rewriting programs, neither of which contradicts each other, but which ceaselessly recode the findings of each in an incompatible language. The requirement for an alternation between these languages arises from an acknowledgement that no synthesis between them is today conceivable, and also that, as has already been observed, either one in isolation is misleading. It is therefore unnecessary to suppose that because *Dialectic of Enlightenment* mobilizes non-Marxist forms of explanation, it thereby constitutes a move beyond Marxism or a renunciation of the Frankfurt School's essentially Marxist programs of the 1930s (an interpretation which makes it difficult to account either for Adorno's later work, particularly in *Negative Dialectics*, or for the uses the radical student movement made of this early text along with its predecessors).[56]

For the perspective of natural history, which seems to be a theoretical alternative based on other kinds of explanations, is in fact rather a kind of *defamiliarization*, a view of the same phenomena (including their explanations) as it were from the epicycle of Mercury.

> Mind arose out of existence, as an organ for keeping alive. In reflecting existence, however, it becomes at the same time something else. The existent negates itself as thought upon itself. Such negation is the mind's element. To attribute to it positive existence, even of a higher order, would be to deliver it up to what it opposes. (MM 328/243)

This essentially anthropological perspective on consciousness clearly feigns a view from the outside, from the Martian observer; and subsumes any concrete historical content of the mind at whatever stage it has been observed in. Within any one of those stages, a certain technological level of consciousness goes on 'reflecting' the division of labor, solving 'such problems as the evolution of the mode of production has posed', generating a certain intellectual class, throwing out a subsidiary web of ideology whose functions are consistent with the class arrangements in question. The anthropological perspective has little to say in the analysis of this concrete moment, little to add to the findings of a more properly socioeconomic theory; it intervenes when we are tempted to eternalize the idealist perspective on the object – mind or consciousness: a perspective required provisionally for its local analysis, but one which must then be redissolved into the larger materialist vision of natural science before it begins to imply the independent or autonomous existence of 'entities' – such as mind or culture, or indeed politics or economics themselves – which are rather to be considered moments in a dialectical totality. Natural history thus intervenes at those moments of methodological contradiction we have already examined, in which the 'critique of culture' or the 'sociology of ideas' (or, in another way, ethics as such) prove impossible to establish as separate non-contradictory disciplines.

But of course the anthropological perspective itself – such as the resonance of the notion of 'mimesis' – implies a different code or vocabulary from the socioeconomic, and tends to stress domination rather than production. These are the resonances of *Dialectic of Enlightenment* that have often been taken by its readers to reflect Nietzschean or Weberian, often even Social Darwinistic, presuppositions. According to our hypothesis here, however, which is essentially that of a rewriting strategy, there is nothing particularly exclusive in the choice to read a particular mode of production as a way of dominating nature, provided this new description serves as a reminder of natural history rather than a new theory

in its own right: following Adorno's methodological rule, then, 'domination' must itself next be unmasked as an essentially social and historical
concept, and the contents of this whole historiographic line must then
be reversed and rewritten again in social terms. But if nature is absolutized
as a first or fundamental code, then it decays into ideology even more
rapidly than do the more obviously produced and class-bound ideologies
of history, and is dismissed rudely in the next chapter, 'even where it
takes itself for the bedrock of Being, as the projection of the wretched
cultural wish that in all change things must stay the same' (ND 361/368).
Thus we rejoin the basic differentiation with which we began, a dialectic
of history in which even the laws of its change are modified at each
stage, and that other kind of 'dialectic' – called, of enlightenment – in
which repetition is a monotonous law of its seeming enlargement over
time. But how can we tell if this repetition is a doom or an anxiety
that feeds a wish-fulfillment?

Indeed, at a time when the relationship of ecological to socialist politics
is very much on the agenda practically, and when also within Marxism
the question of nature (and of natural science) has been significantly
raised again in a variety of ways (after the relative disinterest of most
of so-called Western Marxism in science), this new dialectical double-
standard and alternating discursive relationship suggested by Adorno not
merely problematizes conventional views of the Frankfurt School as hostile to science (a critique of reason, but also a call to natural history!)
but also suggests a new and suggestive strategy and paradigm.

The ultimate terms of any vision of history in the light of nature
are, however, those of the ceaseless stream of the generations themselves,
the perpetual transformation of the river of organisms into which one
never steps twice, the dizzying perspective of Kafka's *Josephine the Mouse-
Singer*, and the omnipresence of ephemerality and death – what is signified
by the untranslatable German word *Vergängnis*, with which indeed this
section on natural history, and the entire chapter on Hegel's World Spirit,
significantly concludes. But such a language, which reduces the dust of
human events and actions to the swarm of the non-human, would deem
to lead us out of history altogether, whether natural or social, into the
realm of metaphysics itself. It is indeed to that realm that Adorno now
turns in the concluding 'model' of *Negative Dialectics*.

Twelve

Adorno's final movement comes closest to a kind of 'literary' text – in other words, one which has to be read thematically rather than philosophically – with the result that each reading will be just 'slightly distinct' from the rest. What accounts for this imperceptible difference is no doubt the content of the chapter, which stages incompatible positions on 'metaphysics' – positions that are untenable and unavoidable all at once, and inconsistent with one another; the resultant rhythm is thus quite different from the rotation of the concept itself in the 'Freedom' chapter, in which differences were internally generated by the object of study; or the momentum towards natural history we observed in the chapter on world spirit. Yet even Kant's three transcendental ideas turned out to project very different kinds of internal dysfunction: the paralogisms were not at all the same as the antinomies, while the impossibility of the ontological proof ended up a very different matter from either. We must not therefore approach this final model with the expectation of drawing the same kinds of conclusions or walking away with the same kinds of results in hand: those were in any case distinct in the earlier two models – the structural doctrine of the radical impurity or heteronomy of ethics constituting something more fundamentally substantive than the methodological call for an alternation between social and natural history.

The 'Metaphysics' chapter, however, does seem to involve Adorno's own paralogisms: death is everywhere and omnipresent, perhaps above all in this late capitalist society after Auschwitz; but on the other hand we seem to have eliminated the very thought of it from the fabric of everyday life. Kant's supreme value for us lies in the way in which he embodies the last possible demand for metaphysics in modern secular society; but he is also the first positivist and provides an arsenal of arguments for the elimination of the metaphysical as such. Metaphysics is not, as Comte thought, a breakdown stage in the secularization of theology; rather, it embodies its own specific value – truth – but then in that case perhaps theology is better still in so far as its supreme value – the body – is materialistic and transcendental all at once. As for some putative 'third stage' in thinking, the dialectic, it is indispensable only on condition that it ultimately abolish itself: this final, logical stage in 'negative dialectics' seems to me the only moment in which Habermas's fear – that this profound critique of reason and rationality might end up in the cul de sac of irrationalism – seems potentially justifiable; even though what cancels the rational and dialectical thought in Adorno is not the instinctual, nor even the lure of false immediacies, but rather materialism and the bodily wish.

What I wish to retain of this short but bewilderingly suggestive chapter is above all a certain tension between two kinds of temporality in Adorno's thought and experience: these are the temporality of the constitutively incomplete, of gratification by way of unfulfillment, and the temporality of survivorhood, or of uneven devolvement: the temporality of Proust and the temporality of Auschwitz (or of philosophy itself). Both are thus forms of temporal experience that exclude any mirage of full presence, of ultimate satisfaction, reconciliation, or historical consonance – the one by way of the future, the other by way of the past; the first of these odd ec-centric forms finally seems to turn on the experience of the individual subject, or happiness, while the second very much involves the experience of history and its 'end' – whether in catastrophe or in achieved revolution and utopian society.

For the philosophical appeal to death and suffering in Adorno is a paradoxical one that has nothing of the mystique of Heidegger's 'being-unto-death'; or any particular morbid fascination with the thing itself. What seems to have happened to Adorno, rather, is not merely the fact of Auschwitz – which, horrifying as it may be to imagine, includes no foolproof guarantee of a response any more than any other atrocity in history, which we can sometimes grasp and sometimes not – but the peculiar way in which he experienced that fact: in other words, the way in which his own life-experience mediated the thing itself. This is also to be understood against a certain distance in his identification with Judaism; as a 'half-Jew', for example, Adorno seems to have felt perfectly secure in returning to a now Hitlerian Germany during summer months throughout the 1930s. The specific form, then, in which he lived the news about Auschwitz could be called 'unexpected survivorhood': what seems to have horrified him was not that he himself was in danger after the fact, or that he also might have been swept into the camps and gassed, however Jewish he did or did not feel himself to be. Rather, it was the idea that by the same kind of accident (and even without knowing it at the time) he himself proved unexpectedly to have outlived those who were herded into the gas chamber. This, then, is an experience of 'death' and 'mortality' which is transmitted not by some vivid imagination of the death anxiety, but rather through life itself, and the guilt of living on, the gift of life as sheer accident, the emptiness of a peacetime existence which is somehow felt to have taken the place that should have been occupied by someone else, now dead. *Das Leben lebt nicht*. This famous sentence, which we have earlier read (not incorrectly) as designating the maimed and damaged nature of human living under late capitalism, now can also be seen to express the gratuitous survival of existence, its aimlessness and pointlessness, after genocide; it being understood that, unlike those contemporary ideologues who manipulated the Holocaust in function of their anti-communism, for Adorno as for Horkheimer, 'they have nothing to say about fascism who do not want to mention capitalism' (the 'state of exception' of Nazi Germany remaining very much a part of the logic of monopoly or state capitalism, according to the various economic theories of the Frankfurt School).

What must now be observed, however, is a structural homology between this form of 'unexpected survivorhood' in guilt and retroactive anxiety and that equally notorious survival of philosophy as such, with which one of the most famous sentences Adorno ever wrote confronts us on the very first page of *Negative Dialectics*: 'Philosophy lives on because the moment to realize it was missed' (ND 15/3). This complicated proposition, which inscribes the failed revolution in the advanced capitalist countries at the same time as it endorses Marx's vision of the eventual coincidence of theory and praxis in a socialist society,[17] also serves as the philosophical basis for that systematic refusal of immediate forms of practice and political relevance implicit in the Frankfurt School's defense of the autonomous moment of critical theory as such. What so often seems to be special pleading and the defense of intellectuals and of the contemplative as privilege and class luxury has its source here, in a vision of necessary historical unevenness that greatly transcends and problematizes Bloch's or Trotsky's, ending up abolishing even the concept of the necessary in history. Yet a certain private guilt surely still clings to this distance from life (as it also clings to the exercise of artistic autonomy), as witness the luminous fable of 'Shaw on his way to the theater, showing a beggar his identification with the hurried remark, 'Press'!' (ND 356/363).

I have suggested in the Introduction that this critical and contemplative

distance from praxis[18] became another kind of praxis in its own right
with the emergence of the new academic spaces in the 1960s, and with
Adorno's embrace of an anti-positivist vocation to struggle within the
disciplines of restoration Federal Republic Germany; which is to say
that the social role of the intellectual can be seen to undergo a profound
mutation within his own personal career: from *émigré* to professor. The
rhythms of this historical unevenness – which seems to confirm the tendential vision of triumphant positivism forecast in *Dialectic of Enlightenment* by its very remoteness from the paradigms of any Marxian social
dialectic – in our own time proceed to abolish both of these 'positions',
on the one hand by transforming the memory of Auschwitz into Jewish
neo-ethnicity and nationalism; on the other by suppressing the last imaginable Archimedean space for critical theory or negative thinking in the
submergent flood tide of a now omnipresent 'cynical reason' (Sloterdijk).
('Society seems intent, by a deathly elimination of tension, on making
a noteworthy contribution to entrophy' (MM 160/123).

The other form of temporal non-coincidence – separated from this
one by a *'presque rien'* that transforms it altogether – is what seems to
have borne for Adorno the name of Proust, who first wrote out the
'identity of identity and non-identity' in the realm of the existential and
registered the peculiar property of experience never to be fully lived
for the first time but only in its reexperience: something which both
affirms and denies all at once the possibility of experience to be fully
gratifying. Something like this seems for Adorno to have been the other
dimension of metaphysics as such, at one and the same time the contemplation of death and the mediation on the possibility of happiness:

> What metaphysical experience is like can best be felt perhaps by those who
> are reluctant to derive it from so-called primal religious experience, in such
> Proustian forms as the happiness of the naming of villages such as Otterbach,
> Watterbach, Reuental, or Monbrunn. You have the feeling that if you ever
> go there, you will reach fulfillment, as though that really existed. Once you
> go, however, that promise retreats into the distance like a rainbow. Yet you're
> not really disappointed; rather, you have the feeling that you can't see it
> now because you're standing too close. (ND 366/373)

Yet this embodiment of gratification through its own failure is not fundamentally different, in Adorno's allegory of the existential, from despair
itself, the promise of gratification being still equally maintained within
its denial. Indeed, Adorno nowhere touches the outer limits of metaphysical speculation with so transcendental a formulation (whose genuine affinity with Benjamin and Bloch is a rare event in his work) as in the
affirmation of happiness as a 'waiting in vain', a *promesse de bonheur*

that, unfulfilled, can also be said to be at one with nihilism and the negative: here passages from Berg's *Wozzek* and *Lulu* join the literary expression of Proustian anticipation. As can be imagined, pages in *Minima Moralia* also rise to these occasions, most notably the childhood reminiscences such as 'Heliotrope' (MM 234/177): 'When a guest comes to stay with his parents, a child's heart beats with more fervent expectation ... '[59] The religious and salvational analogies, however, are important above all in the way in which they once again activate the familiar 'ban on graven images', to which we will return in a moment. Politically, however, the obvious ambivalence must be noted of a conception of inevitable non-fulfillment that stills desire (a reproach that this same 'ban on graven images' would nevertheless go a certain distance towards forestalling). Wisely, however, Adorno generally takes pains to sunder this existential and metaphysical dialectic (along with ethics itself) from a political materialism: 'that no one shall go hungry any more' (MM 206/156). Only after this is in place can we entertain the Utopia of '*Sur l'eau*': '*Rien faire comme une bête*, lying on water and looking peacefully at the sky ... ' (MM 208/157).

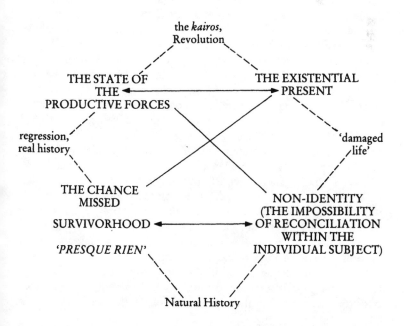

the *kairos*, Revolution

THE STATE OF THE PRODUCTIVE FORCES ⟷ THE EXISTENTIAL PRESENT

regression, real history

'damaged life'

THE CHANCE MISSED

NON-IDENTITY (THE IMPOSSIBILITY OF RECONCILIATION WITHIN THE INDIVIDUAL SUBJECT)

SURVIVORHOOD ⟷

'*PRESQUE RIEN*'

Natural History

The diagram is premature to the degree to which it anticipates what we will discover in *Aesthetic Theory*: namely, the resolute (and very orthodox) insistence on the significance of productivity and the forces of production. Far more than the possibility of revolution or achieved systemic transformation of the social totality (about which it is a schoolboy philosophical debating point to say that it is presupposed by the conception of the missed opportunity) the conception of productive forces can alone, in Adorno as well as in Marx himself, underwrite a concept of history which, in the full complacency of celebrations of its 'end' in a First World fat with commodities, beats its wings urgently in the debtor nations of the Third World. A reading of loops and regressions in the real historical world is possible only at this price, while the 'existential' realm of the maimed and damaged subject (we are still here in the domain of the anti-hero and of 'anomie') takes its meaning and resonance from situations of under- and over-development, in relative autonomy from the longest *durée*, the mindless biological stratum of natural history itself.

From such a 'world-view', it would seem that transcendence is utterly absent; indeed, of this final chapter of *Negative Dialectics* it might well be said that it deals with the metaphysical only by way of the ban on its image and on its overt expression: at its most routine, then, this can result in a mystical formula of the 'not this ... not that' kind. At its most energetic, however, we seem on the point of touching those ultimate boundaries with the non-thinkable which Kant surveyed and carefully marked out, leading Hegel to observe that if he could think them as barriers and limits he had already thought his way beyond them. Hitler, however, made metaphysics materialist, and included the mortal body irrevocably within any such speculation; but at a time when, 'after the decline – long ratified in secret – of the objective religions that had pledged to rid it of its sting, death itself has now been rendered utterly alien by the socially determined decline of continuous experience as such' (ND 363/370). Meanwhile, 'the idea of absolute death is hardly less scandalous for thought than that of immortality' (ND 364/371): Adorno does not thereby imply secret religious impulses (of the type of the later Horkheimer) but rather simply, with Kant's immortality thesis as well, that we know all about our own death but, unable to imagine it, never include its knowledge in our conscious action: our projects thus presuppose our own immortality, even though this last is not merely unthinkable for secular beings such as ourselves, but perhaps always was. The conclusion towards which the force of this paralogism is then impelled is not a leap of faith, but rather the critique of positivism, the denunciation of the anti-metaphysical 'current situation' in which this impossible and contradictory tension in thought cannot even itself be felt with the scandalous force it merits. The dialectic is then precisely this step above the impossible thought which takes its very impossibility as its own starting point, instead of a desperate attempt to solve it anyway with non-rational means.

So it is that even metaphysics itself and the 'last things' bring us back to a critique of this society and its magical spell: 'Kant's epistemological question, "How is metaphysics possible?", yields to a question from the philosophy of history, "Is it still possible to have metaphysical experience?"' (ND 364–5/372). It can of course also, as has been suggested above, be answered in the language of *natural* history:

> [The indifference of contemporary consciousness to metaphysical questions] conceals a horror that would take men's breath away if they did not repress it. One is tempted to the anthropological speculation whether the evolutionary dialectic that led to consciousness, including that of death, does not contradict an equally evolutionary animal constitution that prevents people from bearing such consciousness in the first place. (ND 388/395)

The perspective of human – that is to say, socioeconomic – history, however, discloses something like a web of actions within which something like a conspiracy, with agents, is embedded (my language, rather than Adorno's). The narrative will now turn on the fate of philosophy, whose index is its metaphysical function – or, in other words, what used to be called *truth*. But this traditional preoccupation does not distance Adorno from poststructuralism as greatly as might be imagined, since his theme also is the impossibility of 'truth' in our own time, the enfeeblement of the category itself, the debility of such mental operations and judgements.

It is a theme whose verbal enactment leads him to some of his most magnificent and contemptuous formulations: 'Even if it were a fact, it could not be the truth that Carnap and Mises are truer than Kant and Hegel' (ND 377/385). It is a paradox that turns on the life of dead cultures and approaches the Gadamerian preoccupation with the 'historical effectivity' of tradition from a non-historicist perspective, even though the perspective of social history necessarily binds thinking to its historical function and context. So Kant's 'block' – the critique of all the metaphysical illusions and pretenses of the more 'transcendental' uses of the mind: 'a system of stop signals' (ND 380/388), as Adorno calls it in passing – is evidently part of a larger social process and 'ruse of history':

> Socially there is good reason to suspect that block, the barrier erected against the absolute, of being at one with the necessity to labor, which in reality holds mankind under the same spell that Kant himself transfigured into a philosophy. The imprisonment in immanence, to which he honestly and brutally condemns the mind, is the imprisonment in self-preservation, as it

is imposed on men by a society that preserves nothing but the taboos that
are no longer necessary anyhow. (ND 381–82/389)

Kant is, however, also the place in which the metaphysical impulse is
for one last instant preserved and animate, less in the three great transcendental Ideas than in the impossible conception of the things-in-themselves
as a *mundus intelligibilis* (to which Adorno here devotes a remarkable
subsection).

The paradoxicality of this approach (which, however, began with the
by now well-known first sentence of *Negative Dialectics*) lies in the way
in which philological or historicist questions about the intellection of
the philosophical canon are here transformed into the occasions for a
thoroughgoing critique of the social order and late capitalism: as though
the old rhetoric of relevance had been dialectically inverted, a palpable
contemporary 'irrelevance' thus becoming the most burning and relevant
fact of the matter in the current situation. We have already noted that
only a commitment to a Marxist view of history can differentiate the
stance of these sometimes querulous complaints from that of the (generally right-wing) *laudator temporis acti*; what may now be added is another
type of reproach, namely that of a certain philosophical self-referentiality
inherent in this perspective, which risks turning all of Adorno's analyses
(on whatever topics) back into a purely formal reflection on the limits
and possibilities of contemporary philosophy – that is to say, on Adorno's
own practice. This optic, more than most others, underscores what is
modernist about Adorno's writing (particularly since it at once raises
the great central modernist issue of representation). It seems to me to
pose the strongest general objection for his philosophy as a coherent
position; and can probably not be parried from the outside, but only
by way of a certain philosophical solidarity with that position (something
that must today, as I will explain in conclusion, take the form of postmodernism theory).

But metaphysics, on this most desperate and negative recuperation,
then itself turns into something else – namely theology, about which
Adorno's most outrageous propositions assert its twofold relationship
to materialism, by way of the emphasis on the body and also by way
of the *Bilderverbot* or ban on graven images, to which we now return
and which has the additional advantage of emptying 'theology' here of
all its theological content. The idea had already been developed in the
luminous final pages of the methodological section of *Negative Dialectics*,
where even the most unacceptable dualisms of Kantian idealism (the raw
'sensations' organized into intuitions and concepts by the categories),
along with Hume's related doctrine of 'impressions', are celebrated as

the last epistemological quiver of the somatic element before that element is totally expelled. It lives on in knowledge as the latter's unrest, that it sets in motion and continues to reproduce, unassuaged, in its progress; the 'unhappy consciousness' is no mere delusion of the mind's vanity but rather inherent in it, the one authentic dignity conferred on it by the separation from the body. This dignity is the mind's negative reminder of its physical aspect; its very capacity to feel it is alone the mind's source of hope. (ND 203/203)

And of wishing and desire, of need [*Bedürfnis*], one would want to add as well, since it is with this that *Negative Dialectics* itself concludes: the affirmation of the deeper affinity between philosophizing and sheer bodily need. At this point, however, what is affirmed is something more paradoxical – namely that genuine materialism must be somehow 'imageless'. To evoke the ban on graven images, even by way of everything that Proust has now come to mean – whose whole expression of landscape, most notably in its climactic pages on Venice, turns on it – is perhaps not as useful as an account of the interference of images themselves that would be more congenial to the subjects of an image-and-spectacle society. Even the phenomenological threatens to convert an internal experience into a mere image of this last; while vulgar materialism, as a philosophy in its own right, is characterized by its external relationship to our deeper materialist experience – that is to say, by a conversion of that into an image, or at least a representation. Adorno's materialism thus wishes above all to elude the representational; in it fulfillment and the somatic realization of the object world must somehow exclude the intermediation of the image:

> Consciousness that interpolates some third thing, the image, between itself and what it thinks, unwittingly reproduces idealism; a corpus of representations is substituted for the object of knowledge, and the subjective arbitrariness of such representations turns out to be that of hierarchy and domination. The materialist longing to grasp the thing wills precisely the opposite of that; the full object can be conceived only in the absence of images. This absence of images converges with the theological ban on graven images. Materialism secularizes that, by excluding the possibility of giving any positive vision of Utopia: such is the content of its negativity. It is at its most materialist outer limit that materialism unexpectedly coincides with theology. It longs for the resurrection of the flesh. (ND 207/207)

As with modernism itself, here representation touches its outer limits, something like an aesthetic Kantian block: *mais il voulait cela dans un autre monde ...*' (*La Condition humaine*) ... 'but not here, not now!' (*A Passage to India*) ... Were these ideas possible as philosophy, then at this point Adorno would finally be at one with Bloch: but they are not: and *Negative Dialectics* concludes more modestly with the wish that, as its ultimate act, the dialectic would cancel itself out altogether. Here, then, the mystique of nature and the 'non-identical', which we will find looming larger in *Aesthetic Theory*, seems again to confirm Habermas's foreboding about the ultimately anti-rational thrust of this philosophy.

But in fact, the ban on graven images ought to exclude the vocation of all such representational metaphysics from philosophy, which – now aware of its historicality – can overtly conceive of itself as an instrument for taking the temperature of History itself: not in the sense in which it might somehow positivistically 'reflect' its moment of history, but rather in that this moment remains alive in it, just as in works of art, where we are asked to grasp 'the poem as a sundial of the philosophy of history' [*geschichtsphilosophische Sonnenuhr*] (NL 60), a sundial that marks the stages of collective self-realization and contradiction, but as it were from within the experience of history and not, by adding up the signs of material progress, from the outside. 'A message in a bottle' (PNM 126/ 133)? Perhaps as well; and such was the way in which Adorno characterized Schoenberg's music which, unheard, carried in it the secrets of the twentieth century on to some unimaginable future. But it is surely in his tribute to his teacher Siegfried Kracauer that, in virtually Dantean accents, we find expressed a lesson we must now ourselves apply to what Adorno left us:

> From the very beginning I learned, under his direction, to grasp [Kant's] work, not as some mere epistemological theory or the analysis of the preconditions of scientifically valid knowledge, but as a kind of coded text from out of which the historical position of Spirit was to be deciphered, with the vague expectation that in doing so something of truth itself was to be won. (NL 388)

PART II

Parable of the

Oarsmen

One

The central tension in Adorno's aesthetics is that between his formal project of desubjectifying the analysis of aesthetic phenomena and his commitment – inevitable, one would think, in any attempt to prolong the traditional framework of philosophical aesthetics – to the description of aesthetic *experience*: some last remnant of absolutely subjective categories which the desubjectifying impulse cannot wish to dissolve. What happens, of course, is that under these circumstances aesthetic experience retreats into the ineffable and the unsayable: since anything that can be said or formulated or thematized about it at once falls into the force field of the desubjectifying dialectic and is transformed into symptoms and evidence of *objective* processes:

> The spirit of works of art is objective, and that without any recourse to philosophies of objective or subjective spirit as such; the very content of the works is this objective spirit, and it passes judgement over them: spirit of the thing itself, that appears by way of appearance. Its objectivity can be measured by the power with which it infiltrates appearance. (AT 135/129)

The concrete detail of *Aesthetic Theory* is then the unexpected, unforeseeable result of the encounter between these two contradictory impulses, which must first be characterized in some more general ways. The project of desubjectifying our thinking about aesthetics can be seen in a variety of frameworks, of which the largest historical one is surely the turn of contemporary philosophy away from what are now known as 'philosophies of the subject' – that is to say, from the earlier modern attempt to ground truth in consciousness, the transcendental subject, and a variety of other subjective experiences and phenomena. This radical turn away

from and against subjectivity can be genealogized in a number of narratives, which alternately begin with structuralism, with Heidegger, with
Nietzsche, or even with Hegel or with Kant himself. It is objectively
ambiguous, in so far as the case might also be made that this tendency
in contemporary philosophy thereby replicates the tendencies and interests of the modern state and of monopoly capitalism: these last can be
seen as having a stake in the planification of the individual, the reduction
of individual and subjective choice in the era of organized society, the
penetration and colonization of the older autonomous ego, but also of
the Unconscious and desire, by the forces of the market.

The difficulty in affirming this other reading, this counter-interpre-
tation, of modern philosophy's objectivizing project, lies in the fact that
no reaffirmation of the subject or of subjectivity can be offered in opposition to it: since those various regressions and reversions to myth and
to archaic forms of subjectivity are not political responses to the power
and development of late capitalism, on the one hand; and since they
are probably all marked and maimed by its objectifying tendencies, on
the other – being, in other words fully as much symptoms of that process
as they are forms of resistance to it.

Within the world of culture, this anti-subjective project of contemporary thought – which should now be identified as contemporary interpretation in the broadest sense, rather than that of contemporary philosophy
alone – can also be described in a very different language, as an essentially
materialist repudiation of idealism and its ideologies. This description
does not, however, evade the negative and even paranoid scenario I offered
a moment ago, which can always subsume and invert it: materialist intellectuals thus being seen, by a Hegelian 'ruse of reason', as being unwitt-
ingly mobilized in the service of objective social processes. What this
second framework does offer, however, is a displacement of the first
one into the realm of culture and ideology, of texts and 'daily life', of
the superstructure and its dynamic (as opposed to an infrastructure which
more immediately generates thought and its categories in its own likeness).

The materialist kinds of cultural studies which have developed in the
contemporary period can thus be seen, if you like, as a component in
some vaster tendential project of liquidating the older subject and effacing
its archaic ideologies; but if one believes in the priority of the material
dynamics of culture, not only is it difficult to imagine the commitment
of intellectuals to a different project than this one; there is also a perspective in which it is assumed that such demystifying interrogation will
also ultimately reveal and unmask those very social and political forces
of late capitalism which might have found the anti-subjective cultural
project useful in the short term. At any rate, Adorno's various targets

among traditional and modern aesthetic categories – the notion of genius; the conception of the work as subjective or lyric expression; the various psychologies of the aesthetic (from Aristotle to reception theory); traditional psychoanalysis as well as conventional readings of Kant; the 'religion' of art (in art-for-art's-sake as well as in the notion of the compensatory function of the cultural sphere); the centrality of 'intention', even the philosophical (and Hegelian) reappropriation and dissolution of art in the service of meanings of various kinds – these have all intermittently been the targets of contemporary literary and cultural criticism, from the New Criticism on. Even the ultimate turn-of-the-screw of contemporary theory is not absent from Adorno's speculative explorations; namely, the position that Language, in whichever forms, is not subjective, and that language-centered analyses offer the most effective repudiation of older subject-centered categories.[1] In this sense, *Aesthetic Theory* offers a recapitulation, if not a summary, of the concerns and commitments of a varied tendency of contemporary criticism and theory today, probably the dominant one.

On the existential and ideological level, finally, there is surely a sense in which the moderns are all, in one way or another, eager to escape the kinds of interiority bequeathed us by traditional bourgeois culture and its values: the cultivation of subjective refinements and of heightened ethical discriminations enabled by social exclusion and class privilege, the fetishization of Experience as a kind of spiritual private property, the aesthetic individualism which becomes a privatized substitute for the life and culture of groups in business society.[2] It is not clear how much of this T.S. Eliot had in mind in his famous 1919 statement 'Poetry is not a turning loose of emotion, but an escape from personality. But, of course, only those who have personality and emotions know what it means to want to escape from these things.'[3] This concluding pointed sentence, of course, rechannels the significant anti-subjectivizing impulses of high modernism (shared by Adorno) into an equally period-characteristic conservative disdain for the 'anonymous' and 'inauthentic' masses (something that Adorno's analysis of the so-called Culture Industry has often been accused of as well). However, Adorno's dialectic can also show us how the unseating of the subjective can be pursued within the mind:

> The notions of subjective and objective have been completely reversed. Objective means the non-controversial aspect of things, their unquestioned impression, the façade made up of classified data, that is, the subjective; and they call subjective anything which breaches that façade, engages the specific experience of a matter, casts off all ready-made judgements and substitutes relatedness to the object for the majority consensus of those who do not even look at it, let alone think about it – in other words, the 'objective' itself. Just

how vacuous the formal objection to subjective relativity is, can be seen in the latter's most intimate field, aesthetic judgement. Anyone who, drawing on the strength of his precise reaction to a work of art, has ever subjected himself in earnest to its discipline, to its immanent formal law, the compulsion of its structure, will find that objections to the merely subjective quality of his experience vanish like a pitiful illusion ... (MM 84/69–70)

This is a defense of the objectivity of the subjective which clearly holds fully as much for artistic production as for its reception. That this herme-neutic impatience, this passion for breaking through to some real, material world beyond subjectivity and beyond texts, can be explained in terms of the status of intellectuals and its contradictions does not empty it of truth-content on other levels: it would not be the first time that the ideological vested interests of a group also – by some 'preestablished monadic harmony' or 'ruse of reason' – expressed the objective tendencies of the social system itself. At any rate, Adorno's 'objectification' of the aesthetic seems to me to satisfy other contemporary demands raised not merely by the contradictions of the aesthetic in our time, but also, as will be argued in greater detail later on, by the dilemmas of contemporary historical consciousness.

Two

But now we must register the contradiction in Adorno's thought, and the presence in *Aesthetic Theory* of a very different element which may well, in the context of the desubjectifying tendency that has just been described, look like a remnant or survival of just that 'philosophy of the subject' against which the other tendency was directed. This is the conception, and the organizing absent presence, of genuine aesthetic *experience*: full and achieved experience or listening (music being always, in Adorno, the ultimate test case of the aesthetic), the engagement with 'form'; the achievement, on the aesthetic plane, of ideal comprehension or *Verstehen*: and just as this last term introduces some relationship to history into aesthetic experience, so also does another language – the approach to the 'truth content' [*Wahrheitsgehalt*] of the work – lend it a seemingly traditional philosophical dimension.

The differentiation of aesthetic experience was, of course, always one of the central preoccupations of philosophical aesthetics as a discipline and a tradition: Aristotle on the one hand, and Kant and his successors (including the Lukács of the early and late aesthetics) on the other. Hegel, however, marks the onset of a very different approach, which aims at transforming art into philosophy and subsuming it altogether under considerations of 'truth- content' (with the result that something like the historical 'end of art'[4] becomes thinkable). As for Kant, Adorno's dealings with him are brilliantly unprincipled and suggestive: some guerrilla raids into the *Critique of Judgement* turn it inside out and rewrite it as a virtual Copernican revolution of the new anti-subjective aesthetic (where Kant is traditionally supposed to have virtually invented the issue of the differentiation of aesthetic experience as a subjective 'object of study' in the first place); other forays, however, identify and denounce Kantianism as the anticipation in advance of the whole manipulative program of the Culture Industry (the schemata, which persist in Kant's description of Beauty, becoming the prototype of 'degraded' Hollywood stereotypicality, and the source of that bad familiarity which characterizes 'popular music' and its fetishization of hearing).

But *Aesthetic Theory* is not at all a return to such traditional theorizing of aesthetic experience; in many ways, indeed, it challenges the very conception and ideal of a philosophical aesthetics (just as *Negative Dialectics* can also be read as a challenge to the very structure of the traditional philosophical project). The status of Adorno's stubborn commitment to some notion of 'genuine aesthetic experience' therefore demands clarification; along with the very form of this posthumous book, whose discursive or generic status remains unclear, and which often implicitly or explicitly raises the disturbing question whether we really need a 'philosophical aesthetics' any longer in any form, and whether that 'genre' or form of thinking has not somehow, at least in our time, become contradictory and impossible.

Adorno's thinking about these matters takes place on two distinct axes, which often intersect, but cannot be combined or conflated. On the one hand, he systematically distinguishes between 'art' in general and the experience of individual works: this opposition is then clearly the space in which the practices of contemporary literary criticism and theory conflict with the project of a traditional aesthetics, and not only in Adorno's own work. At least in the force field of the modern, literary criticism has tended to conceive its mission as the identification and description of what is unique in specific works, of their incomparability and radical *difference*. But the formal vested interest of traditional aesthetics lies in identifying what is common to all genuine works of art and their experience, and producing some generic concept of the 'artistic' within which the specificity of unique works, from Greek tragedy to Joyce and Picasso, dissolves away. (Contemporary criticism has, however, often been willing to entertain the possibility of a different kind of general or generic concept, in which various distinct works – by the same author, or from the same period, or in the same genre – somehow participate; but this kind of aesthetic thinking – historical rather than eternal – descends from Hegel rather than from Kant, and has also tended to disrupt and problematize the traditional constitution of aesthetic philosophy and its 'object of study' in a different way.)

Contemporary theory has therefore tended to fasten at once on the individual texts, and to elude the larger question of 'art' or the 'aesthetic' altogether, often by assimilating it to psychoanalytic questions of desire in general, or to dynamics of a textuality evident across the board in other, formerly philosophical or disciplinary, realms such as those of politics, anthropology, or sociology. But Adorno has his reasons for wishing to retain a question and a problem that seems otherwise to have become an anachronistic embarrassment: 'Art can never be completely subsumed in the various works of art, in so far as artists always also work on art itself, and not merely on their individual works' (AT 272/261). The distinction between art and the individual work of art remains, in other words, a dilemma, in so far as it marks a relationship as well as an opposition. It will become clear later on, indeed, that the dilemma is also a productive one, since it is by way of this very conflictual coexistence of art and the art-work – of work on an individual object which is also work on the nature of art itself (as in T.S. Eliot's conception of that 'slight' modification or alteration by the new work of the entire preexisting 'ideal order' of 'existing monuments') – that history enters the aesthetic and that Adorno is able to deploy his remarkable conception of the profound historicity of all individual works of art.

But more is at stake, in the difference between art and the individual work, than the *interpretive* access to history: in it is also inscribed the social, and the very experience of class struggle, as it is transmitted through the primal myth of Adorno's aesthetic theory – namely, the 'Sirens' episode from Book XII of the *Odyssey*. Evoking the pain and the contradiction of that repression of the self and of nature which the 'dialectic of enlightenment' holds out as the price of self-preservation, Adorno and Horkheimer describe Odysseus's twofold solution, the twin yet mutually contradictory possibilities of salvation:

The first he prescribes for his crew. He plugs their ears with wax, and they must row with all their strength. Whoever wants to survive must not give ear to the enticements of what will never come again [*des Unwiederbringlichen*], and he is able to do this only by being able not to hear them. It is an eventuality for which society has always made arrangements. Fresh and intent, the workers must always face forward and ignore the incidental [*was zur Seite liegt*]. They must doggedly sublimate, through redoubled effort, the impulse to diversion. They thereby come to incarnate the practical realm. – Odysseus, the feudal baron for whom others labor, reserves the second possibility for himself. He listens, only bound impotently to the mast; the greater the temptation, the more strongly does he order his bonds tightened, just as later on the bourgeoisie will forbid itself happiness all the more single-mindedly the closer it approaches by virtue of their increasing power. What is heard remains for him without aftermath; he can only move his head to demand release; too late, however; for the crew, who hear nothing, know only the danger of the song, but nothing of its beauty, and leave him at the mast in order to save him and themselves. They thereby reproduce the very life of the oppressor together with their own, while he himself can no longer step outside his own social role. The bonds with which he has irredeemably shackled himself to praxis at one and the same time sunder the Sirens from it; their temptation, thereby neutralized, becomes a mere object of contemplation, it becomes Art itself. The prisoner is attending a concert, listening motionless just like the audience at concerts later on in history, and his enthusiastic call for freedom already sounds like applause as it dies away. So it is that already in prehistory art appreciation and manual labor become disjoined. (DA 34/34)

This remarkable retelling of Hegel's master/slave dialectic reproduces its ironic twist (the 'truth' of the slave turning out to be the master, while the truth of the master '*only*' turns out to be the slave): in effect, Odysseus experiences Art, while his unhearing laborers learn something more profound about the 'individual work of art' to which they themselves are deaf: namely, *das Unwiederbringliche*, what cannot be called back from the past; the work's 'truth-content'.

But Adorno's conception of the individual work will be dealt with later on: for the moment, it is the generic concept of art which concerns us, and about which this passage has revealing things to imply: above all, the sheer guilt of Art itself in a class society, art as luxury and class privilege, a ground bass that resonates throughout all of Adorno's aesthetic reflections without a break, even where its vibration has become a virtual second nature in our sensorium, so that from time to time we no longer hear it consciously. This culpability irreparably associated with all artistic activity is, then, the deeper motive for the radical separation, in Adorno, between Art in general and the individual works: for what these last do, what they 'work on' in the artistic process, is to engage this universal sense of guilt, to address it with lacerating acuity, to bring it to consciousness in the form of an unresolvable contradiction. The individual works of art can never resolve that contradiction; but they can recover a certain authenticity by including it as content and raw material, as what the individual work of art must always confront anew, in all its virulence. In this sense, the guilt with which all works of art are suffused will be one of the mediations by which the otherwise monadic work is profoundly and internally related to the otherwise external social order (but only one possible mediation among others, as we shall see shortly).

It is also the deeper reason why a philosophical aesthetics in our time is not merely impossible, but intolerable. For it is not merely the radical difference of the individual work that general theories of beauty, or of art, or of the aesthetic, both miss and repress; it is also the will to the transaesthetic, to a truth beyond the work and a worldly referentiality in some more general sense, the vocation of Joyce or Aeschylus, of Dante or of Po Chu-yi, to engage the world itself and to be something more than mere 'art', that remains unregistered and invisible in the accounts of a traditional philosophical aesthetic. This is the moment, then, to sound for the first time the major theme and paradox of *Aesthetic Theory* – a principle that will return later in our exposition for fuller development, but whose first provisional formulation speaks to this issue: 'Where art is experienced purely aesthetically, it fails to be fully experienced even aesthetically' (AT 17/9).

As for the guilt of art in general, however, all this needs to be inverted and rearranged: the universal transformation achieved here by a philosophical aesthetics at its most successful and powerful turns all the individual works, in their difference and their various transaesthetic aspirations, back into one long uninterrupted 'aesthetic experience', thereby ejecting us brutally into a social world in which, in the midst of torture and misery, the unjustifiable luxury of art appreciation becomes an irrepressible and unavoidable conviction of every moment. Yet what we have said about contemporary theory also implies that the converse, a framing of the works that goes straight for their 'truth-content', is no less an evasion of this objective guilt, which is a fact of our world; for the metaphysical innocence of that theoretical intercourse with individual works of art, Adorno's formula might well be reversed in order to stress the way in which, when art is experienced only transaesthetically, in the apprehension of its truth content, this last is also missed, and its transaesthetic vocation is itself lost to such experience.

Two final remarks about this as yet provisional motif: first, it will be the form, taken in the aesthetic realm, of what Adorno elsewhere calls the 'determinate negation', the only authentic form of critical thinking in our time – in other words, a consciousness of contradiction which resists the latter's solution, its dissolution either into satiric positivism and cynical empiricism on the one hand, or into utopian positivity on the other. To succeed in thinking art as both aesthetic and anti-aesthetic at one and the same time is to achieve, in this area, the determinate negation. One's second thought, however, must be the awareness that it is very precisely from this dual position that Adorno's unremitting repudiation of political art springs: for it is not only the idle pastimes of the aesthete that are rebuked here, but also the impatience and philistinism of the militant. But we need not yet take a position on this supplementary opinion and consequence, which is also more complicated and paradoxical than it may look in this bald form.

These remarks, however, are all premature: for our first, exploratory concern here has been the status of the concept of Art in general in Adorno, and thereby the relationship of his discourse and form to that of traditional aesthetics: the twist and unexpected reversal in his position can then be characterized as follows – the preoccupation with the nature of art, the very foundation of aesthetics and also the least interesting topic in a situation in which only the individual works of art are interesting and authentic, must none the less be maintained and prolonged, because it is primarily in the area of art in general, as social activity, that the profound culpability of the aesthetic can be registered and identified. *Aesthetic Theory* is thus still an 'aesthetic', as it were, by its negative side, and owing to its commitment to a social perspective in which the inconsequentiality of the aesthetic is an inescapable fact of life.

But we must now turn to the other axis of Adorno's thinking about art, which is in dialectical tension with this first one, in which Art in general finds itself opposed to the individual works. In a second perspective, however, Art in general, now very much including the individual works and indeed precisely consisting of them, will be opposed to everything which is not art; or, more exactly, to everything 'cultural' in the general sense which is not 'really' art. This, the working premiss of *Aesthetic Theory*, must at first be laid out as scandalously and as baldly as possible: all art is 'great art'; there are no degrees in the aesthetic experience or even partial, promising, middling, incomplete aesthetic experience; there is only the thing itself, or else its absence; that is, in this area, the only kind of experience worth talking about, as long as one adds the embarrassing proviso that in case it cannot really be talked about at all in any expository propaedeutic sense; either you know what it is already, or no one can tell you. In this sense, *Aesthetic Theory* presupposes a primitive accumulation of the capital of aesthetic experience; it speaks to you about experiences you have already had, its sentences allude to the already known, the already familiar; and it stands or falls on your agreement with and interest in those descriptions. A brilliant essay in literary criticism might well open up possibilities of reading, or rereading, some hitherto opaque, dull, or exasperatingly perverse text; thereby enabling the emergence in you of some new reading experience (as though, no doubt, for the first time) and even disengaging the formation of some new aesthetic or poetic within your mind. *Aesthetic Theory* does not do that, and does not want to – in that sense also it remains within the confines of the philosophical aesthetic as an a posteriori clarification of what has already been felt.

But we might as well acknowledge our embarrassment with this first peremptory methodological decision: art is by definition 'great art'. What must first be noted is that this position also immediately excludes all the traditional questions about value, which is here presupposed in advance (in a kind of reversal of Northrop Frye's methodological decision to consider all types of narrative, whatever their putative 'value'). Value will come back, however, in another, more historical and social form. Meanwhile one does not so easily exorcize the mocking spirit of the arch-adversary Brecht, the tempter (and the corrupter of Benjamin) whose scenes flash up into the memory, most notably the drunks in *Mahagonny* gazing with wonderment at the player piano and exclaiming, '*Das ist die ewige Kunst!*'

It should be added that Adorno systematically makes a place for something that has tended to be suppressed altogether in the development of contemporary mass and commercial culture – namely, the practice of 'lighter' forms of art (as in the expression 'light opera'): composers like Lehar are as technically expert and admirable in their own way as the 'masters': '"Light" art as such, distraction, is not a decadent form' (DA, 121/135). But it is a space within a specifically bourgeois culture, which the tendential development of that culture obliterates:

> Light art has been the shadow of autonomous art. It is the social bad conscience of serious art. The truth which the latter necessarily lacked because of its social premisses gives the other the semblance of legitimacy. The division itself is the truth: it does at least express the negativity of the culture which the different spheres constitute. Least of all can the antithesis be reconciled by absorbing light into serious art, or vice versa. But that is what the Culture Industry attempts. (DA, 121-2/135)

The famous remark about the 'two halves that don't add up' does not therefore refer to high art and mass culture, but only to high art and light art, whose initial differentiation is itself eliminated by commercialization.[5] Meanwhile, a place is also made for a certain kind of traditional form, as the role played by fairy tales (or archaic late products like the *Struwwelpeter*) suggests. But here too one looks in vain for any politically reassuring traces of populism: indeed, the fundamental mediation on this new opposition – between mass culture and traditional or 'folk' art – is bleak, but also historiographically complex and 'unlinear'. The fundamental social relations in folk art 'are those of masters and servants, gainers and losers, but in an immediate, not wholly objectified form' ('Wolf as Grandmother', MM 272/204). What was ideological about these older forms is revealed in hindsight by the ideological structure of the new mass culture:

> The film has a retroactive effect: its optimistic horror brings to light in the fairy tale what always served injustice, and shows dimly in the reprimanded

> miscreants the faces of those whom integral society condemns, and to condemn whom has from the first been the dream of socialization. (MM 272/204).

Brecht himself had recourse to the traditional and the archaic for ends not terribly different from this one.

But as a matter of fact, these positions of Adorno – so easily reducible to 'elitist' opinions, to 'aestheticism', or to a social mandarinism which looks outmoded and culturally alien from within the mass-cultural democracy of the postmodern superstate – are probably better dramatized as moves against a variety of other imaginary or ideal-typical protagonists. In what follows, at any rate, the various positions become characters, and their abstract ballet turns out to be transferable to areas very different from art.

The initial move, which separates some genuine experience of art from everything that is *not* that, seems to be inherent in any philosophy organized around the experiential, which must necessarily reach its constitutive limit in what it is not ('determination is negation'). But in the case of 'experience', a peculiarly paradoxical situation is confronted, since virtually by definition what is not experience cannot be known or formulated, so that such philosophies are unable to include an account of their own boundaries. Interesting non-reflexive strategies therefore emerge: in Merleau-Ponty's phenomenology, for example, the experience of the body finds its Archimedean point outside itself in the peculiar borderline exceptionalities of the so-called 'phantom member' – that is, the continuing sensations 'in' limbs which have been amputated. Only by way of the absent presence of such withdrawn zones is Merleau-Ponty able to organize his descriptions of the full phenomenological body.

In other existentialisms, the problem of the borderline appears in two related but distinct areas: that of meaning and that of death. Only from another, external standpoint can the situational meanings inherent in any life-project be revealed as sheer constructions without natural foundation: but that standpoint – not given within the life-world of the existential philosopher, for example – tends to veer into positivity, so that its absence of meaning now slowly turns into a concept and a philosophy in its own right – namely, the so-called 'absurd'. Meanwhile, in Sartre, death – another constitutive limit of this kind – ceases to be something we can contemplate like an energizing mystery within life (as is still the case in Heidegger's *Sein-zum-Tode*) and becomes the meaningless other side, an event by definition outside life and which to that degree, as it were, ceases to concern us. (Heidegger's 'solution' to the problem of limits, as Habermas is only the latest to have insisted, reverts to a mythic history, by setting the 'outside' of our fallen world of the existent in repressed and forgotten Ur-time, as a genuine experience and presence of the mystery or the question of Being of which we have, in historical time, lost even the memory.)

So it is that, approaching the description of one of the constitutive features of art as play, as riddle and enigma, Adorno finds himself rehearsing the argument from the 'phantom member' and recommending 'the study of unartistic people', of people 'without artistic sensibilities', *amusischer Menschen* (AT 183/177):

> It is quite impossible to explain to them what art is; and if it were possible to do so intellectually, they would still not be able to square this insight with their experience. For them the reality principle is so powerful as to repress aesthetic behavior completely. Urged on by the official cultural approbation of art, such insensitivity to art frequently shades over into aggression, and this plays no little role in the general tendency today towards the 'deaestheticization' of art [*Entkunstung*, literally 'de-arting' – that is to say, the stripping from art of its conventional artistic features and signals, such as *Schein* (aesthetic illusion and fictionality), along with the attempt to rejustify such aesthetic activity by passing it off as something else, as in happenings, advertisements, certain forms of political art, etc. – *FJ*].

The explanatory features introduced here – the 'reality principle', the 'official cultural approbation of art', the relationship to 'aggression' – open up a variety of social and historical forms into which the 'non-artistic' [*Amusie*] can develop into (and which we will examine in a moment). But this first global privative position is determined by the sheer logic of Adorno's inquiry (as we have argued above); what can be observed in this passage is the way in which it now becomes rhetorically staged within the text as one kind of *reader*: very precisely the one to whom we have already made incidental reference – namely, that reader who approaches *Aesthetic Theory* with no previous experience of what the aesthetic is, and is here dramatized as a reader who is unable, for whatever 'natural' or 'constitutive' reason, to 'have' aesthetic experience in the first place.

Anthropologically, of course, such a reader is inconceivable: a being utterly without negativity (in the Hegelian sense), so completely mired in the immediate that its consciousness would eschew even that relative and minimal distance from the world which we attribute to the 'higher' animals. Fantasy, the capacity for fiction or for the mental entertainment of images of what is not (and even what is not yet, or what is past), is thus not some incidental, supplementary adjunct power of human consciousness but virtually its constitutive feature. But once again, as I have suggested above, attempts to 'define' consciousness (one thinks of the way in which Sartre's definition of consciousness as negation and distance necessarily passes through a description of the 'imaginary') find themselves positing this inconceivable privative position to get about their business. In the same way, descriptions of language at some outer limit need the fantastic and internally contradictory representation of non-linguistic beings – such as the Grand Academicians of Lagado in Swift, whose plan to abolish language and substitute the 'things themselves' (carried around for just such communicative purposes) might have served Adorno as a figure for some quintessential positivism.

Adorno's privative term will thus very rapidly take on what the narrative semioticians call the features of 'surface manifestation', becoming a 'lifelike' character (or several) with the appropriate social and historical determinations (something that already begins to happen in the passage cited, as we have observed above). But at the outset the '*amusischer Mensch*', the person bereft of all aesthetic sensibility, is something like the Other in the text: that ultimate non-reader against whom one argues, or, if that fails (as it must by definition), whom one vilifies and ridicules in order to ratify one's solidarity with the 'proper' reader, who is thereby encouraged to assume – against this Other – the perspective constructed by the text itself. It is tempting to imagine that all texts – at least in the earlier stages of genres in formation: that is, in the process of institutionalization – find themselves obliged thus to include the 'bad' or 'undesirable' reader in the form of just such privative positions: these do not, of course, have to be anthropomorphic 'characters' in a narrative but are most dramatically visible as such – as, for example, in those works of science fiction or of occult genres which systematically include the Rationalist, the Skeptic, the Non-believer, *within* the text in order to confute him and thereby to neutralize undesirable readings.

In a sense, of course, Adorno's non-artistic position has already achieved 'actantial manifestation' in a primary narrative: in the form of Odysseus's oarsmen in the 'Sirens' episode, whose ear-stoppers make them over into people who know that art exists but can have no conception of its experience or powers. It is certain that in some larger social sense, as the class allegory of the Sirens makes explicit, these non-artistic people are identified with the laboring masses. They reappear in another astonishing passage of *Dialectic of Enlightenment*, when Adorno and Horkheimer make the (improbable) suggestion that one might suddenly switch the entire Culture Industry off, without anyone caring:

> Such closures [e.g., of the movie theaters] would not be reactionary Luddism or machine-breaking. The disappointment would be felt not so much by the enthusiasts as by the slow-witted, who are the ones who suffer for every-

thing anyhow. Despite the films themselves, which are meant to complete her integration, the housewife finds in the darkness of the movie theater a place of refuge where she can sit for a few hours with nobody watching, just as she once used to look out of the window, when there were still private homes and 'free time' after work. The unemployed of the great cities find coolness in summer and warmth in winter in these temperature-controlled locations ... (DA 125/139)

This populism (which we probably owe to Horkheimer) is clearly rather different from the conservatism of the same period, with its analyses of 'mass man' or of the inauthenticity of mass industrial culture (Heidegger's *das Man*', or Ortega's 'revolt of the masses') to which it is nevertheless, ideologically related: here, however, the 'marginals' of contemporary radical rhetoric already make their appearance – in the persons of women and the unemployed, and not least in the pathos of those ultimate victims, the stupid or retarded, to which Döblin's *Alexanderplatz* is the monument. The comforting darkness of the great movie theaters then becomes the after-hours resting place of the oarsmen of Odysseus, who pay no more attention to the mesmerizing images on the screen than they did to the Sirens' song.

But what if they did? At this point, Adorno's negative or privative position – non-Art, the quality of people radically unable to have aesthetic experience in the first place – splits in two, as it begins to enter real history; and with this bifurcation in his figures, the notorious conception of the Culture Industry itself begins to appear. For alongside those who have no conception of artistic experience, a place must now be made for those who think they do, and a characterization and an analysis of *ersatz* art must now be devised for all those viewers and listeners who, believing themselves to be engaged in cultural experience, still turn out not to know what art is and never to have achieved 'genuine aesthetic experience', and never even to have known they were deprived of it in the first place.

The 'Culture Industry' does not play a major role in *Aesthetic Theory*, but has already been negatively presupposed by it: indeed, the earlier text poses the most serious philosophical problem for the later project as a whole – namely, how to deal with the exception or the possible middle ground, with a kind of 'aesthetic experience' which is neither 'genuine' (an apparent 'art' which is obviously not 'great art', in Adorno's sense) nor is it non-art altogether. The chapter on the 'Culture Industry' in *Dialectic of Enlightenment* confronts this structural problem in advance, by excluding the dilemma of theorizing a kind of art which is not 'really' art (nor is it 'bad art' exactly, since that is a non-concept) and a real experience which is not really aesthetic, even though it is not anything

else either (in Kant's terms, it is also neither practical nor epistemological).
To say, as Adorno also does here, that this mass-cultural experience is
in fact that of the commodity form is also to stress that it is objective
(it is not a 'pseudo-experience), but not yet to articulate the relationship
of this new code (commodity fetishism) to the traditional aesthetic categories rehearsed here.

Three

But it is difficult today to discuss the notion of the Culture Industry, surely Adorno's single most influential – and also provocative, and even notorious – concept, without including something like the history of the 'fortunes' of this concept in the discussion. Although first outlined, in *Dialectic of Enlightenment*, in a language that wished to combine the sociological and the philosophical, this Ur-text (along with *Minima Moralia*) can also be reread (or rewritten) as work in an older literary genre: namely, that travel literature produced by Europeans as a result of their often horrified contact with the new North American democracy, and in particular with the originality of its political, social and cultural forms, which unlike those of Europe came into being independently of the class struggle with an aristocratic *ancien régime*, whose influence persisted in the Old World, at least until very recent times, in the marks and the survivals of a pre-bourgeois conception of culture (even where, as in Bourdieu's 'distinction', such aristocratic forms and categories were adopted and restructured by the bourgeoisie itself). But the anthropological shock of the contact of these Central European mandarins with the mass-democratic Otherness of the New World was also uniquely conditioned by an unexpected historical conjuncture: the simultaneous rise, in Europe, of Hitlerian fascism.

Today this conjuncture has come to seem less paradoxical and contingent: if indeed it is so, as the historians now seem to suggest, that the Hitlerian moment was in fact Germany's long-postponed bourgeois revolution, and that its violent and petty-bourgeois social, political and cultural *Nivellierung* had as its objective result the destruction of the last remnants of some surviving aristocratic forms, then the two historical phenomena – American mass democracy, the Nazi interregnum in Germany – are closely related. But it was the originality of Adorno and Horkheimer first to have linked these two phenomena culturally, and to have insisted, with an implacability that must surely be counted as a form of political commitment, on the indissociability of the Culture Industry and fascism; and to have mingled their American and their German examples and illustrations throughout their exposition in a provocative fashion that could not fail to scandalize. That the Second World War concluded with the victory of the Culture Industry over its Nazi competitor and rival is then grasped as variation within a single paradigm, rather than the victory of one paradigm over another.

The concept of the Culture Industry thus originally masked and expressed – via some new philosophical stylization and abstraction – one of those Tocqueville-Dickens-Trollope voyages to the United States, whose generic familiarity has always allowed American intellectuals to discount them as so much snobbery and aristocratic prejudice. But for other, left-wing American intellectuals – less wedded to notions of American exceptionalism – the Adorno-Horkheimer critique could also lay the basis for a cultural critique of capitalism itself, by way of that identification of mass culture and the commodity form which has already been mentioned: and in the United States this cultural critique was established independently of the modernist aesthetic values on which it depended philosophically in Adorno and Horkheimer, yet in a situation where, by the 1950s, artistic modernism had become hegemonic and canonical and had conquered the university system. In the ensuing years (shortly to become the 1960s) several of these variables changed and, along with them, the very situation of cultural critique itself. It seems fair to assert that this field of study, with its motivations and values, has remained since then associated with the left in this country (it is only in very recent years that the hitherto episodic forms of right-wing cultural critique have won any legitimacy).

But the American left, as it was reborn socially in the 1960s, also rediscovered its older populist traditions and began to reformulate its cultural positions in an essentially populist idiom. Meanwhile, the essentially European traditions of aesthetic modernism, now canonized in the academy, ossify and are felt to be 'academic' in the bad sense; the repudiation of this kind of modernism by the populist left then merges with an anti-intellectualism which in American business society has paradoxically been a political tradition here on the left as well as on the right; while finally modernism itself, as an artistic movement, for whatever larger systemic and socioeconomic reasons, comes to an end during or shortly before this period (and this means the dissolution of that moment in which, as Adorno describes it, 'art [read: modern art, technically advanced art] was by definition politically left' [AT 377/360]).

But now another feature of the new mass culture of the 1960s (prolonged into our own historical period) must be reckoned into the description: so-called popular culture now becomes technically advanced (very much in the spirit of Adorno's description of modernism, as we shall see later on). The formulation is no doubt inaccurate, and undialectical, in so far as it suggests that the 'technologically advanced' was there already, but that finally mass culture made its way to it. What really happened was, on the contrary, a simultaneous leap forward both mass-culturally and technologically, in which for the first time the two developments were also consciously interlinked: resulting in the emergence together of what we now call the media and the new media-oriented culture. This development must be stressed, in order to replace *Dialectic of Enlightenment* in a historical perspective and to read it as something which has *become* historical, whatever other claims its arguments may have on us. The products of Adorno's Culture Industry must now be identified as standard Hollywood Grade-B genre film (before the latter's reorganization by *auteur theory*), as radio comedy and serials of a thirties and forties variety ('Fibber McGee and Molly', for example) and, in music, as Paul Whiteman (the proper referent for what Adorno calls 'jazz', which has little to do with the richness of a Black culture we have only long since then discovered); it has something to do with Toscanini as well (whose contemporary reevaluation was in many ways anticipated by Adorno himself),[6] and arguably also anticipates the first television programs of the late 1940s (such as Milton Berle). Whatever contemporary nostalgia may have recently come to invest such artefacts, the structural break between their forms and those of our own mass culture seems obvious enough to warrant our positing a similar and equally historical break between the analytic thinking (or 'determinate negation') inspired by them and the theory contemporary mass culture has seemed to demand.

This last can be characterized in terms of populism to the degree to which it shows increasing impatience with theories of manipulation, in which a passive public submits to forms of commodification and commercially produced culture whose self-identifications it endorses and interiorizes as 'distraction' or 'entertainment'. New conceptions of reading begin to cast a certain doubt on these conceptions of reception; while paradoxically Foucault's description of the universal web of micro-power in contemporary societies (a description more baleful and totalizing than anything to be found in the Frankfurt School) turns out to authorize counter-conceptions of 'resistance' utterly inconsistent with its French source (where resistance is always an atomized but individual, desperate, guerrilla effort doomed to failure). The mass-cultural theories of resistance, of rewriting, of the appropriation of the commercial text by groups for whom it was not destined in that form, would rather seem to reflect some sense of the deeper utopian impulses at work in cultural production and consumption alike – where, as Bloch showed us, the mole of collectivity still burrows away through the frivolous individual gratifications of a privatized and atomized society.

The Utopian origins of such theories are then (via Marcuse) far more evident in the sociopolitical theories of the New Left, where it is precisely commodification, and the consumption desires awakened by late capitalism, that are themselves paradoxically identified as the motive power for some deeper dissatisfaction capable of undermining the system itself. Philosophically, something of this position persists in Habermas, for whom the very promises of the bourgeois revolution and of bourgeois legality and democracy retain potential that can lead to social change and evolution. In any case, ironically, the utopian component of those New Left theories of mass culture which replaced Frankfurt School notions of manipulation by the Culture Industry itself ultimately derives from the other, utopian face of Frankfurt School thinking.

The belated theorization of the new forms of mass culture as so many manifestations of 'postmodernism' now seems to complete these new positions at the same time that it profoundly problematizes them. The technological perfection of mass culture today (in a postmodern 'image' in which high technology is also inscribed as content, and which also, as a commodity form, signifies the technologically new as the very object of cultural consumption) seems indeed to render more plausible the new dignity of all these commercial art-objects in which a kind of caricature of Adorno's conception of art as technical innovation now goes hand in hand with the acknowledgement of the deeper unconscious Utopian wisdom of precisely those consuming masses whose 'taste' it validates. Meanwhile, the virtual disappearance of what Adorno used to oppose to it as 'high culture' – namely, modernism itself – clears the field, and leaves the impression of a now universalized culture, whose logic now describes a continuum from 'art' to 'entertainment' in place of the older value oppositions of high and low.

The Archimedean point of some 'genuinely aesthetic experience' from whose standpoint the structures of commercial art are critically unmasked has thus disappeared; what has not disappeared, however, is still the ancient philosophical problem of true and false happiness (from Plato to Marcuse) and whether watching thirty-five hours a week of technically expert and elegant television can be argued to be more deeply gratifying than watching thirty-five hours a week of 1950s-type 'Culture Industry' programming. The deeper utopian content of postmodern television takes on a somewhat different meaning, one would think, in an age of universal depoliticization; while even the concept of the Utopian itself – as a political version of the Unconscious – continues to confront the theoretical problem of what repression might mean in such a context – in particular, it remains to be determined what political content may be assigned to works whose unconscious meaning alone is political. Such texts might well be social symptoms of a deeper political and collective need or longing without in themselves having any political or politicizing function. Perhaps today, where the triumph of more utopian theories of mass culture seems complete and virtually hegemonic, we need the corrective of some new theory of manipulation, and of a properly postmodern commodification (which could not in any case be the same as Adorno and Horkheimer's now historical one).

In fact, however, the 'Culture Industry' chapter does not propose a theory of culture at all, in the modern sense; and the passionate responses it has most often aroused have tended equally often to stem from this misunderstanding and from thinking that it does. It is enough, however, to reread Raymond Williams's now classic account of 'hegemony' for it to be clear that there is no equivalent concept anywhere in Adorno's work (or Horkheimer's either):

> a whole body of practices and expectations, over the whole of living: our senses and assignments of energy, our shaping perceptions of ourselves and our world. It is a lived system of meanings and values – constitutive and constituting – which as they are experienced as practices appear as reciprocally confirming. It thus constitutes a sense of reality for most people in the society, a sense of absolute because experienced reality beyond which it is very difficult for most members of the society to move, in most areas of their lives. It is, that is to say, in the strongest sense a 'culture'... [7]

The contrast is all the more striking when Williams reverts to his central theme here (for it is of hegemony and not initially of culture that all this is affirmed!), and adds: 'but a culture which has also to be seen as the lived dominance and subordination of particular classes', something that would clearly be appropriate to the matter of the Culture Industry itself, if Adorno and Horkheimer had been able to conceive of it in this way in the first place. But they do not: at least partly because, as *Minima Moralia* is there to testify, the experience of the 'damaged life' – but also of Weimar and of Nazism, and even of the brash and materialistic United States – leaves no place for the stability of this kind of evocation of social reproduction. It will not be until Negt and Kluge that accents echoing those in Williams's passage here find their German equivalent.[8] Indeed, it is also possible that the traditional equivalent, *Bildung*, is too tainted a class concept and too redolent of all the complacency of the 'immature' German bourgeoisie, for Adorno and Horkheimer ever to have been tempted by it.

Thus, the 'Culture Industry' is not a theory of culture but the theory of an *industry*, of a branch of the interlocking monopolies of late capitalism that makes money out of what used to be called culture. The topic here is the commercialization of life, and the co-authors are closer to having a theory of 'daily life' than they are to having one of 'culture' itself in any contemporary sense. For Williams's theory is, despite his seeming nostalgia, a very contemporary one indeed, which corresponds to an acculturation of social life far more thoroughgoing and 'total' than could have been conceived in the 1930s (when, with industrial mass production of cultural goods – so-called Fordism – the process was only beginning). Adorno and Horkheimer remain 'modern' in this sense because although they presciently enumerated a whole range of tendencies in what was to become image-society, they could scarcely anticipate the dialectical transformation of quantity into quality that the intensification of the process would entail. Theirs remains therefore, not a *Kulturkritik* but an *Ideologiekritik*: as in classical Marxism, 'ideology' is still here the central concept and has not yet been modified by the demands of a postmodern social order (as, for example, in Althusser's revision).

Four

At any rate, the Adorno-Horkheimer theory of the Culture Industry provides a theoretical description of mass cultural experience which can scarcely be reduced to sheer opinionated or elitist vituperation against 'bad art'. To be sure, the philosophers' argument commits them to differentiate mass-cultural 'experience' from the genuinely aesthetic type: this is achieved by separating 'entertainment', 'amusement', and even 'pleasure' itself off from what happens in art, which cannot be described in those terms. Indeed, the worst fears of those for whom a Germanic dialectic is virtually by definition humorless in its very essence[9] will be confirmed by the obsessive diatribes against laughter that appear and reappear throughout this book; a somewhat different light is shed on this odd prejudice by the realization that laughter is here conceived as essentially Homeric – that is, as a ferocious vaunting, with bared teeth, over the victim, as exemplified, for example, by Wyndham Lewis's Tyros; while we should also read into the record Adorno's frequent exception – from such denunciations of sheer malicious 'fun' – of the genuinely zany, such as the Marx Brothers, and his otherwise astonishing insistence on the deeper mindless silliness or 'simplicity' [*Albernheit*] of all true art.

The analysis of pleasure, however, takes place within a framework of the theory of the alienated labor process and has been prolonged by any number of contemporary discussions of the commodification and colonization of leisure:

> Amusement under late capitalism is the prolongation of work. It is sought after as an escape from mechanized work, and to recruit strength in order to be able to cope with it again. Meanwhile, however, mechanization so

dominates the resting worker's leisure and happiness, and so profoundly determines the manufacture of amusement goods, that his experiences are inevitably
mere after-images of the work process itself. The ostensible content is merely
a faded foreground; what sinks in is the automatic succession of standardized
operations. What happens at work, in the factory or in the office, can be
evaded only by approximation to it in one's leisure time. All amusement
suffers from this incurable malady. Pleasure hardens into boredom because,
in order to remain pleasure, it must demand no effort and thereby moves
rigorously in the worn grooves of association. (DA 123/137)

This concluding word, 'association', needs to be retained, and the historical weight of its philosophical connotation further developed, since, as
we shall see, it functions as the mediation between the labor process
and whatever pleasurable experience may be attributed to mass-cultural
works in the first place. For even the most implacable theory of manipulation in mass culture (and the Adorno-Horkheimer theory is a good deal
subtler than that) must somehow acknowledge the experiential moment
in the mesmerization of the masses before the television set; if only then
to dismiss it as the fix, addiction, false pleasure, or whatever. The great
definition of art which Adorno and Horkheimer borrow from Stendhal
and make their own – art as the *promesse de bonheur'* – suggests, however,
that for them much will be at stake in coming to terms theoretically
with just such false happiness, just such deceptive pleasure (about which
the utopian positions of a Bloch or a Marcuse will suggest that true
happiness or pleasure is somehow inscribed within this false experience).[10]
    In fact, Adorno and Horkheimer make the only really consequent
and rigorous move open to them: they sunder pleasure decisively from
happiness, while at the same time denying the possibility of either as
some full experience or plenitude in its own right. Pleasure thereby
becomes an evanescent natural release, which can never be sustained:

> pleasure [*Vergnügen*] always means not thinking about anything, forgetting
> suffering even where it is shown. Helplessness is its foundation. It is in fact
> flight; but not, as is often said, flight from a wretched reality, but on the
> contrary flight from any last thought of resistance left open by this last.
> (DA 130/144)

In this form, whatever is left of pleasure in the older sense comes to
invest the position of the ultimate victims, 'the ones who suffer for everything anyhow'. As for the ultimate mystery of sexuality – so often taken
as the very prototype of pleasure in general, and sometimes inconsider-
ately (even by Adorno himself in passing) assimilated to the experience

of art itself – it may be preferable, in true Lacanian fashion, to deny its relationship to pleasure altogether:

> Delight [*Lust*] is austere: *res severa verum gaudium*. The monastic theory that not asceticism but the sexual act denotes the renunciation of attainable bliss receives negative confirmation in the gravity of the lover who apprehensively stakes his life on the fleeting instant. In the Culture Industry, jovial renunciation takes the place of the pain that lies at the heart of ecstasy and asceticism alike. (DA 126–7/141)

Pain as the very truth of pleasure: with this deeply felt paradox we touch the central dialectic of Adorno's conception of experience and his notion of authenticity. The related but distinct notion of happiness also, as we shall see later on, follows this pattern, but as it were on a temporal or historical continuum, very much in the spirit of Bloch's 'not yet': happiness is possible, here and now, only as what does not yet exist, as what is not yet possible or achievable. The Stendhal formula takes on its power when we stress its constitutive incompletion: art is not bliss, but rather the latter's *promise*. The Frankfurt School then rewrite it in their own grimmer idiom: 'The secret of aesthetic sublimation is its representation of fulfillment as a broken promise' (DA 125/140).[11] What is inauthentic in the offerings of the Culture Industry, then, is not the remnants of experience within them, but rather the ideology of happiness they simultaneously embody: the notion that pleasure or happiness ('entertainment' would be their spurious synthesis) already exists, and is available for consumption.

This is, then, one crucial thematic differentiation between 'genuine art' and that offered by the Culture Industry: both raise the issue and the possibility of happiness in their very being, as it were, and neither provides it; but where the one keeps faith with it by negation and suffering, through the enactment of its impossibility, the other assures us it is taking place ('Not Italy is offered, but eye-witness evidence of its existence' [DA 133/148]).

This is then the moment at which we must return to the implication of the word 'association' (already stressed above), but less in the sense of the tradition that emerges from Locke than, rather, in its final twist and solution in Kant himself, and in the theory of the categories and the mental schemata. This is of course the point at which, as has already been mentioned, the stereotypicality of Hollywood and Culture Industry products is, with malicious playfulness, attributed to the *Critique of Pure Reason* as its caricature and ultimate outcome; to be sure,

> Kant's formalism still expected a contribution from the individual, who was thought to relate the varied experiences of the senses to fundamental concepts; but industry robs the individual of his function. Its prime service to the customer is to do his schematizing for him. Kant said that there was a secret mechanism in the soul which prepared direct intuitions in such a way that they could be fitted into the system of pure reason. But today that secret has been deciphered. (DA 112/124)

The Kantian problematic is not, to be sure, exhausted by this particular application and appropriation of its mechanisms: for the question of perceptual schemata (and of their opposite number, something like a perceptual or aesthetic *nominalism*) persists in 'genuine art' and returns episodically in *Aesthetic Theory* as the problem of the 'universal' and the 'particular'. Here, however, schematism, in the Kantian sense, provides the crucial mediation between the labor process and 'degraded' entertainment, which seeks the same – repetition and the familiar – as its very element: Taylorization, the rationalization of the labor process and of mass production, is here to be grasped both in production and reception in well-nigh indistinguishable fashion (but the identification of reception with production is constant in Adorno, and holds for 'high art' as well, which will in some sense also constitute another more self-conscious version of this synthesis, and be characterized as something like a reception of production – but of advanced production, of 'high' technology).

Here we seem to pass beyond a straightforward analysis of mass-cultural artefacts in terms of commodification; or, to be more precise, the emphasis at this point shifts from the emphasis on the ideological dimension of the commodity – that is to say, on the 'religious' mysteries of commodity fetishism – to what may be called its existential or even metaphysical dimension in Marx – namely, the effects of exchange itself, and in particular of *equivalence* as a new form imposed on reality and on *abstraction* in the broadest epistemological sense as a historically emergent mode of organizing the world. This is, of course, the point at which the analysis of the Culture Industry loops back into the larger framework under which it was subsumed: the evocation of the 'dialectic of Enlightenment', of what Weber called rationalization and Lukács reification: the coming into being of 'identity' as a mental operation which, as we have seen in the preceding chapter, is at one and the same time a primary instrument of domination and embodiment of the will to power.

The first chapter of *Capital*, indeed, stages 'equivalence' as anything but a natural process, and shows it to be at one and the same time a creative mental act, an extraordinary cultural invention, which is also a brutal and revolutionary intervention into the objective world: nothing in the senses endorses the conceptual leap whereby the famous coat becomes equivalent 'in value' to the equally famous twenty yards of linen. Nor can a metaphysics of Number – according to which, eventually, one pound of iron shavings is discovered to be equivalent to one pound of feathers – ground this new value *form*, whose historical evolution culminates in the so-called 'general form of value' or money: it has not been sufficiently appreciated that Marx's four stages of value project a whole history of abstraction as such, of which the commodity form is but a local result (and Weber's rationalization, Simmel's intellectualization, and Lukács's reification constitute its global generalization, at the other end of time). Abstraction in this sense is the precondition of 'civilization' in all its complex development across the whole range of distinct human activities (from production to the law, from culture to political forms, and not excluding the psyche and the more obscure 'equivalents' of unconscious desire), whose very different histories the history of abstraction might therefore be called upon to underwrite.

'Equivalence' retains these senses in *Dialectic of Enlightenment*, where it excludes difference and heterogeneity, and 'excises the incommensurable' (15/12), transforming the unlike into the same, banishing the fear of the new and allowing comparable and measurable quantities to be manipulated. On the other hand, Adorno and Horkheimer also dispose of an alternate characterization of this primal process (which constitutes the very dynamic of 'enlightenment' as such, and of science and 'instrumental reason'): as we have seen, they also call it *mimesis*, and thereby open up a thematic alternative to the Marxian doctrine or problematic of equivalence – a second language or code which, intended to incorporate anthropology (since the grandest dialectical move in the book lies as we have seen in its assimilation of myth to enlightenment), secures mimetic activity as a genuine drive or impulse, and thereby draws this whole new theory into the mythic proper, reprojecting it as an anthropological narrative of the transformation of primal mimetic impulses into Western science. Now a 'scene of origins' will be necessary; so that the Ur-motivation of the mimetic is staged as fear and impotence before Nature, which ritual mimesis and, after it, science, are called upon to master (by domination of the self); while the evident break of 'modernity', the emergence of science – in, for example, the emblematic passage from perceptual 'science', '*pensée sauvage*', alchemy, into mathematical and non-representational thinking – is attributed to a mimetic taboo, or 'ban on graven images', which is itself, however, dialectically as profoundly mimetic (in the anthropological sense) as what it seeks to repress and cancel.

Habermas has shrewdly suggested[12] that this alternate mythic conceptuality – the code of the mimetic – is ultimately imposed on Adorno and Horkheimer by the inner logic of their positions: as reason and rationality are for them implacably identified as 'instrumental reason' (as *Verstand* rather than *Vernunft*) they no longer have any positive space for the development of conceptual alternatives to 'enlightenment' and are thereby forced back into a type of mythic thinking of their own. He also stresses the unrealized capacity of the notion of mimesis as interpersonality, and as the space for relations with other people (whom we understand by mutual imitation): this possibility, which for Habermas himself is clearly fundamental, is generally, however, in Adorno and Horkheimer, conceived as something fully as baleful as it might be socially and intellectually promising, let alone productive.

Meanwhile, it seems clear that the theory of the Culture Industry is itself unduly limited and restricted by these rather more metaphysical propositions about the mimetic impulse, which to be sure 'explain' the deeper power and attraction of a mass culture that has none of the power and attraction of Art; but explain it too easily and naturalistically (the schematisms of alienated labor invested by some deeper human 'drive'), thereby forestalling those more complex lines of speculation and inquiry that postmodern mass culture seems to demand.[13] In particular, the matter of repetition in contemporary mass culture has not only become a more complicated and interesting phenomenon than the one Adorno and Horkheimer had in mind: it would also seem to suggest mediations of a type they could obviously not elaborate with the originality of daily life in late capitalism, and in particular with the newer structures of an image or spectacle society (which are also scarcely even foreshadowed in Benjamin's alternate theory of mass culture, staged under the sign of the mechanically reproducible work of art). As for the 'stereotypical', the current revival of the term 'formulaic' to designate some of these mass-cultural structures suddenly opens up analogies with cultural production and reception in non- or pre-capitalist societies, which are equally excluded from the historical framework of *Dialectic of Enlightenment*.

Five

Our inquiry into the way in which Adorno conceives of the negative or 'opposite' of art, however, is still not complete. We have in effect identified not one but two such oppositional terms, which do not quite overlap conceptually: there is on the one hand an absence of art altogether [*das Amusische*], a position occupied by Odysseus's crewmen; and alongside that the somewhat stronger negative term of the anti-art or 'bad art' of the Culture Industry, with its betrayed and victimized public:

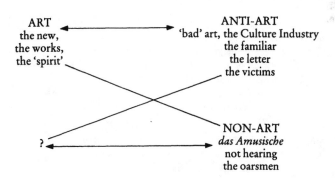

The missing fourth term in this system is secured less by a new form of culture (or its absence) than by a generalized negation of the other three terms that, playing across a range of thematic levels, can itself only be identified allegorically as a character in Adorno's deeper ideological and phantasmatic narrative. This 'slot' constitutes the negation of 'anti-art', for example, not by way of the end of the Culture Industry and the emergence of some new and positive 'negation of the negation'; but rather as the opposite number to the latter's drama of victimization, as the agency of that victimization and the place of the production of the Culture Industry itself. Beyond them, of course, the term expands to include the *philistines* in general, who are not, in Adorno's scheme of things, those who passively consume mass culture, nor are they the oarsmen, who are deprived of the very sense organs for any culture, whether authentic or commercial, but rather those who carry in their hearts some deeper hatred of art itself.

The philistines are not first and foremost, therefore, those who do not 'understand' art or, better still, who do not 'understand' modern art; rather, they understand it only too well:

> What our manipulated contemporaries dismiss as unintelligible secretly makes very good sense to them indeed. This recalls Freud's dictum that the uncanny is uncanny only because it is secretly all too familiar, which is why it is repressed. (AT 273/262)

The philistines in this sense are not to be grasped in terms of categories of taste; their project is a more active one, and their refusal is a gesture that has a social meaning which ultimately transcends the matter of art itself and the more limited sphere of the aesthetic:

> The increasing spirituality [or abstraction] of a henceforth secular art spurs the rancor of those excluded from culture, thereby generating a new kind of consumption art over against itself, while at the same time their revulsion against this last drives the artists themselves on to ever more desperate and imprudent forms of spiritualization. (AT 28/20)

This encapsulated mythic history, whose context is a discussion of the peculiar unpleasurability of modern art (and even its vocation to be resolutely unpleasurable), dramatizes the moment of differentiation of what will become the three distinct positions that come into being over against art: those who are initially excluded (Odysseus's crew), those who come to demand consumer pleasure in the place of what they have been excluded from (the public of the Culture Industry), and finally those who, more keenly aware of the whole process (and of what Odysseus is able to hear), conceive a more generalized reaction to it, which must now be identified: it is none other than the great figure of *ressentiment* most dramatically elaborated in Nietzsche.

For what the philistines 'understand only too well' in the (modern) works they hate and characterize as incomprehensible is of course the deepest vocation of art itself – the *'promesse de bonheur'*, in the form of art's 'broken promise', which keeps the idea of happiness alive at the moment of denying its present existence. It is, then, this ultimate relationship to 'happiness' and to utopian fulfillment which is symbolically at play in the passion of the *'homme du ressentiment'*, and can thereby become manifest on a range of other social levels. In fact, the strong form (or narrative manifestation) of Adorno's philistine is to be found not in the 'Culture Industry' chapter of *Dialectic of Enlightenment*, nor anywhere in *Aesthetic Theory*, but rather in the final chapter of the former work, which deals with anti-Semitism. This extraordinary utopian analysis of anti-Semitism in terms of cultural envy now stages the anti-Semitic passion as the very hatred of happiness itself:

> The rights of man were designed to promise happiness even to those without power. Because the cheated masses feel that this promise – as a universal – remains a lie as long as classes exist, it stirs their rage; they feel mocked. Even as a possibility or an idea they repeatedly repress the thought of such happiness, they deny it ever more passionately the more imminent it seems. Wherever happiness seems to have been achieved in the midst of universal renunciation, they must repeat that gesture of suppression which is really the suppression of their own longing. Everything that occasions such repetition and such repression, however miserable it may be in itself – Ahasverus and Mignon, alien things which are reminders of the promised land, or beauty that recalls sexuality, or the proscribed animal reminiscent of promiscuity – draws down upon itself the destructive lust of the 'civilized', who could never wholly fulfill and realize the painful process of civilization itself. To those who spasmodically dominate nature, a tormented nature provocatively reflects back the image of powerless happiness. The thought of happiness without power is unbearable, because only then would it be true happiness. (DA 154-5/172)

Elsewhere in this chapter (and alongside various alternate explanatory models of more doubtful interest) Adorno and Horkheimer develop their analysis further in the direction of the relationship of anti-Semitism to the archaic – both social and 'natural' – and to their own theme of mimesis, at least implicitly enlarging this conception of a rage at the idea of happiness to include the envy for what is fantasized as the less alienated state of an older community or collectivity (very much in the spirit of their *'Odyssey'* commentary, in which the Enlightenment spirit of Odysseus is read as a series of cancellations and repressions of pre-capitalist forms). Along with Sartre's theory of anti-Semitism, this 'utopian' analysis surely remains one of the most powerful and convincing diagnoses of what has otherwise been attributed to sheerly psychological and irrational impulses (and thereby structurally consigned to what is by definition incomprehensible). This particular analysis is also independent of the psychologizing perspective of Adorno's *Authoritarian Personality*, where the meaning of *ressentiment* as a social act is recontained and reified into a theory of character structure.

The emergence of the 'anti-Semite' as a strong manifestation of the social form of the 'philistine' in general now also makes a little clearer the cultural 'convergence theory' of *Dialectic of Enlightenment*, in which a Hollywood and New Deal USA is structurally characterized as bearing a family likeness to Hitlerian Germany. The deeper continuity is precisely secured by this figure, who, anti-Semite in the Nazi social order, is in the United States identified as the seemingly more benign figure of the philistine of the Culture Industry: both negative embodiments of the deeper *ressentiment* generated by class society itself. Meanwhile, the valorization of art now finds its deeper function in precisely this diagnosis, as the guilty and fragile place of a promise of social and personal happiness persisting within a social order deformed by class and tending towards an ever more universal bureaucratic control. With this larger framework, then, the external positioning of the aesthetic is complete, and *Aesthetic Theory* proceeds to its central topic, which is the exploration of the internal dynamic of art and form.

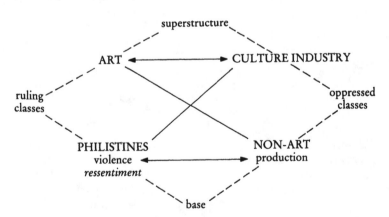

PART III

Productivities

of the Monad

One

The shifting and ambiguous ideological implications of this defense of art against its enemies or its deceptive equivalents are, however, radically changed the moment we complete the move – already anticipated in advance above – from some general notion of art as a process or a value to the individual works of art themselves. This shift in focus – which modifies the whole tenor of the discussion and reveals everything that is still vital and unexploited in what might today be called Adorno's critical method – can be characterized in terms of one of Adorno's great themes, that of *nominalism*, whose multiple significance can even here at the outset be briefly sketched.

Nominalism is for Adorno a philosophical tendency which is at one and the same time a historical event. In aesthetic terms it means the repudiation of the universal: for example, the refusal of the Hegelian objectification of art into genres and styles (a dialectical advance in the form of a strategic withdrawal or limitation: Adorno quite properly mentions Croce as the moment in which this thematic emerges, without yet developing into an exploration of the consequences which then practically ensued in the emergence of what we call 'modern' – that is to say, nominalistic – art [see AT 398/377]). The repudiation of these kinds of historicizing aesthetic universals (Hegel's three great forms of the symbolic, the classical and the romantic, for example) is accompanied by critical mixed feelings about those even more local historical universals or abstractions which are the 'isms' of the avant-garde movements (deployed, much against the spirit of Adorno, in the present book): they still have their truth, but as intellectual signs and symptoms of the *Novum* rather than as stylistic or period terms under which one could subsume the individual works as a particular is subsumed philosophically under a general.

Here Adorno comes the closest to that contemporary (or postmodern) *Bilderverbot* leveled on historiographic narrative itself, on the various stories of art history, on the larger historical paradigms of period and evolution, from which the freshness of the present (including the 'present' of the individual works of art) has always, since Nietzsche, seemed to evaporate. The difference between Adorno and these anti-historical anxieties of poststructuralism lies in the informing presence of an Event (the concept of nominalism implies a causality, identified with the tendencies of history), but also in a migration of history into the work's very form (which now becomes more profoundly social and historical than would have been the case when it merely served as a privileged example of some larger historical or social narrative).

Yet behind the spurious 'universals' of this still historical type, nominalism also tracks the more static universals of the Kantian type, to which reference has already been made above: for us today, such schemata sort themselves out along a wide range of henceforth distinct specializations. They can be grasped as a kind of proto-psychology, in which case the business of aesthetics is reduced to the analysis of various kinds of stimuli, from the machinery of the Culture Industry all the way to Aristotelian catharsis (which Adorno quite consequently denounces – [AT 354/339]). They can, on the other hand, be viewed as the detection of various kinds of conceptual grids and categories within the experience of what we normally call perception: in which case, for Adorno, they are to be denounced as the illicit attempt to transform bodily immediacy into more 'spiritualized' and idealistic forms of abstract thinking, a repression by way of sublimation and a mind-oriented, philosophical dread of what cannot, in aesthetic experience or elsewhere, be philosophized.

Here, then, the work of art is dissolved into sets of abstract patterns, which the universalists are able to draw and exploit in various directions: towards structuralist descriptions, for example, which seek grounding outside the traditional psychological categories; towards metaphysical meanings of the loftier and most traditional high-philosophical type (wherein the individual works – and even, for Adorno, their individual truth-contents – are still replaced by the universals of religious or existential or aestheticizing-religious 'experience'); or finally towards the specific universals of specialized philosophical aesthetics, including such categories as harmony, consonance, proportion, aesthetic appearance [*Schein*], expression, and the like. Such specifically aesthetic or formal categories – which already, as can be seen, span a variety of distinct historical experiences of the aesthetic – are, however, not merely false in the philosophical sense, for they carry within themselves, and within their empty conceptuality, the sedimented experience of specific historical works as such.

Indeed, the project of yet another philosophical aesthetics after the end of aesthetics as a philosophical discipline remains entangled in this dead conceptuality which it cannot jettison but must somehow untangle and provisionally readapt for new purposes, while definitively devaluing and discrediting it. What very different concepts such as proportion or mimesis or expression all illicitly by their very formal nature strive for – and what must be blocked and forestalled in all of them – is the vocation to yield a single-shot 'definition' of the work of art in general (a vocation we already know to be misguided by the very assimilation within it of Art in general and the individual work); something Adorno has taught us to see not as the relationship of the general to the particular, but rather as a deep contradiction and an unresolvable tension within the individual works fully as much as within Art itself.

This means, however, that traditional aesthetic concepts can still be pressed back into service dialectically when the identification of what contradicts and de-universalizes them is systematically secured: thus ugliness must rise up at once against proportion, and the concept of the fragment rebuke the value of harmony; mimesis must be painfully shackled to its irreconcilable opposite, expression, and aesthetic appearance itself – the untranslatable *Schein* – undermined at once at the moment of its triumphant emergence by that omnipresent drive to transcend the aesthetic and to be more than mere aesthetic appearance (an undermining which can also be identified as yet another of the protean forms of what we have here begun to evoke with the name of nominalism). This inducement of a state of war between the traditional aesthetic and formal concepts, then, at once discloses their varied historicity and their deeper situational taproot in specific forms of artistic practice in this or that historical moment.

But in this Adorno must also argue against himself: in so far as his is still an *aesthetic*, in the traditional sense, he also has his single-shot descriptive formal category, which will shortly be identified as that of *construction*, and also has its specifically historical praxis-situation – namely, the nominalist or minimalist moment of aesthetic modernism (from Schoenberg's expressionism to Beckett's theater). Whether his own privileged formal category – which is, to be sure, often released into the local dialectical maelstrom of oppositions with other local formal categories – is as a concept structurally distinct enough from the traditional kinds to sustain this function and this organizational centrality; whether, indeed, it can project its formal claim beyond its own historical aesthetic moment (which is now a thing of the past with enough power to speak to our own very different one) – these are the ultimate problems with which *Aesthetic Theory* confronts us.

The matter of nominalism, however, is by no means exhausted by these conceptual difficulties, which have until now been registered on the side of the 'notion' or the 'idea', as Hegel might have said; they have their equivalent on the side of the psychic subject, whose resistance to universals nominalism also is. Indeed, there is a widespread commitment of contemporary (or poststructural) philosophy to descriptions or even valorizations of fragmented subjectivity, of the 'decentering of the subject', of 'schizophrenia', of the repressive function of the ego or the illusions of personal identity or of biographical continuity, all the way to the 'waning' of the subject, its eclipses, drops in '*niveau*', swoons, breaks, the fitful glimpses of the effects of determination of consciousness by something that is not itself (whether the unconscious, language, or an otherness of doxa and ideology). Such contemporary phenomena or formulations are all, from Adorno's dialectical standpoint, to be seen as so many symptoms of a nominalism that has penetrated subjectivity itself and conferred on a variety of punctual subjective 'experiences' an immediacy that is not to be reduced or defused by their assimilation to something more general, or more abstract, or more intellectual-generic. What this means is not merely that the aesthetic tastes of this fitful post-contemporary subjectivity will be very different in kind from those of the controlled and more comfortable identities of older bourgeois or aristocratic publics: although that is so also, and spells the end of any universal aesthetics or doctrine of aesthetic invariables, the tendency even goes so far as to challenge the very conception of aesthetic unity and of the closure of the work itself (something which poses a crucial threat to Adorno's aesthetic project; the notion of Leibniz's *monad* will be invoked to parry it, as we shall see later on).

Subjective nominalism also means that these fragments of a former subjectivity have now paradoxically become objective, and can therefore be seen as constituting themselves materials, building blocks, the stone and glass and aluminum, of the work's construction (alongside the more traditional aesthetic raw material and artistic languages out of which the work was once, traditionally, thought to be made or formed). As has already been suggested above, this dialectical reversal of the subjective into the objective is – in what it eliminates of false problems, as well as in the new and virtually inexplored interpretive possibilities it opens up – the central heritage of Adorno's aesthetic positions, comparable in that only to some of the more intuitive speculations of the Russian Formalists. The predominant exposition throughout in terms of music is, from this perspective, scarcely a specialized limitation, but rather opens a door wide for speculative analogies of the most creative kind with the other arts.

Finally, we must note what is in many ways the most central sense of the term nominalism as Adorno uses it throughout *Aesthetic Theory* – namely, as an event, and in particular as something that happened to the history of art itself. The historical paradigm remains that familiar one of the emergence of modernity (as we have learned to understand it in Marx's account of the commodity form, and in Weber's account of rationalization) and of modernism (as it is registered in the forms of the artists, most emblematically, from the European perspective, in Baudelaire). This mythic 'fall' – into capitalism and into modernization – was, as we have seen, already paradoxically inscribed in the very title of *Dialectic of Enlightenment*, where a repressive mimetic and self-sublating process of abstraction and control – projected back into the very origins of human history, and beyond Homer all the way to the first forms of the magical domination of nature – now suddenly, in the eighteenth century, seems to know a dialectical leap in which, brutally canceling its older magical and superstitious, overtly mimetic forms, it pursues the mimetic process on a higher level of abstraction, keeping faith with the deeper impulse of mimesis by systematically expunging all traces of mimesis itself, in what Adorno and Horkheimer will call the *Bilderverbot*, the ban on graven images of a henceforth secular, skeptical, mathematizing thought.

What is to be retained in the aesthetic context of these older descriptions of scientific rationality is the way in which each state produces historicity and the past in the very process of canceling it: scientific 'progress' is thus synchronic rather than diachronic, not merely sweeping away its older mode of production as *pensée sauvage*, but with each new act transforming the very precursor steps of its own, now 'rationalistic', scientific activity into superstition and metaphysical survival. Adorno and Horkheimer are of course, in their earlier work, crucially concerned with the way in which the theoretical component of such enlightened science ruthlessly converts its own official philosophies into unenlightened myths; so that even positivism, which more effectively turned all previous philosophy into theology than any Marxian vision of the former's end and realization, then itself, in its Comtean form, became a peculiarly Hegelian or even occult vestige of superstitious error to be stamped out in its turn.

That discussion, however, seeks to dramatize the inherent vanishing point of theory itself, the ultimate black hole into which, as Reason, Munchausen-like, draws itself up by its own pigtail and kicks its ladder away from under itself, it ultimately repudiates the last vestiges of its own theoretical foundations and finds its extreme abstract vocation in the elimination of thinking altogether, as some earlier, archaic, henceforth dispensable stage. This scientific 'nominalism', then, also seeks the abolition of what used to be called subjectivity; to be sure, its dynamic is henceforth intertwined with the 'economic' (in the larger Marxian sense of the labor process and the commodity form, and in particular, as we have already seen, with the emergence of equivalence and the abstractions of 'identity'); nor is the emergence of the 'aesthetic' at the dawn of modernizing Enlightenment – its radical dissociation from the rational and the scientific; the flight of the sensory and the sensible, the representational and the mimetic, into this newly constituted marginal space of rejection and compensation – in any way a secondary or non-constitutive process, but so essential to the description of Enlightenment that henceforward, as we have seen, only the 'degraded' Culture Industry offers a vivid picture of the prolongation of its colonizing logic.

None the less, the temporality we have attributed to science is significantly analogous (just as a caricature is also an analogy) to the historical dynamic of the aesthetic monad; the paradoxes of the first may illuminate those of its opposite number, and in particular the troublesome problem of the 'New' or the *Novum*. For there is a sense in which the aesthetic *Novum* also cancels its prehistory and converts the very techniques on which its innovations depended into outmoded and obsolete technology: if the word synchronic has been insisted on, however, it was evoked in order – more effectively than the older aestheticizing terminology of 'intrinsic' and 'extrinsic' – to exclude or to dispel the illusion that such innovation could be detected and registered from the outside, from the vantage point of some 'diachronic' narrative from which we calmly observe the emergence of the chromatic (in Wagner), or of 'point of view' (in Henry James), enumerating them furiously on our score card as they pass by, conjoined with notations on the various players and dated volumes.

The historicity in question within the individual work, however, includes that past in the moment of canceling it; so that it might be said of it that however idealistic the Hegelian doctrine of *Aufhebung* may well be elsewhere – in a human history of material breaks and convulsions in which the past of individuals and of collectivities vanishes into death without a trace – here alone, within the aesthetic monad, *Aufhebung* remains true, as a well-nigh materialist descriptive concept (much as Adorno will also say, of Leibniz's concept of the monad itself, that it is the inspired, deformed, mystified anticipation of that very peculiar 'material' object which is the work of art alone). The experience of the 'New' is therefore not something which comes to the experience of the work of art from the outside, owing to fresh philological or iconographic information, say (although such information has its role to play in preparing us for that experience): it is at one with aesthetic experience, it is itself in some deeper way the work's 'truth content' (*Wahrheitsgehalt*).

We must pause here to reemphasize a consequence that has already been mentioned, namely, that given the traditional valorization of the 'New' and of innovation in all the modernisms, in effect such an aesthetic assimilates all 'genuine art' to what had hitherto been considered a single period within artistic history, namely modernism 'proper'. The basic problem with such an assimilation is not the most obvious one of periodization (or, in other words, what one does with Bach, or Chrétien de Troyes, or Propertius): emergent money and commercial economies pass their internal logic and their dynamisms on unevenly to the processes of cultural production. The very impudence of the time frame of *Dialectic of Enlightenment* (which describes Odysseus as the first 'bourgeois') suggests that a 'capitalist' cultural dynamic is not to be narrowly construed within the (still rather short) lifespan of industrial capitalism; and also, on the other hand, that that 'modernism' preeminently characteristic of the second or 'imperialist' stage of triumphant European capitalism in the late nineteenth century may also be seen as something like the 'inner truth' of earlier, slower, seemingly more representational cultures. What is more scandalous, and yet no doubt logically consistent with these positions, is their radical exclusion of what may anthropologically be called non-capitalist art: the cave paintings of Altamira were evoked, but as an example of magical mimesis – that is, of the proto-Enlightenment domination of nature – not as some radically different form of art or culture as such from our own. Nor is the status of non-Western music imaginable, except as some Hegelian 'end of art' in our Western sense. The central unspoken proposition – that all great music is bourgeois music[1] – is thinkable (well beyond the current issues of postmodernism and its relation to the great tradition) only as a utopian projection of radically different societies and modes of production in which what we think of as art – and in particular as the 'work of art', no longer socially differentiated in our fashion – would have to be called something else.

Were the atomic structure of society to be transformed, then art would no longer have to sacrifice its Idea – how the particular is possible in the first place – to some social universal: as long as the particular and the universal diverge, freedom cannot exist. Freedom would, however, accord the particular those rights which are today aesthetically in evidence only in the idiosyncratic constraints artists find themselves obliged to submit to. (AT 69/62)

We will return later to the exceedingly characteristic idea that the contemporary artist's freedom is to be found not in free-floating subjectivity somewhere, whether in choice or caprice, but rather in the objective constraints of the material itself. But it would be a mistake to deduce, from the way in which this passage traditionally stages philosophical 'reconciliation' as the harmony between the universal and the particular, that such a vision plays any normative role in Adorno's aesthetics: there indeed such harmony ('the concrete universal') is not merely normative in all the bad senses, but historically unrealizable in a situation (for which we have been using the word nominalism) in which precisely the most authentic works reveal the incommensurability between the particular and the universal, and are therefore all, in the traditional normative sense, determinate 'failures'.

As for Adorno's conception of the *Novum*, a fuller account cannot be given until we have some better sense of the relationship between the 'productive forces' – or what Marx called the 'level of development attained by social production' – and the work of art itself. What has already been implied, however, is that the 'New' is not a temporal concept in the phenomenological sense; and also that its very conception and theorization (at the dawn of the Modern, with Baudelaire) has a great deal to do with nominalism itself: the universal now being the repetitive and the return of the same, whose only resistance – fragile as that may be – would seem to be the unique here and now, without a name, incomparable, the unrepeatable conjuncture, what can be exchanged with nothing else, and what thereby becomes the 'New' by default, since there are no longer any generic categories to classify it under. Yet nominalism in that sense is not merely a form of resistance to the bad Universal, but also a dilemma and a generalized historical situation, a crisis, whose results for the work of art we must now examine.

Two

The most familiar and widely read version of Adorno's account of the crisis of art (or the emergence of modernism) we owe not to him but to Thomas Mann, who appropriated its earlier formulation (in *Philosophie der neuen Musik*) for his novel *Doktor Faustus*. The heart of the matter is there thematized as the crisis of *Schein*, a convenient term for which English has no easy equivalent and which has frequently been rendered as 'aesthetic appearance' or 'show' or, alternately, as 'aesthetic illusion': expressions which tendentially imply the existence of something else *behind* that appearance or illusion and which, besides the obvious presence of an 'original', may also suggest things as diverse as the 'true meaning' of the work, or on the other hand its primary and quite unaesthetic materials, such as oil paint, or words, or bodies wearing costumes and make-up. What is troublesome about these versions is not so much the implication that in a given situation *Schein* might vanish away and utterly evaporate, abandoning its spectators to the idle activity of staring at pieces of smeared canvas or witnessing, with no little embarrassment, a little group of people striding around a platform waving their arms improbably and opening their mouths (the well-known defamiliarizations of art itself in Flaubert and in Tolstoy).[2] Such moments of the eclipse of illusion (or the sudden wakeful disintoxicated demise of our 'belief' in it) are on the contrary useful as a kind of aesthetic version of the theory of the phantom member – the moment when we step outside the thing and have some more vivid sense of what it really was.

The difficulty is, rather, that such a vaguer sense of 'aesthetic illusion' as mere adornment, as an outer ornamentation superadded to some thing itself, then encourages speculation as to what an art would be like that

had the courage to throw off such 'illusions' and to be what it really
was in the first place. As a matter of fact, this is exactly what seems
to happen in the artistic history of the new or the modern (a process
which for Adorno, as we have seen, can be conceived as extending back-
wards into the *ancien régime*): each successive form or generation then
repudiating its immediate past as an affair of romance, lies, the grossest
trumpery, in contrast to which its own offerings draw their novelty
from a more passionate vocation for truth and a greater commitment
to exactitude and detail. Here already, but in restricted form, we see
the 'ban on graven images', the anti-mimetic impulse, deployed as a therapeutic instrument against a limited past. Nor is this generational critique
of *Schein* or aesthetic appearance always staged in terms of that value
called realism: 'truth' – or, more recently, 'authenticity' – will work
equally well; neither seems quite so bound to any normative aesthetic.
Yet even 'realism' can be used against itself, as when only yesterday
Robbe-Grillet attacked the ideological illusions at the heart of Balzacian
realism in the name of some more revolutionary commitment of the
nouveau roman to 'reality'.

The crisis of *Schein* can thus, properly restricted, be pressed into service
as the primary motor-power of the modernist aesthetic 'permanent revolution' or the ceaseless fashion changes of artistic innovation in modern
times. But for some outside observer – or, at least, for the aesthetic historian whose sense of the ever more rapid dynamics of this process opens
a certain bemused distance from it – it is the end or vanishing point
of the momentum which becomes a matter for speculation, returning us
to the ultimate question of whether an art utterly divorced from aesthetic
appearance is conceivable, or on the contrary (the great Hegelian concept
of the 'end of art' itself) whether the suspicion that attaches to *Schein*
will not finally result in the abolition of art altogether: a *Bilderverbot*
that triumphantly annihilates all its graven images without a trace.

The deeper motive for the stigmatization of aesthetic appearance we
have already learned: it is the ultimate social guilt of art itself, as that
was revealed nakedly and without comment at the very dawn of 'Western'
culture in the story of the Sirens' song. But this 'original sin' is evidently
intensified in class society by rationalism and secularization (Enlightenment in its narrower historical sense), with the result that the only place
where 'aesthetic appearance', 'aesthetic illusion', lives on comfortably,
with a clear conscience, is the Culture Industry. Genuine art, which
cannot abolish *Schein* altogether without destroying itself and turning
to silence, must none the less live its illusory appearance and its unreal
luxury status as play in a vivid guilt that permeates its very forms, and
is sometimes oddly called reflexivity or self-consciousness. 'Fiction', how-

ever – another powerful proper name for *Schein*, which inflects its meaning in instructive directions – is evidently, in a variety of styles and forms, the principal commodity the Culture Industry has to sell (the poststructural variant is called 'representation'): still, endless talk shows, quiz programs, game shows, lotteries, mock courts, and even the news itself, suggest not so much that appetite for truth that Dziga Vertov's documentaries hoped to arouse as well as to satisfy in a socialist society, as rather some secret worm eating away even at the gratifications of the fictional and representation in mass culture: the crisis of *Schein* now extending even into that commodified and degraded precinct in which it was to have been safely practiced.

The substitute term 'fiction' is, however, more suggestive when we try it out on areas outside its official domain, where all the conceivable internal and external permutations of storytelling in novel and film are only too familiar (from the anti-novel to the documentary). What, however, would a non-fictional architecture be?[3] unless it is simply a matter of some resolute functionalism for which decoration and embellishment are very precisely the fictional elements to be expunged. Meanwhile, a non-fictional painting, far from being unimaginable, is the very foundational concept of a henceforth stereotypical history of this art, in which storytelling is tracked down, denounced and exterminated to the point only the painterly materials themselves – and even after them, only their abstract idea or 'concept' – remain the object of aesthetic contemplation. (Such was at least, until yesterday, the hegemonic master narrative of a certain modernist tradition.) But fiction's other identity – *Schein* – still presumably lives on in these rudimentary materials, at least when appropriately framed by the museum and the institution of the viewing experience. Adorno's own account of 'abstraction' is rather different from this one and may serve as an initial staging of his own idiosyncratic dialectic, which will be described at greater length shortly; for it focuses, not on the opposition between the commodity form and 'great art', but rather on their identity:

> Baudelaire neither struggles against reification nor does he simply offer a representation of it; he protests against it by way of the very experience of its own archetypes, the medium of such experience becoming poetic form itself. This is what lifts him authoritatively above all late Romantic sentimentality. The historical originality of this work lies in the way in which the overwhelming objectivity of the commodity form, which absorbs all remnants of the human into itself, is syncopated with that objectivity of the work of art which is prior to living subjectivity: the absolute work of art thereby coincides with absolute commodification. The residue of abstraction in the concept of the modern is the tribute levied on this last by the commodity

itself. If what is consumed in monopoly capitalism is no longer use value, but exchange value, by the same token the abstractness of the modern work – that irritating indeterminacy about its nature and function – becomes the very index of what it is. ... From its very beginnings, aesthetic abstraction, in Baudelaire still rudimentary, and a kind of allegorical reaction to a world itself become abstract, was something like a taboo on graven images. The taboo is specifically directed against what the provincial Germans hoped to salvage under the slogan *Aussage* [message], namely some meaningfulness still left in appearance; after the catastrophe of meaning, appearance itself becomes abstract. (AT 39–40/31–2)

What is sacrificed, on this analysis of abstraction, is less the 'fictive' dimension of the work than, rather, its 'meaningfulness' or, if one prefers, the pretense that the particular and the general – the thing and its meaning – are still in any, even distant, way 'organically' or experientially related. Nominalism here dissociates the remnant of lived immediacy itself from its 'universal', which has now become the universal equivalence and abstraction of the commodity form: the work of art, however, stubbornly holds on to both, in order to preserve the truth of their contradiction. With such an account, we are evidently far enough from those questions of *Schein* with which we began; unless we have to do here precisely with an extraordinary mutation in aesthetic appearance itself, in which the omnipresent power of the commodity form is now paradoxically pressed into the service of that aesthetic impulse it sought to master (and, in what is called the Culture Industry, succeeded in doing so). What is paradoxical here, however, is that in this case the modern – or, for Adorno, the work of art in general – is coterminous with the power of the commodity form, so that to evoke some 'aesthetic impulse' that preceded this situation (the taste for beauty, for example) becomes a logical non sequitur.

Commodification, however, is only one of the alternate codes in which Adorno dramatizes the crisis and the agony of aesthetic appearance. Its related Marxian thematics – the question of the dynamics of production – will be dealt with in a later chapter; here, it is appropriate merely to stress the philosophical relationship between commodification and that language of nominalism which has already been touched on and which – far more than 'non-identity' – constitutes something like the primary 'key' of *Aesthetic Theory* (in so far as one can assign priorities in a text as variable and atonal as the great 'pieces for orchestra' of the second Viennese school that looms so large within it). The commodity form, then, is to the situation of nominalism as the false universal to the bereft particular: the former's empty abstraction determines a heterogeneity of isolated data – whether in the world or the self – that can no longer be made to *mean*, if one understands 'meaning' in the traditional way as the subsumption of a particular under a general.

The ultimate and fundamental aesthetic medium in which this situation is explored – that of music – returns us to the crisis of aesthetic appearance (or *Schein*) in a way which now concretely mobilizes all these analytic categories. To ask the question about the fictionality of music – whether a non-fictive music is conceivable? how a music might be imagined which would resolutely attempt to confront the guilt of the fictional and the original sin of aesthetic appearance and to absolve itself of it? – to raise such questions in the musical realm is now to begin to identify *Schein* and 'fiction' with the *time* of the work itself; it is to pose issues of the whole and the part in a new way, which at once engages the historical 'psychic subject' that can or cannot hear and remember such relationships (the 'fetishization of hearing') and also at once problematizes the very concept of a 'whole' or overall form in terms of which particulars might be perceived; it is finally to make unavoidable the primacy of construction as such, which the dynamics of other artistic media might well inflect in the direction of more partial aesthetic categories: in language, towards that of *expression*, or in painting, towards that of *mimesis*.

Such oppositions, inherited from various moments of traditional aesthetic reflection, reemerge and disappear in various permutations throughout *Aesthetic Theory*: *Schein* versus *Ausdruck* (expression), for example (AT 168/161); or the mimetic versus the constructive (AT 72/65); or montage versus meaning (AT 231–3/221–3). These oppositions are in Adorno to be read as shifting constellations: that is, no definitive terminological solution or philosophical resolution is to be derived from them – the bias or the tendency towards the valorization of something like a concept of construction is evident, but the term itself should as far as possible not be reified or privileged (something that would turn Adorno's book back into a traditional aesthetics). Meanwhile, each oppositional conjuncture is historicized, on two levels: the opposition between montage and meaning, for example, expresses a specific historical moment in the development of modern art; but it also emerges at a specific 'historical' or narrative moment in Adorno's text, so to speak, and is thereby as situational and as provisional in the text as it is in some 'external' history of form.

Finally, all of these oppositions can be mobilized within the discussion of a specific artistic medium: in music, for example, the opposition of *Schein* and expression designates the historically crucial moment of expressionism and of the breakthrough year 1911: the moment in which the nominalist impulse to absolute expression of the subject collides, in the most archetypal of all confrontations, with the ultimate inner formal commitment of the work of art to some remnant of *Schein*. If it is understood that, in music, this last corresponds to time itself, to the length of the work, to the sheer duration of musical development; if it is also understood that for Adorno 'expression' is somehow always the expression of suffering, the cry of pain, sheer dissonance as such – then the dramatic nature of this confrontation or contradiction will begin to be clear, as well as the relevance of the 'problem' of a non-fictive music raised above. Fictionality, in music, is then simply temporal duration, which is also the *Schein* or aesthetic appearance of the musical work. How much time do you need for something properly musical to happen? Are a few notes already 'musical' in that sense? Would the utterance of a single musical 'sentence' – that is to say, an intelligible phrase or theme, melody or tune – be enough? The sonata form, however, speaks against this, implying that the phrase or theme is not really uttered, even for the first time, until it is somehow (after suitable variation) repeated and confirmed:

> The reprise is the very crux of the sonata form. It endowed what was decisive since Beethoven – the dynamics of thematic development [*Durchführung*] – with a retroactive confirmation, like the effect of a film on a viewer who stays on after the ending and watches the beginning all over again. Beethoven mastered this by way of a *tour de force* which became his trademark: in the optimal moment of the final reprise, he presents the result of those dynamics and of that process as the ratification and justification of the earlier moment, of what had already been there in the first place. This marks his complicity with the guilt of the great idealistic systems in philosophy, with the dialectician Hegel, in whom finally the very essence of the negations, and thereby of becoming itself, flows back into the theodicy of the already existent. By way of the reprise, then, music – itself a ritual of bourgeois freedom – remains, like the society in which it exists and which exists in it, in thrall to mythic unfreedom. It manipulates the cyclical relationship to nature in such a way that what returns, by virtue of the simple fact of its return, seems greater than itself, and becomes metaphysical meaning proper, or the Idea.[4]

The sonata form, then, works to produce an Idea or a feeling of necessity which is socially ideological, and confirms and justifies the totality of what is: at the same time – and in so far as Adorno's thought has a metaphysical dimension, which will become clear when we discuss the relationship between art and nature – this ideological function and mendacity of the sonata form is itself but a distorted historical reflection or manifestation of the deeper metaphysical dilemma of all art:

> how a making can disclose something which is not made; how what is not even true to its own concept can have a truth content. One could grasp

this only if the content were somehow distinct from its appearance and in a form of its own. (AT 164/157)

How there can be something like a 'natural truth' of the *constructed* will then be the central issue of this metaphysical dimension of Adorno's aesthetics, which will be dealt with in a later chapter.

Here, however, in our immediately musical context, the problem becomes rather that of the authenticity of constructed musical time, and the tendential reduction of expressionist music to a few brief instants is only the outward symptom of this ultimate crisis in aesthetic appearance, and but the formal result and end-product of a whole musical nominalism which eschews the intelligibility of the lengthy and elaborated musical phrase. It does so, however, less in the name of some ultimate musical point or note than in the name of the dissonant cluster, whose formal drama lies in the fact that even it needs some minimal time in order to register its expressive pain. Even the most facile philosophical dialectic reminds us that dissonance still needs consonance to be registered as such; but if we think of that consonance as a habit of the ear, and as a traditional musical culture of the first shocked listeners, then we are led to reflect on the 'aging of modern music' and the paradoxes of a *Novum* which, like any other event, has it in itself to become ancient history.

If, on the other hand, we think of the consonance that dissonance still needs as a framework in time, a minimal duration apt to set in place the preconditions for its own violent cancellation, then we register the historical situation of the crisis of *Schein*, which must perpetuate itself as even the briefest of temporal extensions in order for its truth – not *Schein* itself, but its very crisis, its guilt, its inauthenticity and impossibility ('poetry after Auschwitz') – to come to expression. Adorno's disillusionment with the 'solution' to this expressionist crisis – later Schoenberg and the twelve-tone system, from which the very idea of consonance, and along with it the authenticity of dissonance, vanishes altogether – has been discussed elsewhere. What may be observed here is the interesting historical trajectory whereby his commitment to this moment of extreme expressionism is then unexpectedly fulfilled thirty years later by the forms of Samuel Beckett; the secret history of what it would be frivolous to think of as nothing but Adorno's personal tastes then stands revealed as a discontinuous spark that leaps from expressionism to minimalism. On the other hand, if it is a question of disengaging those tastes with some precision, it must be added that the purity of Webern's minimalism is equally repugnant to him; Berg's radical impurity – the true model, rather than either Schoenberg or Stravinsky, for

the orgiastic later compositions of Thomas Mann's Leverkuehn – he
seems much to have preferred. An impure minimalism, then! – which
oddly absorbs bits and pieces of a degraded mass culture all around it.

A rather different philosophical conception of the history of modern
art thereby strangely displaces the more conventional one that runs from
Baudelaire to some exhaustion of the modern (for example, to the impasse
of Schoenberg's twelve-tone system, to use a kind of formal shorthand).
This alternate history – in which modernism is transformed back into
'great art' in general – now finally makes the ultimate function of the
omnipresent motif of nominalism clear; for the latter is required philosophically to ground the former. From the perspective of the dilemmas
of nominalism, indeed the historical position of Beethoven, for example,
'whose music is no less haunted by the nominalistic motif than the philosophy of Hegel' (AT 329/315), is metamorphosed from that of a pre-
modern classic into the very showplace of the most modern dialectic
of *Schein* and construction:

> The power of the crisis of aesthetic appearance can be measured by the fact
> that it strikes even that music in appearance least inclined to the values of
> illusionism. Even in such non- or anti-illusionistic music, the very sublimated
> forms of fictive elements die off, not merely expression (as of non-existent
> feelings), but also fictions of structure itself, such as that of total or overall
> form, which here emerges as being unrealizable. In great music like that of
> Beethoven, but probably well beyond the confines of the temporal arts as
> such, the so-called primary materials, those ultimate building blocks that analy-
> sis reaches in its ultimate stage, turn out to be virtually empty of content
> and in themselves vacuous or worthless [*nichtig*]. Only in so far as they asymp-
> totically approach nothingness can they fuse together, in their becoming,
> as a whole. Yet as distinct formal components, their deeper impulse is always
> once again to turn back into *something*: whether a motif or a theme. This
> immanent nullity of its most elementary determinants draws all integral art
> down towards the amorphous, whose force of gravity increases proportionally
> to its degree of organization. Only the amorphous confers the power of inte-
> gration on a work of art. It is in the very moment of formal completion,
> at the greatest distance from the formlessness of nature, that the natural
> moment, that of the not yet formed and of the unarticulated, returns in
> strength. On the closest inspection of a work of art its most objectivized
> forms and images are transformed into a swarm of elements, texts dissolving
> into sheer words. When you think you have the basic details of a work
> of art firmly in your hands, they suddenly melt away into the indeterminate
> and the undifferentiated: such is the nature of artistic mediation. Such is also
> the way in which aesthetic appearance takes up its presence in the structure
> of works of art. The particular, the very life element of the work, flees the
> viewing subject, its concreteness evaporates under the micrological gaze. Pro-

cess, which has in every work of art coagulated into the appearance of an object, now begins to undermine its status as a static thing, and flows away again to where it came from. (AT 154-5/148-9)

What is being proposed is a good deal more scandalous than the simple opinion that Beethoven is not a particularly melodic composer; it is, rather, that his greatest themes or phrases are never anything more than an appearance of something like 'melody' in the first place – this last existing no doubt only in the Culture Industry as a kind of fetish. Rather, the functional power of the great themes is proportionate to the artificiality of their construction, which is motivated by the functional demands of the form (they must be modifiable here, susceptible to variation or the appropriate modulation there, serviceable by way of minimal reconstruction as transitions or as bridge-passages – in short, they come to sound like prefabricated architectural components or Le Corbusier's modular units); and yet, and for those very reasons, they come before us as meaningful aesthetic form, or *Schein*. Beethoven's is thus a minimalism fully as much as Beckett's, but one which *looks* organic and Romantic, and with the promise of late-Romantic lushness already stirring in it like an alien mirage. Adorno's Beethoven is thereby, like Pierre Menard's rewriting of Cervantes, exactly the same as the 'original' and yet a radically different historical text. ('To compose the *Quijote* at the beginning of the seventeenth century was a reasonable undertaking, necessary and perhaps even unavoidable; at the beginning of the twentieth, it is almost impossible,' etc.)

Anachronistic as it may seem, therefore, Beethoven's music is *montage* and as non-fictive as Eisenstein or Juan Gris: montage, the most consequent campaign 'against the art work as a coherent structure of meaning [*Sinnzusammenhang*]' (AT 233/223), is also the moment of triumph of the constructional principle itself:

> The aesthetic constructional principle, the peremptory primacy of the planned whole over detail as such and the latter's relationships within the microstructure, now stands as the correlative [to this seeming surface disorder]; in this sense, and in terms of its micro-structure, all modern art may be considered montage. (AT 233/223)

But the corollary of this doctrine of the worthlessness of the elementary components of the work, and the illusory nature even of their seemingly meaningful or harmonious combinations, turns out to be a modification in the subjective power attributed to the artist (let alone the 'genius'). It is a conclusion we will explore more fully when we deal with the dynamics of productivity; still, some initial consequences need to be

drawn here, for paradoxically the constructional materials are meaningless
or *nichtig* only in terms of human agency, of the composer or the listener.
In reality they have their own meaning within themselves as a historically
specific material or technique, which dictates its own formal development:

> How intimately related technique and content really are – conventional wis-
> dom notwithstanding – was demonstrated by Beethoven himself in the remark
> that many of the effects normally attributed to the genius of the composer
> are in fact the results of little more than adroit manipulations of the diminished
> seventh. (AT 320/307)

The relationship of the part to the whole, therefore, redolent not merely
of traditional aesthetic theory but also of a form of aesthetic taste and
a type of classicizing aesthetic practice which is today utterly alien to
us, recovers an astonishing and well-nigh postmodern relevance when,
as supremely in *Aesthetic Theory*, it is reformulated as a historical crisis
and an unresolvable structural contradiction. It is therefore appropriate
to conclude this section on nominalism and construction in Adorno with
a lengthier final *mise au point* on Beethoven himself:

> Beethoven confronted the antinomy [between unity and particularity], not
> by schematically extinguishing the individual component in the spirit of the
> prevailing practice of the preceding century, but rather – very much in kinship
> with the developing bourgeois natural sciences of his own time – by depercep-
> tualizing it and stripping it of its qualities. He thereby did more than simply
> integrate music into the continuum of a new kind of becoming or process,
> thereby preserving musical form from the intensifying threat of empty abstrac-
> tion. For the individual moments, as they sink in value, begin to interpenetrate
> each other and thereby to determine the very form itself through the very
> process by which they themselves tendentially disappear. The individual com-
> ponents in Beethoven are (but on the other hand are also not) the very impulse
> towards total form, in so far as they can have their existence only by way
> of that whole that allows them to be in the first place; whereas in and of
> themselves they tend towards the relative indeterminacy of the basic tonal
> relationships and thereby towards amorphousness. If you hear or read his
> exceedingly articulated music closely enough, it comes to resemble a conti-
> nuum of nothingness. The *tour de force* of each of his great works lies in
> the way in which – as though taking Hegel absolutely literally – it determines
> the transformation of a totality of nothingness into a totality of Being –
> yet only as appearance [*Schein*], not with any claim to absolute truth. Yet
> even this last is at least suggested, by way of the immanent rigor which is
> the work's ultimate content. The latently diffuse and intangible, on the one
> hand, the supreme power that compels it to form together into something,
> on the other – these are the two poles of nature itself at work. Over against
> the daimon, the composing subject, who forges and flings great blocks of

material, there stands the undifferentiation of the tiniest unities into which each of his movements becomes dissociated, ending up no longer even as raw material but rather as the abstract system of tonal relationships themselves. (AT 276/264-5)

In fact, the problem of Adorno's minimalism is at one with the ambiguity of his very enterprise. If *Aesthetic Theory* is ultimately the expression of Adorno's personal aesthetic experience, and thereby projects his own limited biographical 'taste', then its philosophical positions become relativized in a more than historical fashion, and the work shrinks to the status of a document (albeit one of extraordinary intelligence and resourcefulness). If, on the other hand, more universal truths about the work of art are, for whatever reason, to be generalized from minimalism as a unique and privileged moment in the history of art, then we find ourselves unexpectedly back within a more traditional philosophical aesthetic, which still seeks to deduce the general from the particular in a manner peculiarly unacceptable for postcontemporary thought.

Characteristically, to be sure, this minimalism also includes a critique of minimalism (just as its framework denounces 'isms' in the first place). Thus the movement of detail evoked above in the analysis of Beethoven – the becoming 'anti-essential' and non- or anti-foundational of detail as such, its consequent and modern refusal of any internal self-justification, what Hegel would have called the loss or tendential impoverishment of its 'content' – is elsewhere identified as the very 'death wish' of detail itself (AT 450/421); while the triumph of Adorno's central principle of construction – in Constructivism as a historical avant-garde movement – spells the end of art itself: 'in fact, Constructivism has no place left for invention [*Einfall*], for the unplanned and the involuntary' (AT 450/421). The fact that Adorno, like Hegel, goes on to fantasize an art beyond the end of art, or even several, is intriguing enough: the conception of models developed in *Negative Dialectics* returns briefly in the supplementary fragments to suggest that artists may continue to invent and project models of art in a situation in which art-works can no longer concretely be realized (AT 452/423) (hence the stimulation postmodern painters find in theoretical writings about art, which seems today to have replaced the practical stimulation that used to be afforded by the work of other artists). In another place, indeed, Adorno prophetically suggests a return of the tonal after the most implacable forms of atonality, under whose hegemony it once again becomes strangely new: something that seems in fact to be happening in postmodern music (AT 62/54).

Yet the proper use of the doctrines of minimalism and of construction would appear to be those that seek to do without their fatal positivity:

not norms, then, but rhetorical features and parts of the constructed or reconstructed representation of a contradictory situation, pushed to the limit, in which the impossibility of art is not the occasion for pathos, but rather the deconcealment of an articulated structure that is in fact a concrete historical contradiction. What is then achieved, and the effectiveness of praxis, can thereby be measured and evaluated only after the fact. In art also, the slogan 'pessimism of the intellect, optimism of the will' is the only truly energizing ethic.

Three

But with this contextualization of Adorno's judgements, which 'sets them in motion' dialectically and rewrites them into the form of a situation and a contradiction, we again confront the issue of the status of the historical dialectic in the author of *Negative Dialectics*, and in particular the old problem of correspondence or reflection (or even, if you prefer, of base and superstructure): the essentially linguistic question of how the relationship between the cultural or aesthetic act and the social situation is to be expressed. *Aesthetic Theory*'s ingenious philosophical solution to this problem – the concept of the work of art as a windowless monad, which will be examined in the next chapter – in fact, for all practical intents and purposes, leaves it intact. The monad is, in other words, at one and the same time a reflection and not a reflection, just as the work of art itself is social and non-social all at once – or, better still, social through and through by virtue of its very antisociality (see below). This is of course the classical form of the Hegelian dialectic, the identity of identity and non-identity.

What complicates the classical formulation is that there are two forms of non-identity to be confronted, rather than one: Nature, the absolute Other, on the one hand; but also society, a very different kind of other from the first, and certainly nothing like the 'second nature' of the tradition, even though it is often evoked in the language of ontology as the 'totality of what is'. The reflexes of the well-known Great Refusal, then, are, here – where society is in question – peremptory and absolute (and go a long way towards explaining Adorno's hostility to left politics – unless, indeed, it is the other way round): '*denn wahr ist nur, was nicht in diese Welt passt*' [nothing complicitous with this world can have any truth (AT 93/86)]. But this imposes a very different kind of negativity from the classical form of non-identity (and introduces the supplementary terminological difficulty one always has when explicating the Frankfurt School – namely, that the words 'positive' – associated with positivism – and 'affirmative' – as in Marcuse's 'affirmative character of culture' – are always for them negative in connotation).

There fatally reappears, then, that dualistic alternative present in all radical thought: the differentiation, under whatever form or in whatever terminology, between the positive and the negative, the progressive and the reactionary (or regressive), what resists and what submits, between the radical (or the utopian) and the ideological, between refusal and complicity. Adorno's concrete analyses include these judgments and are inseparable from them (even the stigmatized political word 'progressive' reappears, albeit in the rather different context of the development of productive forces, which we will examine later on). That such judgements are at one with the old problem of correspondence and reflection (or of the base-and-superstructure model) seems evident, since only a distance between the work of art and the social could allow them to come into play in the first place; that the old correspondence model is complicitous with the doctrine of the autonomy of the work of art may at first seem more paradoxical – yet Peter Bürger has shown us persuasively how it was the very doctrine (and institution) of aesthetic autonomy that liberated the possibility of such political judgements in the first place.[5]

Here is Adorno's most incisive statement of the matter:

> Art is social, not merely by virtue of its process of production, in which at any given moment the dialectic of productive forces and productive relations is at work, not even only in the social origins of its contents and raw materials. Rather it becomes social by virtue of its oppositional position to society itself, a position it can occupy only by defining itself as autonomous. (AT 335/321)

What I want to show, however, is that this seemingly clear-cut oppositionality is in Adorno a good deal more complicated and dialectically variable.

Take for example the reading (or the rewriting) of Kant's circumscription of the aesthetic as 'disinterested interest' or 'purposefulness without a practical purpose' [zwecklose Zweckhaftigkeit]. This, historically the classical first form of the doctrine of aesthetic autonomy, is reissued by Adorno with a powerfully dialectical modification:

> The shadow of the most passionate practical interest must be associated with the concept of the 'disinterested' if it is to be anything more than mere indifference, and there is reason to think that the dignity of a work of art can be

measured against the very strength of the interest from which it has been wrested (AT 24/16).

(He will elsewhere [AT 396/375] interpret 'disinterest' as a suspension of that drive to self-preservation which was identified as the source of the will to power of the dialectic of enlightenment.) But almost at once this 'positive' reevaluation of disinterestedness becomes dialectically problematized:

> As soon as the art work takes up a position with respect to the negativity of reality, however, the very concept of disinterestedness is modified. Works of art involve in their very nature a relationship between interest and its denial, contrary to both the Kantian and the Freudian interpretations. Even the contemplative relationship to the work of art, wrested away from the objects of action, is lived as a repudiation of immediate praxis and thereby as being itself a form of praxis, a refusal to play the game. Only those works of art which can be felt as modes of action [*Verhaltensweise*] really justify their existence. (AT 25–6/17)

What therefore began as a suspension and a negation of the fallen praxis of a business and commodity society here slowly turns around into a higher form of praxis, which now annuls the earlier concept of 'disinterestedness' or 'purposelessness' and becomes a higher form of interest and a more authentic *telos*.[6]

The other – and antithetical – component of Kant's formula, the nature of that 'purposefulness' or interest-like quality that the art-work does seem to possess, is the object of even more complex dialectical transformations, since it seems most closely affiliated to the dynamic of the social itself, and thereby, as an impulse, the most dubious and contaminated:

> The Kantian notion of 'purposefulness', which secures the link for him between art and the inner essence of nature, is in fact most closely related to *Technik* [a term which in German associates the twin connotations of *technique* and *technology*]. The way in which works of art 'purposefully' organize themselves so as to distinguish themselves from mere being, is called technique; only through technique do they acquire this illusion of 'purposefulness' (AT 321/308).

By thus transferring Kantian teleology from nature to human science, Adorno deliberately introduces into the very heart of the aesthetic the dynamic of 'enlightenment' and the original sin of Western rationality and domination which he was concerned elsewhere to denounce. The later adventures of this perverse resocialization of the Kantian aesthetic will be traced below, in the dialectic of the aesthetic 'forces of production'.

What seems more immediately instructive for Adorno's practice of the dialectic itself will be the prolongation of this theme in the cognate concept of reification [*Verdinglichung*], which plays an equally crucial and equally ambiguous role in his analysis of the work of art.

For reification is, in Adorno's aesthetic, first and foremost a positive, that is to say a valorized, concept – a reversal of its conventional position in the Marxist tradition.[7] There it designated not merely the substitution for human relations of thing-like ones (money, the 'cash nexus') but also – in the form of so-called commodity fetishism – a peculiar pathology of the material in which the former solid things of a world of use values are transmogrified into abstract equivalencies which none the less now project the mirage of a new kind of libidinally invested materiality in the commodity: in this sense 'reification' is virtually at the other extreme from matter itself, which it seems to transform into strangely spiritualized objects which none the less seem more thing-like than the things themselves.

As a materialist Adorno cannot ground his anti-capitalist aesthetic – whose context is that well-nigh universal commodification of the world already diagnosed in *Dialectic of Enlightenment* – in convenient forms of anti-material spirituality, which he plainly loathes and which is included in the denunciation of all forms of 'inwardness' and subjectivization that runs through *Aesthetic Theory* as one of its philosophical programs (to be more closely examined in its proper place). Nor does he have recourse to those conceptions of praxis whereby a Gramsci or a Sartre, in their very different ways, sought to cut the Gordian knot of the dualisms of idealism and materialism and to replace them with something else. What results, therefore, is a restless series of transfers whereby reification – for Adorno absolutely essential to the work of art – changes its valences as it passes from the social to the aesthetic (and vice versa).

'What is called reification gropes, where it is radicalized, towards the language of things. In effect it tries to move back towards the Idea of that nature extirpated by the primacy of human meaning' (AT 96/89). By a kind of ruse, then, the radicalization of the force that destroyed nature is pressed into the service of its at least ideal reestablishment. But this is no mere local strategy: 'reification is essential to works of art, and at the same time contradicts their nature as emergences [*Erscheinendem*]; their thing-like character is no less dialectical than their status as what is to be contemplated and observed [*ihr Anschauliches*]' (AT 153/146). But it is a deadly counter-poison:

> works of art are negative a priori by virtue of the very law that condemns them to objectification: they kill what they objectify by wrenching it from

its living immediacy. Thus their own life feeds on death. This is in fact the qualitative barrier beyond which the modern begins. Works of art mimetically abandon their images to reification, their deathly principle. The hope of successfully escaping this principle is the moment of illusion in art which it, since Baudelaire, seeks to shake off, without thereby resigning itself to becoming again mere thing among things. The heralds of the modern, Baudelaire and Poe, were as artists the first technocrats of the aesthetic. Without the homeopathic ingestion of the poison itself – reification as the virtual negation of the living – the pretense of art to resist subsumption under 'civilization' would have remained a helpless pipe-dream. By absorbing into art, since the beginnings of the modern, objects alien to it that can never fully be transformed by its own internal formal laws, the mimetic pole of art yields to its counter-principle, and this all the way up to the emergence of montage. (AT 201/193)

At this point, then, reification is borrowed back from the social, in order to permit the aesthetic a continuing and ever more precarious existence in a wholly reified world – from which, however, the counter-poison somehow protects it. But in a final moment, reification seems to have been transformed into a more active weapon (against itself); arguing for and against that property of art still called *Geist* or spirituality, Adorno stresses the produced or constructed nature of the work of art, 'which specifically includes the objectivity of its spirit. Aesthetic reflection must sanction that as the expression of the work's objectivity at the same time that it seeks critically to dissolve it' (AT 274/263). Such passages, in which critical and receptive activity seem to become independent of the work itself and to be endowed with a supplementary power and function not implicit in the art-object, are rare enough in Adorno, who rejects the exploration of reception in the general spirit of his anti-subjective program; by the same token, his very project of a belated aesthetics (whose problematic nature and internal contradictions have already been touched on) can also be read as a displacement and a repudiation of the autonomy of literary criticism and interpretation that has come to be affirmed in the present moment of the hegemony of the theoretical. None the less, the sense of the passage is clear: the commodity form must somehow be made available and tangible in order for the activity of its dissolution to have any point: the work must designate itself as a commodity in order to acquire the means of escaping that status. But none of these formulations is quite so peremptory and astonishing as our final one: 'art remains alive only through its essentially social powers of resisting society; *unless it submits to reification, it becomes a mere commodity*' (AT 335/321; emphasis added).

Four

Whatever the orthodoxy of Adorno's Marxism, it can be argued that of all Marxist aestheticians he is the most faithful to Marx's own method, or mode of *Darstellung*. To be sure, the great formal architectonic of *Capital* is no longer historically available to him, like some earlier moment of sonata or symphonic form which, undermined by nominalism, can no longer be reconstructed as such. But *Aesthetic Theory* stubbornly keeps faith with the methodological lessons of the 1857 Preface to the *Grundrisse*: that while one category – production – may have structural primacy over all the others, in the writing it must never be allowed to become the dominant theme or motif; it must never, to switch to the language of poststructuralism, be allowed to organize the terms around itself into a specific code (or 'private language'). So in Marx the category of production rises and sinks, sometimes becomes the terminological partner of lesser categories (distribution, consumption), sometimes disappears from sight altogether, and at other moments, with a thunderclap, is revealed as the very motor of history itself. The concept is here still held at a certain mediate distance from the term which is its name, and which threatens to absorb it altogether into a linguistic identity that approaches the condition and dynamic of poetic language at the same time as it marks the triumph of conceptual reification (we have already observed the intimate relationship between the two).

So it is that this aesthetics can speak a variety of speculative languages, none of which ever finally freezes over into Adorno's 'method', which might then be laid out in the theoretical handbooks with a convenient tag, like Lukács's, Bloom's, Macherey's, Bakhtin's, or Derrida's. We have just seen, for example, that reification plays as fundamental a role in

Adorno's formal analyses as it does in Lukács's thought, and is often more intricately related to his readings than anything in Lukács's own expositions: one does not, for all that, turn to Adorno as the primary source for 'reification theory'. The history of aesthetic situations is here as omnipresent and inescapable as in Sartre; but Adorno does not, as Sartre did at least twice in his life, try to write a 'linear history' of those.[8] The contradiction between parts and wholes is as exhaustively rehearsed as anything in contemporary bourgeois theory, from the aestheticians to the New Criticism; but that dynamic is never codified as a doctrine, about whose formulations endless philosophical argument might be generated: at the last moment before codification the problem is always enlarged, its terminology transformed, and we turn out *also* to have been talking about something else, which needs a different kind of development.

Proving equal to Adorno, therefore, doing right by him, attempting to keep faith with the protean intelligence of his sentences, requires a tireless effort – always on the point of lapsing – to prevent the *thematization* of the concept of production, to use Paul de Man's suggestive phrase. That the notion of production somehow underpins the valorization of construction in Adorno, authorizes it and grounds it, is not wrong but only misleading: rather than a logical process, in which deeper presuppositions are reached and then unfolded in their own name and right, it seems more prudent, for the moment, to think of the one as something like a modulation of the other, which takes us into a different conceptual or sonorous dimension altogether. In that case, the method might be Marx's, but the philosophical form something closer to *Finnegans Wake*.

In so far as *Aesthetic Theory* is also in certain respects an abstract writing up of concrete analyses worked out elsewhere, the more immediate reference for this doctrine of the aesthetic categories will appropriately enough be Adorno's *Versuch über Wagner*, his first full-length musical monograph (written in exile in 1937–8) and a splendor, in which an ideal mimesis of Benjamin's book on tragic drama produces what stands in Adorno's own work as the equivalent of the older critic's virtually contemporaneous 'On Some Motifs in Baudelaire' – a description of the simultaneous emergence of modernism and mass culture.

The dialectic of Wagnerian form – which draws its remarkably 'modern' innovative technology from the relatively untutored simplicities of the composer's essential dilettantism – throws up a virtual textbook opposition between construction and expression, where the driving insistence of the second of these impulses interferes with the architectonics of the first, as it is exemplified in the first Viennese school, with its elaboration of sonata-form temporality. But expression is also not an autonomous category, and knows its own idiosyncratic fate in Wagner, where its 'moment of uncontrolled intensification can scarcely tolerate the mid-space of temporal consciousness and is released in the form of external gestures' (W 35/39), by which Adorno means the Wagnerian leitmotivs, as these seem, sometimes with a virtually cartoon-like larger-than-life crudity, to dramatize the peremptory movements of the Wagnerian characters themselves. But even in terms of this still minimal account of the 'gesture' in Wagner, it is clear that this cannot persist as an auton-omous category either, but must enter into tension and contradiction with the category of 'expression' from which it seemed to derive:

> the problem is compounded by the fact that the moment of expression, which is supposed to lead from one gesture to another in the basic sequence (in the most famous of all, that of the *Tristan* Prelude, the expression is 'yearning' or 'longing'), in fact excludes all repetition of the type of interpolated tonal dance forms and calls out for that very thoroughgoing variation against which the gestural character of the leitmotivs originally struggled but which can be replaced by the Wagnerian principle of 'psychological variation' only in the most rationalistic fashion that does violence to the musical forms them-selves. (W 37/42–3)

What happens, therefore, to the abstract aesthetic categories is that they become transformed into the instruments by which a concrete musical (or productive) situation is measured and characterized. They do not finally themselves (even historically) become harmonized into this or that more comprehensive or dialectical theory or aesthetics as such; rather, it is their very immediate incompatibility and contradiction that describes the technical and historical problems whose solution will constitute the *Novum* of the new work. This, then, is a rather different relationship between the general and the particular than is conveyed either by the traditional philosophical subsumption of species under genres, or by the nominalistic transformation of a particular into the generality of a 'unique style': here the notion of the historical situation, problem, or contra-diction itself mediates between the general and the particular, between the eternal aesthetic categories and the unique and incomparable text.

There are evidently deeper reasons why this richest of all explorations of the modern should finally come to us from music, rather than from the verbal, visual or architectural areas in which prophets and ideologues of the modern have been most vocal and strident. For music seems to be the art in which the distance between producer and ideal consumer is the minimal imaginable, and tendentially abolished: as a composer, Adorno seems to have been able to hear musical works as though he were composing them – from a specialist or expert's standpoint, which has always alternately intimidated or irritated the critics of the other arts, for whom other equally authentic positions of reception seemed available and worth defending against it.[9] Here, however, it is as though there is no outside: a paradoxical outcome indeed for an art that, more than all the others, seems to have its *esse* in its *percipi* and to enjoy little existence of its own beyond the moment of hearing it.

On the other hand, it is precisely this tenuousness of musical object-hood, this more thoroughgoing passage of the artistic object into the sense organ itself – from which for a time it seems indistinguishable – that suddenly seems to put a different face on the old subject–object problem, without 'solving' it by violence, abandoning it as false or meta-physical crux, or projecting a mirage of reconciliation or spurious atone-ment between the poles. Yet this new projection of the work of art also issues from that field in which sheer technical knowledge – and an evolutionary development of that knowledge seemingly as rigorous as what happens in the natural sciences – is massively preponderant and inescapable throughout the entire history of music (as distinct from the local role some more exact knowledge of the metric potentialities of a given language or the psychophysiological dynamics of color or optics may have played in key but discontinuous moments of the history of poetry or painting).

The musical experience thus permits the coordination of a very special account of the subject–object relationship with an emphasis on objective technical dynamics: from this unusual conjuncture will miraculously emerge, reborn long after its tiresome ideological exhaustion in the various ideologies of the modernisms, the concept of the New.

The first of these issues – which will take the form of a reinvention of Leibniz's notion of the 'windowless monad' – constitutes an outcome to the subject–object dialectic which will also 'solve' the traditional Marxian dilemma of base and superstructure, or of the 'correspondence' of the aesthetic work to social reality (or its 'reflection' thereof). The aesthetic translation of Hegel's great formula – the identity of identity and non-identity – is peremptory: 'if the work of art is experienced in a purely aesthetic fashion, it is not even aesthetically properly appre-hended in the first place' (AT 17/9). The doctrine of the aesthetic auton-omy of the work of art is the correct one; but it is true only if grasped as the very opposite of an aestheticizing doctrine, or a kind of philosophi-cal 'art for art's sake'. The work is social and historical through and through: only thus can it become autonomous. The religion of art, the glorification of the cultural and the aesthetic, is a social conduct and an ideology that has nothing to do with the work of art itself.

To put the problem in a somewhat different way: it is clear that every work of art is 'of the world' and that everything about it is social – its materials, its creator, its reception, art itself (or culture) as a leisure class activity, and so forth; as a thing in the world it is social, yet the most important thing about it is not 'in' the world at all, in that sense. As a thing-in-the-world it is either a luxury item, which can be set in opposition to real human need and suffering (or some deeper infrastructural reality of human experience and social life) or else, as some small fragment of the world, it can try to 'reflect' other larger segments of that reality, doing so in either a frivolous or a socially responsible way.

From these standpoints, then, the work of art might be, so to speak, 'more' or 'less' social; 'more' or 'less' historical. But it is precisely that kind of measurement that Adorno thinks nonsensical, when one has to do with 'genuine' works of art. The bad ones: kitsch, decoration, the applied arts and handicraft, Culture Industry products – all these, being already things and commodities in the social world, are fair game for such evaluative exercises; nor is the deeper guilt of art and culture itself denied, rejustified or rationalized away at any moment, as we have seen in Part II. But what we saw there also was that the true work of art is something radically different from both these sets of things (art objects, or the institution of art).

It is to solve this peculiar problem – how we are to think about something every part of which is social but which itself is somehow not social – that the doctrine of the monad is invoked:

> The work of art is what rationalistic metaphysics at its very height proclaimed to be the principle of the world, namely the Monad: a force field and a thing all at once. Works of art are closed off against each other and blind, yet in their very hermetic closure they represent what lies outside themselves. Thus have they traditionally offered themselves, as that autarchic principle of life that Goethe was wont, in synonymity with the concept of the monad, to call entelechy. It seems conceivable that the more problematical teleological concepts became in the world of organic nature, they grow even more intensively appropriate for the work of art. As the moment of an overarching system of relationships in the spirit of a given age, intertwined with history and society, works strain beyond their monadic condition without ever being endowed with windows. (AT 268/257)

Entelechy, the mind–body problem, the doctrine of the soul as the inner form of its external parts: such idealistic references raise the deepest suspicions about the tendencies of Adorno's monadology only if we fail to grasp the crucial historical distinction that for him, those older problems – consciousness, the soul, creation and cosmology – are precisely idealistic and false, but that their pseudo-solution in an older metaphysics – most specifically now this one of Leibniz – can be reread as the distorted and mystified solution to the very different materialist problem of the work of art, where it alone has validity:

> That society 'appears' in works of art, with polemic truth and also ideologically, is a fact that can easily lead to the mystifications of the philosophies of history. Speculation can all too easily fall prey to some doctrine of a preestablished harmony between society and the work of art that has been conveniently arranged in advance by the world-spirit. But theory cannot capitulate before this problem of the relationship between art and the social. The process which is completed and brought to fulfillment in works of art is to be thought of as having the same meaning as the social process in which they are embedded: they represent it, following Leibniz's formula, in windowless fashion. The configuration of elements in an artistic whole obeys immanent laws which are related to those that prevail in the society outside. Social forces of production and social relations of production return in the very form of the work, divested of their facticity, because artistic labor is also social labor; works of art are also the products of social labor. Nor are the productive forces within the work of art distinct in and of themselves from those in society, but only by virtue of their constitutive absence from the concrete social order. One can scarcely imagine anything performed or invented within the work of art that does not have its equivalent – in however latent a form – within social production itself. (AT 350/335)

So it is that the doctrine of the monad – and above all the windowless closure that constitutes it as an idea (and has nothing philosophically to do with current discussions of 'open' and 'closed' works) – at once permits the most sweeping affirmations of the sociality and the historicity of art:

> It is the historical moment that is in the work of art constitutive: the most authentic works are those that give themselves over to their historical raw material without reservation and without any pretense to floating above it somewhere. Works of art are in this sense unconsciously the historiography of their own epoch; history is not the least form of knowledge they mediate. That is precisely why they are incommensurable with historicism, which seeks to reduce them to a history external to them, rather than to pursue their genuine historical content. (AT 272/261)

But at this point a caution must be inserted: a price must be paid for that separation from the world that endows the monad with its capacity to be as profoundly historical and social as history and society itself. It cannot be *political*, something which will come as no surprise to readers familiar with Adorno's views on socialist realism (or on Sartrean *engage-*

ment) as well as with his deep antagonism to Brecht. 'Praxis' is thereby dispatched in what will by now have become a familiar thought-figure: 'Praxis does not lie in the effect of the work of art, but rather encapsulated in its truth-content' (AT 367/350). Adorno is in any case very clear about the separation of the three levels of the historical, the social and the political (in a way which paradoxically reconfirms the tripartite scheme of *The Political Unconscious*):

> Social struggles and class relationships are expressed and articulated through the very structure of the works of art; such political positions as these may take, however, are in contrast *mere* epiphenomena, which generally hinder the formal elaboration of the work and finally even impair its social truth content. (AT 344/329)

The political vehemence such statements and positions of Adorno frequently arouse on the left (this one is an obvious provocation) should not lead anyone to forget that there has never been any kind of left consensus on the possibility, or even the desirability, of a properly political aesthetics; nor even on the immediate political effectivity of the most 'committed' works of art. Meanwhile, the futility of the discussion becomes clear when you realize how easy it is to move allegedly 'political' works over into another, more respectable category, as Adorno often does with the parts of Brecht he likes.

But the spirit of these remarks, and the methodology they inspire, is clear enough. The informing presence of society within art and language is all the greater when it is indirect and invisible, 'all the more complete, the less any representation of the ego and of society is made thematic, and the more involuntarily it crystallizes such a representation out of itself' (NL, 55).

Almost the basic question about this cultural politics, then, would be why these views do not simply settle back into a stereotypical Romantic opposition between the individual and society: they cannot do so precisely because society is already within the 'individual', sapping and undermining an individuation and an individuality for which it is itself responsible. And this will oddly, paradoxically, for good or ill, be the reason given for the repudiation of overtly political art:

> For the theory of committed art, as it is current today, presupposes a superiority and an invulnerability to the basic reigning fact of life of exchange society – namely, alienation between human beings and also between objective spirit and the society that it expresses and judges all at once. The theory of commitment demands that art speak directly to people, as though the immediate could realize itself immediately in a world of universal mediation. (NL 120)

Five

Adorno has, however, another, equally provocative way of turning the tables in this situation: 'the social thinking on aesthetics', he observes with feigned astonishment, 'has customarily neglected the concept of productive forces' (AT 69/62). And it is certain that very few Marxist aesthetics have taken the concept of economic production – rather than the conventional ones of class affiliation and struggle, ideology, or political position – very seriously, despite the extensive use of a rhetoric of production in the 1960s and 1970s. Certainly no one – least of all the cultural Stalinists themselves – has had the audacity to suggest a relevance for aesthetics of the even more vulgar-materialist notion of sheer economic productivity (that is to say, the primacy of productive *forces* – machinery and technology – over production *relations* – class positions and consciousness, collective versus authoritarian organization of the shop floor, and so on). Yet it is precisely this conception of production that for Adorno will subsume both the historical and the social dimensions of the work of art, whose relationship to history is marked and dated, as it were, by the advanced character of its production process, while its essential sociality is given in advance by the collective social nature of production itself.

I want to overemphasize this matter of productive forces for a moment, not merely because it is the least familiar or traditional feature of Adorno's aesthetics, but also because it at once reopens the possibility of conceptualizing the 'New' or the *Novum*, so central in all modernism, discussion of which we have found ourselves obliged to suspend heretofore on the merely negative injunction that, whatever else it was, it was not a temporal or a phenomenological concept. This now clearly has something to do with modernization, in the sense in which, from the very onset of capitalism, new and more productive machinery has driven out its predecessors and made them obsolete: a historical paradigm which is surely very much akin to Adorno's own vision of the history of artistic 'progress', where the new ruthlessly annihilates older forms and conventions, and where – particularly in the history of music – something like scientific and technological invention is at one with artistic construction.

The paradigm is a familiar one and constitutes the fundamental master narrative of all the ideologies of the modern, from the Russian Formalists to Pound and passing through the most varied manifestos of the most artistically dissimilar avant-garde movements: what is unique in its rehearsal by Adorno is the philosophical appeal to the only economic theory capable of providing an adequate grounding to what otherwise becomes an ever more frantic story of styling changes and the dynamics of fashion – namely, Marxism itself:

> In many authentic manifestations of the modern, the level of industrial content was strictly avoided thematically, owing to the mistrust against the pseudometamorphoses of machine art, but none the less in them – and perhaps above all in them! (in Klee, for example) – made its irresistible dynamics felt, negatively, by way of the reduction in the permissible or the tolerable and in the intensification of construction proper. This feature of the modern has changed as little as the very fact of industrialization itself as a force in people's daily lives: hence the extraordinary appearance of an invariable that the aesthetic idea of the modern has taken on. To be sure, the aesthetic realm affords no less developmental space for this historical dynamic than does industrial production itself, which has in a century been transformed from classical nineteenth century factories to automation, passing through the period of mass production proper. The formal process of artistic modernism draws the power of this its historical content from the fact that the most advanced types of material production and organization at a given historical moment are not limited to the immediate area from which they derive. In a fashion still inadequately analyzed by sociology, their influence is felt even in those areas of life most distant from them, and penetrates deeply into the zone of a purely subjective experience which is unaware of such influence, against which it thinks itself sheltered. That art alone is modern which, according to its own specific modes of experience and by way of the very crisis of experience itself, absorbs what the most advanced state of industrialization under the then dominant relations of production has made current. Yet this involves something like a negative canon, the taboo on what such modernisms repudiate in their procedures and their technique: a specific set of negations which in fact turns out to form something like a canon of what remains to be accomplished. (AT 58/50)

These final remarks deserve special emphasis, for they supply some unexpected clues to the enigmatic nature of the 'New' in art – that 'blind spot' of the modern, 'as empty as the immediate here and now of the thing before us' (AT 38/30) – about which Adorno's technological rhetoric risks suggesting that it is somehow in the mint shininess of streamlined or futuristic machinery that the perpetual *Novum* of great art is to be sought: an impression instantly tarnished by the memory that nothing becomes quite so quickly antiquated as such once 'advanced' equipment.

The problem is meanwhile compounded by the fact that aesthetic phenomena – being cultural; that is to say, formations of a superstructure that is only a functional part of the whole it claims to be the equivalent and the substitute for – are also ideological. The 'New', therefore, is also an ideological compensation, as well as an aesthetic value and a historically original category of capitalist production. Thus, in a slashing paragraph of *Minima Moralia*, Adorno suddenly outdoes Benjamin in his identification of the 'cult of the new, and thus the idea of modernity' as a 'rebellion against the fact that there is no longer anything new' (MM 316/235). The whole of the modern now becomes (very much in the spirit of Benjamin's own essay 'On Some Motifs in Baudelaire') 'the first consciousness of the decay of experience'. The New here becomes sensation, in its most garish media senses ('in a statement at the time of the first pogroms, Goebbels boasted that at least the National Socialists were not boring' [MM 319/237]); and the lurid light shed back by modern politics on modern art now virtually causes the 'truth-content' of the latter to pale away into little more than a repetition which, like artificial stimulus in general, wishes it were a new experience: 'not for nothing were Poe, Baudelaire, Wagner addictive types' (MM 320/238). This drug, however, no longer looks much like the art demanded by the avant-garde, 'a music that astonishes the composer like a new substance that appears in the chemist's retort'.[10]

How one is then to 'remember' the 'New' none the less remains the nagging doubt at the heart of this aesthetic value. Detemporalizing what seems an irrevocably temporal concept demands that we restructure the problem to which it responds in some less immediately phenomenological or experiential way, if that is possible. The worry clearly turns on the status of formerly 'new' works of the past, thereby reawakening that complex of issues that swarm around the term 'historicism', whatever immediate meaning one decides by fiat to limit that to. But as so often it is a mistake to confront the mystery of our understanding [*Verstehen*] of the past in the Cartesian manner, reconstructing its a priori possibility as it were deductively from zero – that is, from an imagined starting point in which the past does not yet exist and we are, as it were, as yet without memory altogether. We must rather begin from the fact and the premiss that we do occasionally 'understand' the past in some stronger sense: that, from time to time, we have been able to have the conviction that we 'know' what Lenin was thinking on the occasion of this or that intervention; that we sense what the Paris of the 1830s felt like as a life-world; that we know how Lu Xun's first writings must have struck his contemporaries; that we can feel the excitement of the outbreak of World War I in the various European capitals or the intellectual animation of the devisers of the first vernacular *canzoni*.

Such moments of conviction about the past, unverifiable, ephemeral, and subject to endless sober revision and fresh doubts, may be metaphysically illusory; but can be examined in their own right for what they contain and what goes on in them. I have tried to show elsewhere, following Collingwood, that they involve the reconstruction of a situation and a problem or a question, whose 'answer' then takes on the value and the freshness of an act in which we seem to reparticipate.[11] Adorno's aesthetics does not pose such issues of historicism or *Verstehen* as such: but his conception of art as production is usefully consistent with this view, and affords it additional possibilities of development.

What the present passage suggests, for example, is that our most intense approach to what is 'new' about the old involves a sudden intuition of taboos and constraints, negatives, restrictions, prohibitions, reluctances and aversions. But these are not inherited dogma or aesthetic moralism, and have nothing to do with the respectable tastes and unexamined aesthetic good conduct of the conventional public sphere. They are *new* taboos; indeed, what is new about the *Novum* is less the work itself (whose most spankingly new innovations, in all their self-conscious Sunday pride, may well come to seem the most pitiably antiquated thing about it) than these new prohibitions, about which it would therefore be better to say, not that they tell you what not to do, but rather that they spell out what is *no longer* to be done; what you cannot do any more; what it would be corny to do again; or about which something (Socrates' Daimon) warns you that it is somehow not quite right and ought to be avoided, for reasons you yourself do not quite understand and may never fully grasp.

Such taboos can bear on the widest range of aesthetic materials: a certain kind of sentence, for example, which one had better no longer indulge in, a feeling or an emotion which may be real enough and very widespread but which had best from now on be left out (so that it becomes interesting to see whether you can think of characters who have never had such feelings and could not imagine them); a boring sound combination, a narrative whose structure makes you impatient, a philosophical argument which one would be embarrassed to repeat, no matter how true it may be. The New, then, is what happens when one excludes those things, providing what results is something other than silence. This is, of course, a reasoning that leads to minimalism by its very internal momentum, and in which minimalist values are somehow structurally inscribed: but more often in the history of modern art the devaluation of the older aesthetic technology, the obsolescence of a whole range of now prohibited contents and forms, has felt like a liberation to which invention responds with a flush of new forms that seems very rich indeed.

There is therefore no insurmountable problem about sensing what it was Beethoven could no longer allow his instruments to do; the problem is now the other way round – how we are to prevent ourselves from attributing what he did find to make them do to the sheerest subjectivity or 'genius'. 'The subjective component of the work is itself a piece of objectivity' (AT 69/61). How to demonstrate this, how to undermine our tendencies to subjectivism in some persuasive and definitive way – without thereby capitulating to positivism – is, as we suggested at the very outset, one of the most fundamental vocations of *Aesthetic Theory*.

That the raw material of the work of art is historical through and through is a useful lesson that we cannot learn often enough, which may not, however, fully complete that particular task. Those of us who learned our modernist historicity from Proust, for example, will appreciate Adorno's corrective rewriting of the doctrine:

> Proust (and after him Kahnweiler) took the position that painting transforms our very mode of seeing and thereby the objects themselves along with it. As authentic as may be the experience to which this doctrine corresponds, the formulation may well be too idealistic. Precisely the reverse of this formulation may not be altogether unconvincing either: that it is the objects themselves which have historically changed, so that the human sensorium adapts to those changes and painting ultimately invents the appropriate indices for them. Cubism could in that sense be interpreted as a reaction to a new level of rationalization within the social world itself, which geometrizes that world's nature by way of new forms of planification; it may be seen as the attempt to make available this new situation, which is in itself hostile to the experiential, to and for experience itself, just as Impressionism had done in the preceding, not yet wholly planified stage of industrialization. This would then mark what is qualitatively new about Cubism with respect to its predecessor: that whereas Impressionism sought to reawaken and to rescue the vitality paralyzed within the commodity world by means of its own internal dynamic, Cubism despairs of doing so and embraces the heteronomous geometrization of the world as its new law and its new order, in order to secure some new guarantee of objectivity for aesthetic experience. (AT 447/418)

But even the example of the visual arts still leaves the door too far ajar for some differentiation between the objects out there and the 'techniques' that are invented to register their modification. Yet it was that very distinction Proust's aesthetics sought with such paradoxical novelty and force to obliterate, inventing, *avant la lettre*, 'defamiliarization' as a concept whose first effect is very precisely intellectual defamiliarization. In Adorno, where the tendential distinction between subject and object is somehow not yet even available, music will, as always, perform this function more adequately. Here is Adorno's lesson on the fugue, for example:

> The fugue is bound to tonal relationships; its very invention is somehow called forth by the *telos* of the transformation in which modality is set aside and tonality comes to reign supreme over an imitative musical praxis. Specific procedures such as the real or tonal answer constituted by a fugal theme make musical sense only in a situation in which an outmoded polyphony sees itself confronted with the new task of transforming the older homophonic center of gravity of tonality, of integrating tonality into polyphonic space, of making room for contrapuntal and harmonic progressions in musical thought together. All the peculiarities of this new form – the fugue – can be deduced from this objective necessity of which the composer seems by no means to be conscious. The fugue is the specific organizational form of a polyphony become tonal and thoroughly rationalized; this is the general meaning of the form, beyond any of its individual realizations, without which it would not, of course, exist in the first place. The tendential loosening of the fugal schema, and even the eventual liberation from it, is therefore inscribed in advance within it. Once tonality is no longer binding, the fundamental categories of the fugue – such as the distinction between *dux* and *comes*, the stereotypical structure of the fugal response, and above all the reprise-like motif that facilitates the return to the dominant key – lose their function and become technically false. But the moment the articulated and dynamized expressive needs of the individual composers no longer long for the fugue (itself far more complexly differentiated than later ideologies of musical freedom were willing to suppose), this form has, *qua* form, become objectively impossible. (AT 297–8/286)

The composing subject need not, therefore, be conscious of the historical situation of productivity as such, any more than the great inventor-entrepreneur (Edison) of a certain stage of capitalism need worry particularly about the system itself as a whole. Yet in that the composer-inventor, by composing, registers the objective needs of the system – Adorno uses the word desire [*begehren*], but it is the composer's whole sensibility, his 'expressive needs', and even those developed to their most elaborated level of intensity ('articulated' [*differenzierte*] and 'dynamized' [*dynamis-*

ierte], that do the 'desiring' for him – this receptivity of the 'creative subject' is not simply the irrational opposite number of a rationality that would more consciously 'know' where it was in history. It is not some form of creative 'intuition' which is being opposed here to a different, more intellectual, form of self-consciousness. Rather, the immanent technical operations of the 'creative spirit' are themselves what Hegel would have called 'objective spirit', but what it is better in the present context to identify as the collective productivity of a society at a given moment of its development.

> By virtue of the infinitely minute and differential nature of his artistic choices and decisions, the individual artist in fact assumes the role of the executor of the collective objectivity of spirit itself [*Geist*], his own personal role vanishing into that in the process; something implicitly recalled in the traditional conception of the genius as passive-receptive. (AT 402–3/381)

This is perhaps the moment to register the fresh new light Adorno's productivism casts on his similarities and dissimilarities with the positions of Benjamin. The latter may be seen as equally 'productionist' from two relatively distinct standpoints: an emphasis on technology, and on the well-nigh allegorical value of the modifications of urban machinery for the transformations of the psyche (as in his essays on Baudelaire): alongside a rather different (and more Brechtian) stress on the role of 'productivity' in the work of the advanced artist – a position essentially laid out in 'The Author as Producer'. But what this essay seeks to affirm is quite different from Adorno's identification of the most advanced forms of social production *within* the work of art. For Benjamin is looking for a link and a form of class solidarity that might connect modernist vanguard artists with an industrial proletariat. He discovers it by affirming not the identity of the two productions, but rather the identity of the advanced character of each one, taken separately. Thus the artist's class solidarity with the values and attitudes of the factory worker passes through the high productivity embodied by each; whence the sympathy each may have with the other. The comparison thus yields more or less the results one might have anticipated: from Adorno's perspective, Benjamin's dialectic is either too external (the allegorical machinery) or too mediated; from Benjamin's, Adorno's dialectic is too idealistic in its immediate identification of industrial production and inner form.

But the model of productive forces alone (in Marxism a 'vulgar' or reductive conception of production) is at length completed by its orthodox complement, the notion of the *relations* of production (from class relations down to the articulated component positions of these, either in the labor process or in those expanding and contracting spaces for agency opened in business which were touched on in the analogies between the artist and the vanishing entrepreneur). The concept of productivity in Marx mediates between these 'levels' in such a way that it can only tactically be assigned to one or the other on any specific occasion: 'advanced' may here designate state-of-the-art machinery, or on the contrary what bourgeois thought generally considers to be expert scientific and technological knowledge and the experience of skilled workers (the true epistemological capital which alone explains the miraculous resurgence of this or that 'advanced' industrial power after the thoroughgoing wartime destruction of its material equipment). The so-called creative subject also incorporates this fund or level of collective competence, below which it falls only to its aesthetic peril. But to analogize artistic productions in these terms – as a socially average advanced productivity read in terms of labor rather than in terms of machinery – at once introduces hitherto unmentioned complications and contradictions which are no less central for Adorno's aesthetics.

Six

For when one passes from the concept of productive forces to that of productive relations, all the negative and diagnostic themes traditionally associated with Marxism reappear: first and foremost the division of labor itself, as deeply inscribed in the individual work of art as were the state of productive forces. It is at this point that what has been loosely referred to as 'creative subjectivity' proves to subsume two very different things: the mental operations of the composer, and that very different part of contemporary mutilated subjectivity which is the maimed and shrunken 'self', which tries to 'express' its subjective suffering through the work, in a situation where that suffering and the very 'subject' itself (with all its feelings of consciousness and precarious personal identity) turn out in reality to be part of the work's raw material and its content. This is the other sense in which 'the subjective component of the work is in reality a piece of objectivity' (AT 68/61) and in which the 'subjective' in art is never truly grasped until we reach a standpoint from which it is revealed as part of social and historical objectivity, a 'method' Adorno rather inadequately characterized as 'second reflection', as we shall see. (It will be more appropriate to deal with the implications of this view of subjectivity all together in a later chapter).

For the moment, only the contradictions involved – their various formulations are familiar in Marxian social science, but less so in the aesthetic forms Adorno gives them here – need be briefly enumerated. The division of labor, for instance, determines a process which is best not thought of in its traditional bourgeois form as an opposition between the individual and the collective, but rather as a tendential collectivization in which previous forms of individuation are recast, problematized, fragmented

and often threatened in their very being (*Dialectic of Enlightenment* recurs
to this situation throughout in its systemic form, while *Minima Moralia*
stages it from the standpoint of the subject). Yet it is an objective and
dialectical process, which should neither be surrendered to the rhetoric
of conservative pathos – for the loss of individuality is not something
necessarily always to be deplored in and of itself – nor too frequently
saluted with the triumphalist accents of socialist realism, as though collectivization *always* meant the rebirth of true cooperation in Marx's sense.
The process is primarily a matter of the increasing, and increasingly complex, collective nature of social labor (as though the primal 'division
of labor' were a kind of infernal machine that redivides and rearticulates
itself *à la* Luhmann in a well-nigh infinite momentum); and only then
a social matter of what Weber called bureaucratization, which in our
society essentially designates the collective organization of the business
firm and the multinational industry; it is also a political fact of life for
oppositional groups in a situation, prevalent since the 1970s, where the
very cultural image of either the isolated romantic rebel or the solitary
anomic victim have virtually disappeared, and virtually all so-called 'marginal' or opositional groups have collectively, in one way or another,
mobilized and acquired an institutional framework.

But this tension or contradiction in modern society is reinscribed in
the individual work of art in the form of the distinction already referred
to between the collective character of advanced artistic technique and
the remnants of individual isolation and subjectivity that become the
former's content and raw material at the very moment they seem to
demand the work as their last remaining possibility of subjective expression. Indeed, postmodernism – if there is such a thing – may then be
theorized as the moment in which that older subjectivity – now fully
collectivized – disappears altogether; so that the tension that constituted
Beckett's minimalism fully as much as Schoenberg's expressionistic
moment – the silent cry of pain – evaporates, leaving advanced collective
productivity and technology free to 'express' nothing but itself: a process
whose end-product is at once no longer works of art but commodities.

But the distinction between productive forces and productive relations
can also be rehearsed as a dialectic and as a contradiction in its own
right, in a reversal of priorities whereby it is precisely the primacy of
the productive forces which secures a momentary aesthetic triumph over
everything that is repressive in productive relations or in other words
in class society:

Every intelligible unit of collective forces transported within the work of
art – units that look subjective [in so far as they embody the know-how

of the individual creator] – marks the potential presence within it according to the degree of socially average productivity: monads include all that in windowless fashion. This can be most strikingly observed in the artist's reactions to criticism and in the corrections he makes in response to it. Through such improvements, to which he feels compelled, often enough in conflict with what he considered the work's initial impulse or inspiration, he functions as an agent of society, whether consciously or not. He embodies the social forces of production, without thereby feeling in any way bound by the censure dictated by the relations of production, which he himself also feels able to criticize on the basis of his own professional expertise [*métier*]. ... This is why every true artist is obsessed with questions of technique and method; here the fetishism of the means has genuine legitimacy. (AT 71–2/65)

Despite the pathos of maimed subjectivity, therefore – and because that suffering is itself of a piece, dialectically, with the injustice of the social or class system in general, that is, with the *relations* of production – the artist who puts his blind trust in technique and in the *forces* of production – often, for example, altering the original content of a work for what seem to be superior technical reasons – is the more authentic.

Yet the forces of production are also finally the place of rationalization, in the Weberian sense or in the sense of what the Frankfurt School rebaptized as 'instrumental reason'. We have already to a certain degree recapitulated this dialectic as it turns on reification and the commodity form:

In the rationalization of the means there lies in art, as everywhere else, the *telos* of their fetishization. To the degree to which control over means becomes absolute, to that degree they tend objectively to become ends in themselves. (AT 439/412)

Adorno's valorization of productive forces thereby becomes a poisoned gift, or a Trojan horse, in a situation where these carry instrumental reason or the baleful 'dialectic of Enlightenment' at their very heart. Yet this doctrine is, as I have tried to show, a beneficial one which can liberate contemporary criticism from its subjectivizing tendencies and make possible a new kind of analysis in which the formal and the social or historical, far from being incompatible or antithetical, are at one. Perhaps one should say, then, that it is when the doctrine of productivity becomes wholly positive and undialectical that it begins at once to resonate that other dialectical mirage which is the sense of the impending 'end of art'.

It is appropriate therefore to end this particular discussion negatively and to reformulate its essential lesson in a paradoxical reversal. For what the doctrine of productive forces really has to teach contemporary criticism is not how to identify aesthetic success, but rather how to diagnose aesthetic failure: 'There are many indications that in works of art metaphysical untruth can be identified by mistakes or ineptitude in technique' (AT 195/187). This observation – which opens a bridge between traditional ideological analysis and technical or formal interpretation – will not be fully measured, however, unless we remember that Adorno is never, in *Aesthetic Theory*, concerned with 'bad' art as such: the technical flaws he has in mind here are rather those to be detected in ambitious and advanced aesthetic production (the example that most frequently recurs is the music of Richard Strauss [AT 319/306]). The proposition is further strengthened, and perhaps paradoxically transformed or dialectized beyond recognition, by a different kind of reminder: that

> what is ideological and 'affirmative' about the idea of fully achieved works of art must be corrected and rebuked by the fact that in that sense there are no achieved or 'successful' works of art. If those were really capable of existing, it would mean that reconciliation [*Versöhnung*] was really possible in the midst of the universal absence of reconciliation that endows art with its vocation in the first place.' (AT 283/271)

The 'achieved' work of art draws its deepest truth from contradiction as such, and from its unreserved commitment to it – something which virtually by definition guarantees that it cannot be achieved or complete or successful in the sentimental sense of a traditional normative aesthetics. But this unexpected conception of the necessary failure of all authentic works was in reality always implicit in the doctrine of productivity, and even in the conception of the 'New' that is implicit in it. 'Every masterpiece', Gertrude Stein once remarked, 'came into the world with a measure of ugliness in it. ... It's our business as critics to stand in front of it and recover its ugliness.'[12] Here is Adorno's version of the same conception of the New as ugliness and as scar:

> Every meaningful work leaves a mark or a trace on its material and its technique; what constitutes the modern as a kind of logical necessity is the obligation to track down that mark or trace, and not the flair for the latest fashion. This obligation, concretely realized, can be called the critical moment within modern art. Those marks on the material and the artistic procedures – to which every qualitatively new work then commits itself – are in reality scars, they are the places in which the preceding works failed. As the new work goes to work on them, it ends up turning against those who left such traces behind themselves. (AT 60/52)

This is the sense in which one is tempted in general to characterize Adorno's aesthetics as an aesthetic of scars: in his implacable insistence on suffering fully as much as in his implacable identification of authenticity - in philosophical thought as well as in art - with contradiction as such, in its most acute and unresolvable form. None the less, there remains an open question - which *Aesthetic Theory* seems to raise more naggingly than the earlier, more local monographs and critical analyses - as to whether these two things - individual suffering and systemic contradiction - are finally, in Adorno, always one and the same. A further examination of the various polemics against subjectivism in *Aesthetic Theory* will not necessarily answer that question, but will be justified if it ends up confirming it as a deeper problem in Adorno's thinking.

Seven

Productive power, we have observed Adorno to say, 'is, deeply embedded within the technological processes, the true subject, which has coagulated into technology' (AT 69/62). Meanwhile, his approving citation of Adolf Loos's remark 'that ornaments cannot be *invented*' (AT 46/39) implies the far more sweeping corollary that aesthetic innovation is not to be seen as invention – let alone 'creation' – but rather very precisely as discovery, as an activity which, analogous to the natural sciences, seems to locate and to register ever new and hitherto unsuspected features in the thing itself – that is to say, in the artistic raw material (something which, as we shall see shortly, has very interesting implications for the notion of artistic *intention*).

These positions are now familiar; but they also imply the possibility, and indeed the obligation, to reread or rewrite the text, and demand a kind of estrangement effect or *ostranenia* by which what looks subjective in the work can somehow, by a dramatic enlargement of perspective, be revealed as objective in its deeper essence. In spite of Adorno's insistence on commitment to the objective logic of the work, therefore, there remains an open space in his aesthetics for the critical gesture and the act of the critical transformation of the text: something he only fragmentarily, and seemingly with great reluctance, theorized as 'second reflection'.

There will therefore be a certain ambiguity in the positions on subjectivity we are about to outline: they often present themselves as historical and philosophical analyses of what subjectivity is, or thinks itself to be – that is, its objective illusions (or even its ideologies); at the same time, however, they can also be read as methodological clues and indications of how one is to objectify these seemingly subjective components (or 'moments', to use the Hegelian term) in our reading of the works themselves.

Adorno's first published book, on Kierkegaard, to be sure, provocatively denounced the concept and the experience of bourgeois 'inwardness' in a famous passage that assimilated the bourgeois soul to the *interior* of a Biedermeier household.[13] This can also clearly be taken as an aesthetic judgement and a sentence passed on certain kinds of 'spiritualizing' art, which, however, were they works of great quality, could presumably in another sense be reobjectified and their more objective 'truth content' historically and philosophically disclosed. Once again the ideal of a kind of liquidation of the ego is variably situated: sometimes in the works themselves as their objective tendency, and sometimes in our relationship to them, as when the objectivizing spirit of Hegel's aesthetic is celebrated for the way in which, anticipating Constructivism long *avant la lettre*, 'it sought the subjective success of the art-work precisely in those moments where the subject vanishes from it' (AT 92/85).

But as we have shown, Adorno's philosophical procedure does not involve the destruction of older, sometimes even false categories (and the projection of some new hitherto non-existent utopian philosophical terminology or language), but rather a playing through them which mobilizes even their untruth to project its opposite. The category of 'expression' is, for example, both a philosophical and a historical problem (the social position of subjectivity) and an aesthetic value which stands in precarious and antagonistic tension with cognate but incompatible categories such as mimesis on the one hand and construction on the other, but above all with *Schein* or aesthetic appearance – something that will more immediately be appreciated when we remember that for Adorno expression is above all the expression of pain (which takes the aesthetic form of dissonance or a new and sharper kind of ugliness, themselves tendentially in conflict with the value of aesthetic appearance and a fundamental feature of that crisis in *Schein* which as we have seen is at one with the modern itself):

> The antithesis of expression and *Schein* is a primary one. In so far as expression can scarcely be conceived except as the expression of suffering – joy resists expression stubbornly, while bliss, one would think, remains inexpressible – expression constitutes then immanently that moment in which art wards off that utter and complete immanence towards which its formal law tends, by means of one of its own constitutive elements. (AT 169/161-2)

The immediacy of expression, therefore, the impatience of its passion, prevent the work from sealing over into a purely aesthetic object (and thereby ceasing to become art altogether but, rather, a commodity): art remains art only by holding to the anti-aesthetic claims of reality and truth. Yet this truth, secured by the commitment to subjective expression, also threatens tendentially to undermine aesthetic appearance altogether (as we have already seen technically in the shrinkage of expressionistic music into the briefest of instants).

This is not to say, however, that subjective expression in the work of art persists as some foreign body within it, or some alien impulse: it is also transformed and objectified in a peculiar manner, which Adorno characterizes after a fashion that can be said to be *his* version of Benjamin's concept of *aura* (with which *Aesthetic Theory* pursues an endless subterranean dialogue of pro and con): 'Expression is the gaze of the work of art' (AT 172/165). Yet what is most beautiful about this formulation is what it does not yet say, but what we might have deduced from the related figure of the windowless monad – namely, that this gaze is *blind* (AT 174/167), blind both because we see it as an object and because it cannot look back at us, or indeed out at any empirical reality.

But expression is also bound to the dialectic of time, and not merely because its contents – these particular passions, these strong but dated feelings – are always historical. In so far as beyond all specific contents (already, indeed, somehow reduced and de-differentiated by their assimilation to sheer suffering in general – that is to say, paradoxically, to what can never really be 'expressed' in the first place), expression characterizes the historical status of the psychic subject itself, its tendential compression and its ever more onerous historical constraints and unfreedom – to that degree, every moment of expression bears within itself synchronic history:

> The language of expression is in contradistinction to that of meaning something older, yet unresolved: as though the work of art, by assimilating itself to the subject in its structure, repeats the process of that very subject's emergence in the world and its liberation from it. Works of art possess expressivity, not when they communicate subjectivity, but rather when they tremble with its *Ur*-history, and the *Ur*-history of endowment with soul and life: the *tremolo* of willed expressions of subjectivity is an unbearable substitute for this primal historicity. This situation is what circumscribes the affinity of works of art with subjectivity: that affinity persists because that primal history lives on within the subject itself, beginning again and again throughout all history. Only the subject can constitute the vehicle for expression, no matter how mediated it is even where it imagines itself to be the most immediate. Even where what is expressed resembles the psychic subject, and where its impulses are 'subjective' in the conventional sense, these remain impersonal, passing

through the integrated ego rather than emerging from it. Expression in works of art is the non-subjective dimension of the subject itself, less its expression than its impression: there is nothing quite so expressive as the eyes of apes, that seem objectively to mourn the fact that they are not human beings. (AT 172/165)

This peculiar dialectic of a subjectivity that passes back and forth between the two poles of expression and of the psychic subject itself, in which each is alternately subjective and objective in opposition to the other's variability, finds its most dramatic formal rehearsal in an excursus on the lyric, and on its pronouns (themselves variably objective or subjective [AT 249–52/239–41]), which completes Adorno's earlier (and fundamental) programmatic essay on this topic, 'Lecture on Lyric and Society'.[14]

Indeed, the originality of Adorno's observations on language and on style as such lies in his emphasis on the objectivity that speaks through this most subjective of all phenomena (and it is an objectivity to be distinguished from Bakhtin's collective speech as well as from the non- or inhuman dimensions of language foregrounded by poststructuralism). Here that dimension of language alienated to the concept and the social totality is in effect used against itself and redirected:

If in fact lyric content is to be grasped as something objective that operates by way of individual subjectivity – and otherwise what most obviously defines it as a genre, its effects on others besides the monologic poet, can scarcely be explained – this can be so only if the withdrawal of the lyrical work, its interiorization and distanciation from the social surface, is itself socially motivated behind the back of the author himself. The medium for this is, however, very precisely language. ... The greatest lyric constructs are those in which, in the virtual elimination of mere content, the subject sounds through language in such a way that language itself becomes audible. The self-forgetfulness of the subject as it surrenders itself to language as to something objective, and the immediacy and involuntary nature of its expression, are one and the same: and this is how speech mediates lyric and society within itself. (NL 56)

This deeply Benjaminian idea will then be explored in two directions: the first most obviously and dramatically affords a dialectical and utopian 'method', particularly in Adorno's readings here of the way in which Mörike's and George's subjective expression stand as virtual photographic negatives of their experience of the social, which can be read back from them in reverse. The other path, however, tends towards forms of the objective in subjective language that finally lead out of the modern period itself:

In so far as language cuts through the threads that connect it to the subject,
it speaks for the subject that can no longer speak for itself – Hölderlin was
probably the first whose art sensed this. (NL 478)

But Hölderlin's neoclassicism leads back to epic and parataxis, and to
the forms of social and linguistic experience already registered in the
moment of their disappearance in *Dialectic of Enlightenment*:

> This murmur [of the hexameter in the *Odyssey*] is the very voice and intrinsic
> sound of epic speech, in which identity, the fixed and the univocal, mingles
> with the polysemous and the transitory, in order to separate itself from them
> once again triumphantly. The undifferentiated flow of myth is the ever-
> identical; the *telos* of narrative, however, is multiplicity and difference, so
> that implacably rigid commitment to identity in which the epic object is
> fixed serves precisely to ratify its non-identity from the badly identical and
> the unarticulated indifferentiation of sameness. (NL 34)

But this is the very point at which Adorno's intermittent literary analyses
meet the fundamental work in which so much of the dialectical aesthetics
of that period were crystallized – Lukács's *Theory of the Novel*, where
the account of the historical fate of literary form itself prefigures the
other dialectical trajectories – the concept, repression, the subject, technology, the senses – that the Frankfurt School was to explore so luminously.
Here, then, the possibility of realism is itself tendentially excluded 'from
the narrator's standpoint by sheer subjectivism that no longer tolerates
a content that has not been transformed by subjectivity and thus undermines the epic commandment of objectivity itself' (NL 41).

At this point, however, a retroactive rewriting of history, and in particular the history of the relationship between lyric and society, language
and the subject, imposes itself. In an astonishing passage that goes far
towards establishing and clarifying Adorno's essential modernism, he
will thus assert that lyric and its language could only be a modern phenomenon (the argument Lukács made for the novel in his fundamental
work) and that

> its concept, as that is immediate for us and virtually 'second nature', is essen-
> tially modern. In a similar way landscape painting and the idea of 'nature'
> it proposes also first knew autonomous development in the modern period.
> I know I am exaggerating in this, and that you will find many counter-examples
> to oppose. The most powerful one would be Sappho. Of Chinese, Japanese,
> Arabic lyrics I will not speak, as I cannot read them in the original and
> must suspect that translation deploys mechanisms of adaptation that preclude
> adequate understanding. But the properly lyric statements that have come
> down to us from older times are only intermittent and fragmentary, like

those occasional backgrounds in older painting that anticipate something of what will become landscape painting. Such lyric instants do not constitute form. Those great poets of a more distant past that are classified under lyric in literary histories – Pindar, for example, and Alcaeus, but also the overwhelming bulk of the work of Walther von der Vogelweide – are very distant from lyric in its contemporary primary sense. They lack that character of the immediate and the desubstantialized that we have rightly or wrongly become accustomed to seeing as the very criterion of lyric, and that only intense training allows us to transcend. (NL 52–3)

Such essentially historicist positions – never developed elsewhere in Adorno, save for certain reflections on earlier music – suggest the retroactive effects Marx posited for his theory of the modes of production – namely that it was only in the more advanced social formations (above all capitalism) that the implicit 'truth' of the earlier ones came to light. But of course that truth of the earlier formations (here the intermittent presence of lyric) comes to light by fulfilling and abolishing the earlier forms in which it was only implicit.

These varied reflections on the objectivity of language then reach a kind of theoretical climax and codification, thereby returning very much to their Benjaminian inspiration, in the peculiar notion of the 'speech-like character' [*Sprachähnlichkeit*] of the work of art, developed in *Aesthetic Theory*: a notion which, paradoxically, is introduced in opposition to linguistic theories which see the individual linguistic work as a mere example of language as such, as well as to communicational ones which ignore the fact that 'more modern forms of art work to transform communicative speech into something mimetic' [AT 171/164]. The opposition of speech (as what is imitated on this view) and the specific text that imitates it – reminiscent of the great opposition between 'capital in general' and 'the many capitals' in Marx – thus not unexpectedly offers a different way of conceiving the relationship of general to particular:

> Language is hostile to the particular yet seeks the latter's salvation. It mediates the particular through generality and within the constellation of the general, doing justice to its own universals, however, only when these are not static and endowed with the appearance of essential being, but rather concentrated to the extreme upon what is specifically to be expressed [that is to say, the particular]. The universals of language thereby draw their truth from a process antithetical to their own inner logic. (AT 304/292)

Meanwhile, the implications of Adorno's aesthetic positions for practical criticism generally are more wide-ranging than this important local probe into literary method. It has already been made clear that those critical methods somehow defined and limited in advance by an a priori conception of subjectivity are here systematically excluded: reception was bracketed by way of the primacy of construction; psychological studies of various kinds are peremptorily assigned to the manipulative techniques of the objects of the Culture Industry; even Aristotelian catharsis is repudiated (although Freud's treatment at Adorno's hands is sometimes more nuanced,[15] along with what may still seem 'psychological' in Kant).

What is more interesting here is the fate of the various critical approaches to meaning, something all the more strategic in so far as Adorno also – along with his historical critique of philosophical aesthetics – wishes to restage the latter's claims in some new way, and to reinvent a new kind of primacy of philosophy over artistic experience. In general, however, more limited literary-critical doctrines of meaning are here dialectically undermined by an operation which transfers them into the interior of the work of art, as the latter's content. The pretensions of the symbol are thereby historically dispatched:

> Art absorbs symbols by depriving them of what they 'symbolized'; advanced artists have themselves concretely completed the philosophical critique of the symbol. The indices and characteristics of the modern have thereby become absolute in their own right, they are signs whose meaning is forgotten even for them. Their penetration into the aesthetic medium and their resistance to all forms of intention are two manifestations of the same process. (AT 147/140–41)

The crucial word here is 'intention', which marks the first stage of the polemic against meaning. But Adorno's position is to be sharply distinguished from the way in which recent critical debates on this subject have been conducted, and in particular from the twin questions of whether 'intention' could ever be determined on the basis of a text (to which its putative formulation merely supplies an additional text to be deciphered, and not some deeper truth); and whether, even if intention could be established, it would constitute the ultimate bedrock or foundation for understanding. Adorno's is not in that sense a doctrine of understanding (or *Verstehen*), but he is also more historically variable about the detectability of intentions in a given work. What changes everything in his discussion of this matter is that even where intentions can be determined, they are not to be grasped as something outside or behind the text – which gives us hints as to its proper use – but rather as part and parcel of the text itself, fully as much a component of its raw material as the creative biographical subject, who is equally drawn into the work as part of its aesthetic 'ruse of reason'. In fact, the appearance of intention in a given work is generally useful as a negative symptom:

> The distinction between truth and intention in the work of art becomes available for critical consciousness above all where intention stands in the service of the untrue, mostly of those eternal truths which are in reality little more than the repetition of the mythic. (AT 195/187)

What is meant here is surely the Heideggerian thematics (also reaffirmed by Gadamer) about the confrontation of great art with the eternal mysteries of death and being: but such eternal verities are also perpetuated on a garden-variety level by a humanistic criticism mesmerized by the 'human condition'. Here intention passes over into conventional versions of meaning itself, about which Adorno tirelessly insists that whatever it is, it is not the same as what he will call 'truth content': 'understanding, meaning and content are not equivalents' (AT 516/476). Meaning and intention, even in the traditional sense of the idea of the work, 'such as the inherent guilt of subjective moralizing in Ibsen's *Wild Duck*' (AT 515/475), is not 'truth content', since it merely identifies this particular component of the work without disposing of any further means of judging it – whether the judgement be couched in formal language (is the intention realized?), in philosophical language (is it 'true' or 'false'), or in historical and social language (that of the situation itself). The categories of meaning or message are inadequate, not merely because they do not allow for the possibility that, as in Beckett, it is the very absence of meaning that could be the work's meaning, constituting something like a 'judgement on the very nature of meaning itself which includes and develops the latter's very history' (AT 230/220).

They are also, in the conventional use, formally inadequate, yet by the same token indispensable as symptoms:

> No matter how irreducible the content of a work is to its intention – if only for the simple reason that no matter how carefully thought through, no intention is ever destined to be fully realizable in a representation – only a rigid dogmatism would disqualify the category of intention as a moment in the work of art. Intentions have their proper place within the dialectic between the mimetic pose of the work of art and its participation (*methexis*) in the historical dynamic of 'enlightenment' [or instrumental reason]: not merely as subjectively mobile organizing forces that are exhausted in the work itself but also in the form of an objectivity proper to them. ... If the materiality of the work of art constitutes its resistance to empty identity, then their fundamental process essentially involves a dialectic between materiality and intention. Without this last – which is the immanent form of the

identity principle – form could as little come into being as it could in the absence of the mimetic impulse. The surplus of intentions then proclaims the irreducibility of the work to mimesis alone. And the objective bearer of such aesthetic intentions, which synthesizes them with each other, is what is called meaning. (AT 226–7/217)

The category of intention, like that of 'meaning', is thus retained as one of a variety of traditional aesthetic categories without whose interplay and mutually canceling critique the discussion of the work of art would remain empty: there is at work here in Adorno something like what Freud called overdetermination, by which he not only characterized the simultaneous and multiple determination of the dream's final form, but also marked the discovery, in the course of analytic interpretation, that any one of those 'paths' could equally well lead back to the central nucleus of the dream itself. What functions as such a nucleus in Adorno is of course 'truth content' (which has not yet been examined in its own right); clearly the metaphoric spatiality of the Freudian hermeneutic is inappropriate here, where the work's truth content does not lie behind the work somewhere or deep within it as that '*substantificque moelle*' archetypal in the imagery of hermeneutics.

The 'analytic method', however, by which one transcends the play of partial categories towards that truth-content, does make a fitful appearance in *Aesthetic Theory*, where it is called 'second reflection', a term by which Adorno seemed to want to convey something a little more than a second reading or a higher form of reflexivity. For the 'reflection' of a first order within the work surely designates its technological and productive energies, which mark the investment of collective knowledge and labor: this is the level of technique and of social productivity, as that becomes historically differentiated into the dynamic of the work's materials and the intentionalities of its producer (not excluding, as we have seen, the historical status of the subject itself).

'Second reflection', then, presumably means a drawing back from this in such a way that it becomes visible to the naked eye, not merely as features or energies within the work of art but as the work of art itself. The few tantalizing remarks Adorno consecrates to this 'method' – which in another sense is simply the dialectic itself in the realm of aesthetic thinking – suggest that it has the dual capacity to transform what looks subjective in the work into something objective, and to return the appearance of objectivity to its original productive dynamism:

> The truth of the new, or in other words of spaces and positions that have never yet been occupied, is situated in the non-intentional. This is what puts it in contradiction with reflection, the very motor force of the new, and

potentiates it to the second power. Second reflection is thus quite the opposite of its conventional philosophical embodiment, such as Schiller's doctrine of the *'sentimentalisch'*, which ends up heaping further and further intentions on the work of art. Second reflection aims to grasp the procedures and the language of the work of art in as articulated and intensely conscious a fashion as possible, but essentially steers towards blindness. (AT 47–8/39–40)

This 'method', then, has as its rule the effort to avoid conceptual formulations which one might substitute for the work of art; yet it aims at a higher type of philosophical thinking (Adorno will explicitly evoke the Hegelian concept of the *Begriff*) which somehow remains concrete without losing itself in some ecstatic identification with the work itself. It maintains a distance from the work, which it intuits from a broader perspective (my language) and thereby certainly involves the positing of certain new kinds of meaning, whose formulation, however, is a matter of great tact and delicacy. We conclude this chapter with one of those provisional attempts:

What is mediated in the work of art, what makes it something other than its mere presence as an object in the world, must be mediated a second time through reflection, by way of the 'concept' [the Hegelian *Begriff*]. That can be successful, however, only if the concept addresses itself specifically to the details of the work rather than moving away from them into generalities. When, shortly before the end of the first movement of Beethoven's sonata *Les Adieux*, a fleeting association of three bars seems to quote the clatter of horses' hooves, this evanescent passage, which seems almost ashamed of any intellectual recognition, a sonorous expression of disappearance scarcely even identifiable within the context of the movement, bespeaks more of the hope of ultimate return than any general reflection on the nature of this sound itself, a mixture of transience and persistence, could make explicit. Only an aesthetic philosophy capable of securing such micro-logical details in their innermost spirit, within the construction of the aesthetic whole, could be said to live up to its promise. Such a philosophy would, however, also have to be a self-sufficient articulated and mediated form of thinking in its own right. (AT 531/490)

Eight

At length, at the term of this elaborate historical and often technical reflection on artistic form and the thoughts it is possible to think about it, aesthetics – to whose contradictions and historical impossibility *Aesthetic Theory* had so often seemed to testify – reasserts itself, in the abandoned draft preface published at the end of the posthumous volume, and philosophy once again lays claim to primacy over the whole field of aesthetic inquiry. We must therefore in conclusion speculate as to the concrete content of such philosophizing, whose lone and enigmatic watchword – 'truth-content', or *Wahrheitsgehalt* – inevitably raises the suspicion that it may be no more than a euphemism for that doctrine of authenticity whose emptiness and ideological character Adorno so tirelessly denounced in his great adversary Heidegger.

Even more disturbing – and yet another unexpected convergence with the philosophical opponent – is the seeming reappearance of ontology at the heart of Adorno's most probing philosophical attempt to characterize the nature of the work of art, as a contact with non-identity or with nature for which the stigmatized term 'being' often scarcely seems a jarring substitute. It is not, to be sure, a question of accusing Adorno of the kind of reversion to Schopenhauer and to mysticism, if not to religion itself, which Max Horkheimer seems to have experienced towards the end of his life ('the appeal to an entirely other than this world … led finally to a more positive evaluation of certain metaphysical trends').[16] Nonetheless, the ontological account of the work of art would seem to coexist uneasily, in *Aesthetic Theory* taken as a whole, with its relationship to social and historical contradiction – on which Adorno so strongly insists elsewhere throughout the text, as we have seen.

Paradoxically, it is the very will to wrest artistic experience from the aestheticizing language of sheer contemplation, as well as the reemphasized vocation of the dialectic to disqualify the aesthetic monisms of materialism and positivism alike, that leads Adorno to his ontology, in which the peculiar nature of the art-work as something both aesthetically autonomous and anti-aesthetic or profoundly social and historical is to be philosophically characterized:

> The spiritual mediation of the work, by which it is able to stand in contrast to the empirical, cannot be realized without its integration of some properly discursive dimension. Were the work of art purely contemplative [*Anschauung* – 'intuition' – has the overtone of a quasi-visual contemplation], it would remain imprisoned in the contingency of the sensuously immediately given, against which, however, the work in reality opposes its own specific logic. Its quality is determined by the degree to which its concreteness and its articulated development and inner differentiation precisely shed that contingency. The purist, and in that sense profoundly rationalistic, opposition between the visually contemplative and the ideational in reality reinforces that dichotomy between rationality and material sensuousness perpetuated by society itself for its own ideological ends. Art must, on the contrary, struggle in effigy against that opposition with the objective critique it in effect embodies; if art is banished to the sensuous pole alone, the opposition is thereby merely reconfirmed. That untruth which is the deeper critical object of all art is not rationality itself, but rather the latter's static opposition to the particular; if art extracts the moment of the particular as an object of mere contemplation, it ratifies precisely that reified rigidity and valorizes precisely the waste products that social rationality abandons and excludes in order to draw attention away from itself. To the degree therefore that, according to traditional aesthetic precept, the work becomes ever more seamlessly an object of contemplation, to that very degree is its spirituality reified, outside sheer appearance and well beyond the more truly aesthetic event of apparition. (AT 151/144)

It is therefore as a relationship to otherness, nature, or being itself that the work of art can be rescued from the trivializing aestheticism of the doctrine of aesthetic contemplation, with the unexpected additional advantage that art need no longer find itself in opposition to technical rationality but can be seen as incorporating that form of collective social knowledge as well in the process.

In fact these twin results, which seem paradoxically to conjugate the two incompatible temptations of this aesthetic – the metaphysical relationship to non-identity on the one hand, the affirmation of art as advanced social productivity on the other – circumscribe the mystery of the work of art and the philosophical problem it poses:

The metaphysical questions raised by art today turn on the problem of how something 'spiritual', a thing that is made and in the language of philosophy merely 'posited', can also be true. What is at stake in this problem is not immediately the individual work of art at hand, but rather its content [*Gehalt*]. The question about the possible truth of an object that is made is, however, nothing less than that other question about aesthetic appearance and about its possible redemption as the appearance of truth itself. Truth-content, however, cannot be made or constructed. All making in art is one long struggle to say what that made object itself can never be and what art itself can never know: that is what *Geist* or spirit means in aesthetics. And this is where the idea of art as the restoration of a repressed nature submerged in the dynamics of history comes in. Nature, whose imago art aspires to be, does not yet exist; what is true in art is a non-existent. It comes to coincide with art within that Other, which a reason fixated on identities and bent on reducing it to sheer materiality calls Nature. That other is, however, neither a unity nor a single concept, but rather the multiple. The truth-content of art therefore takes the form of the multiple, rather than some ultimate abstraction under which the individual works of art might be subsumed. There is therefore an inseparable relationship between the way in which the truth-content of art is realized only in individual works and the multiplicity of all those realities reason seeks to reduce to so many identifications. The most profound of all the paradoxes of art is probably this: that it can encounter the non-made or truth only by means of the construction and the composition of particular and specifically organized individual works, and never through any more immediate access. Yet the individual works stand in the most extreme tension with their truth-content. To the degree to which such truth appears only within constructed objects without any conceptual form, to that very degree it negates their construction. Every work of art disappears *qua* representation in its own truth-content; the latter causes the work of art itself to sink into sheerest irrelevance, something it is given only to the very greatest works of art to experience. (AT 198–9/191)

The undertones of *Dialectic of Enlightenment* in this passage remind us that the relationship between history and nature – what we have here seemed to detect as an incompatibility between metaphysics (or ontology) and Marxism – was there coordinated with no little philosophical ingenuity as an alternation of history with nature: the process designated by the title was described as the response to some initially hostile and threatening nature which took the form of the latter's tendential domination, and the gradual emergence throughout history of the instrument of that domination – 'enlightenment', or reason, instrumental reason, 'bad' rationality or *Verstand* (in distinction to *Vernunft*), which the authors traced back to the earliest forms of magic spells, rituals, sacrifice, mimetic attempts to control and dominate nature which they saw as earlier forms of 'enlightenment' and of a piece with it (save that the dialectical twist in the transformation of this last into science marks the turning of mimesis against itself, in the moment of the anti-mimetic taboo on graven images). Even the theme of the tendentially repressed, damaged, victimized subject was given in advance by the premiss that Reason or 'Enlightenment' also requires the domination of an inner human nature (in short, a repression of instinct) in order to secure its primacy.

This means, in the context of *Aesthetic Theory*, as the above-cited passage makes clear, that 'the idea of art as the restoration of a repressed nature' will be capable of identifying the presence of nature or being somewhere at the heart of all historical contradictions and conjunctural constellations of social meaning, since the domination of nature is deeply inscribed within them as their ultimate dynamic. Meanwhile, in this sense later and more complex social forms of human drives and motivations – productivity fully as much as commodification (or that 'reason fixated on identities' which is at work in the establishment of exchange value as such) – will all carry within them the primal drive (or original sin) of this first moment of the relationship to nature, which is not merely fear but also the 'instinct' of self-preservation. Yet in the sense in which this properly infinite 'dialectic of enlightenment' which is human history can have no real beginning – that baleful fearful thing henceforth called Nature having been conjured up by human terror of it in the first place – one can also say, as Adorno does here, that 'nature does not yet exist': an uncharacteristically Blochian note in Adorno, and particularly in *Aesthetic Theory*, where the utopian character of art and its commitment to Hope and to the not-yet-existent has decisively receded and is sounded only in a few sober local references.

What we have been calling the ontological motif in Adorno's aesthetics now tactfully recapitulates many of these themes, particularly in his polemics against the aesthetic subject and against subjectivity and subjectivism, which now take on a somewhat different meaning and appearance. For the true place of the subject in aesthetic experience is not to be characterized by its purification (Aristotelian catharsis), nor in its 'reconciliation' with the object, still less in its creative mastery over this last and objective contingency (as for example in Sartre), but rather in a violent eclipse of the subject itself which is, however, sharply to be distinguished from annihilation, submission, the surrender of the subject to what transcends it (as in Heidegger and on some readings of Kant's concept of the sublime), let alone the virtual swoon or momentary obliteration of the human:

> *Erschütterung* [the shock of the aesthetic experience], which is in any case
> the polar opposite of traditional notions of aesthetic experience, is unrelated
> to any particular gratification of the ego, let alone its pleasure. Rather it
> is to be seen as a memento of the liquidation of the ego, which by way
> of such aesthetic shock becomes aware of its own constraints and finitude.
> The experience is also sharply to be distinguished from that sapping and
> weakening of the ego perpetuated by the Culture Industry. For this last such
> a conception as that of aesthetic shock would be an idle vanity, an attitude
> that justifies its deeper motivation in *ressentiment* to destroy art altogether
> [*Entkunstung*]. But in order for the ego to reclaim even the most minimal
> possibility of peering out over the prison that it is in its very nature, it requires
> not distraction but the most extreme form of tense effort: this is what preserves
> aesthetic shock – in any case an involuntary conduct – from regression. Kant
> very correctly posited the strength of the subject as the necessary precondition
> for his aesthetic of the sublime. (AT 364/347–8)

Yet this simultaneous strength or affirmation of the subject in its moment
of involuntary annihilation – a strength which allows it to confront
the experience without lapsing into the various regressive conducts
exhaustively enumerated by the Frankfurt School, from fascism and the
mythic to their various aesthetic equivalents – is also, momentarily, a
surrender of all the scars left on the ego by the dialectic of enlightenment,
most notably the drive to 'self-preservation':

> As Schopenhauer well knew, aesthetic experience is able to break through
> the spell of rigid self-preservation and to project the image of a state of con-
> sciousness in which the ego no longer finds its gratification in its own private
> interests, including that of its personal survival. (AT 515/475)

We should here note in passing how this new utopian account of the
relationship of aesthetic experience to the psychic subject decisively re-
absorbs Kant's two great motifs: that of the suspension of interests, and
also the doctrine of the sublime, which is here and throughout reread
or rewritten by Adorno as precisely this encounter with the not-I or
the Other that is ontologically central to his aesthetics. His account moves
dialectically through the various traditional descriptions, drawing its
power from their critique (and in particular the notion that aesthetic
experience is in any sense to be assimilated to pleasure or the satisfaction
of needs) but also sometimes modifying them in a positive way:

> The traditional mode of relating to art, whatever its relevance, was [not one
> of pleasure or enjoyment, but rather] one of admiration: admiration that
> works of art are what they are in themselves, and not merely for the viewer.
> What was felt to dawn in such works and what overpowered the viewer

was their truth, something that for example outweighs all the other components of a work such as that of Kafka. Works of art were not considered
instruments of enjoyment of some higher type. The relationship was not
seen as any sort of culinary incorporation, quite the opposite: the viewer
vanished into the thing itself: something fully realized only in those modern
representations that erupt out at you as onrushing locomotives used to do
from the movie screen. (AT 27/19)

This otherness of the work of art, which it may perhaps be more accurate
in the light of such passages to formulate as the otherness of its truth-
content, is now finally – in the obligatory yet peculiarly central pages
Adorno feels it necessary to devote to the traditional topic of 'natural
beauty' – identified as the *Ansich*, the in-itself of being or of nature:
'Natural beauty is the trace on things of the non-identical in a world
dominated by universal identity' (AT 114/108).

Several impulses need to be disentangled here: first of all, even the
most evanescent experience of nature registers the mystery, not merely
of the not-I, nor even of what resists identity (either in the ego-logical
or the rationalizing-commodifying sense), but above all of what has not
been *made* by the subject (a paradox already registered above for the
'truth-content' – unmade – of works of art which are 'made' or 'constructed' by definition):

> The experience of nature can only be that of appearance [or better still: *Erschei-
> nung*, of the act of appearance, the event of apparition], and not of some
> raw material for work and the reproduction of life, let alone of the substratum
> of scientific knowledge. (AT 103/97)

This essential distance of nature from the human or from praxis then
accounts for Adorno's unsatisfactory attempt to characterize nature itself
philosophically: 'For natural beauty, as an apparition, is already itself
image [*Bild*]' (AT 105/99), a description whose slippage into precisely
those accounts of our contemplative relationship to nature and to art
that he seeks to discredit it would seem difficult to prevent. We are
here, perhaps, at the closest point in Adorno to the various existential
philosophies: the suggestion that natural appearing or apparition is a
kind of event recalls the Heideggerian doctrine of Being itself as something
that happens; even though the simultaneous effort to endow this event
with the force of negativity and the shock of what is radically not the
subject seems more Sartrean in spirit, and should also be strongly empha-
sized.

But Adorno will then immediately remind us that even in this metaphysical or ontological sense all experiences of nature are mediated histori-

cally and socially: his discussion of natural landscape, for example, modulates almost at once as though by its own inner force of gravity towards that rather different thing he calls 'cultural landscape' (AT 101–2/94–6), in which natural perceptions have somehow become indissociable from cultural and historical ones: 'without historical recollection or commemoration [*Eingedenken*], beauty would not exist' (AT 102/96). To be sure, there is here a reversal from the ontological account of nature to the history of the concept and the experience of the natural, which then at once makes available more familiar dialectical solutions to this tension (where, for example, we intuit nature itself by way of its destruction by capitalism).

Still, as this motif of a contemplative glimpse of nature as image (or better still as the sheer conceptual possibility of such a glimpse) is the crucial pretext for all recent attempts to argue a philosophical *rapprochement* between Adorno and his archenemy Heidegger, it is worth recalling what is incompatible, in Adorno's conception of natural history, with the *Seinsfrage* of Heideggerian existentialism. Even leaving aside the dizzying horror of the organic and Darwinian perspective disclosed by Adorno's notion of 'natural history' (something which might, in a pinch, find its more lofty, 'metaphysical' equivalent in the Heideggerian Being-unto-death), the materialism of the body contained within Adorno's insistence on the idea of happiness and his fleeting evocation of Utopia is very different in spirit either from the mood of heroic fascism in early Heidegger, or the latter's ritual solemnity, as in the wondrous pages on the inauguration of the *polis* in 'The Origins of the Work of Art'. This last is in fact a good deal more political (in all senses) than anything in Adorno, whose physicality here demands at least the courtesy of a comparison with the great Brechtian materialism of the soup and the cigar.

We can also problematize this issue – essentially the tension between history and nature – one last time in a somewhat different way before we engage the crucial matter of the relationship of this aesthetic to 'truth-content'. The dilemma can be dramatically staged by quoting what is surely Adorno's most forthright statement on the historical semantics of aesthetic experience and the social and historical character of the 'truth-content' of great art:

> That a Beethoven symphony is as little accessible to someone who cannot grasp what are often called its purely musical or technical occurrences as it is to someone unable to perceive the echo in it of the French Revolution; and how both those moments mediate each other – is to be reckoned among the tough yet unavoidable problems confronting any philosophical aesthetics. (AT 519/479)

The example will seem less facile if it is augmented by even those scattered observations about Beethoven which have been quoted above; everything that is most admirable about Adorno as an aesthetic thinker and the embodiment of one possible form of the cultural and political intellectual is richly in evidence here. Our concern, however, is with the consistency between this account of Beethoven's historical 'truth-content' and the metaphysical or ontological aesthetic of non-identity which has just been outlined. In what way, in other words, can this aesthetic intuition of the great historical *Novum* of the French Revolution be reformulated in terms of the otherness of the experience of the natural? Thereby a supplementary problem, a third term, is added to the philosophical task Adorno describes above of mediating between formal and historical approaches. Meanwhile a certain mediatory thread is already given by Adorno's historical account of the history of aesthetics, which shifts for social and historical reasons from attention to beauty (still finally Kant's framework) to an emphasis on the constitutive relationship between art and freedom (Schiller, Hegel); perhaps the ontological motif in Beethoven is to be grasped here in some deeper relationship between the experience of political liberation and the dawning sense of freedom in nature itself. But whatever the elements of a solution, it should be clear that Adorno's multiple parameters demand an analysis of extraordinary complexity and range, which he himself failed to articulate theoretically with absolute coherence, all the while projecting the ideal of such analysis with a power that rebukes the ambitions of most contemporary criticism.

Nine

As for truth-content, however, it seems at least minimally possible that it cannot be philosophically described, since it is inscribed in a situation of well-nigh nominalistic multiplicity in which only individual works of art, but not Art itself, have their various truth-contents, which are therefore incomparable, incommensurable and not susceptible to abstract philosophical generalization. To say that it involves the correspondence of the work to its own specific concept [*Begriff*] is not apparently to say very much (except to Hegelians). To insist on the completion of aesthetic judgement and description with a properly philosophical form of judgement is perhaps to suggest a little more:

> The truth-content of a work is not what it means, but what decides whether it is in itself true or false, and it is this conception of the truth of the work in itself which is alone consistent with properly philosophical interpretation and which coincides with philosophical truth (at least in the Idea). (AT 197/190)

The difference between these kinds of truth judgements and Heideggerian 'authenticity' can at least be read off their respective critical practice, by comparing the emptiness of the content of this last (death and Being) with the historical specificity of Adorno's readings. But it should be clear that the notion of 'truth-content' is what enables Adorno to transcend the limits of a whole range of conventional interpretations and hermeneutic schemes and to step outside aesthetic meanings in such a way that they can be historically grasped. This larger capacity of 'second reflection' to foreground meaning in a historical way specifically includes ideological analysis and secures a philosophical innovative and original place for 'false consciousness' within the work's larger historical 'truth-content'. If Beethoven is a privileged example of one kind of truth about formal history, and Schoenberg and Beckett are examples of a more extreme kind of formal solution, here it is the figure of Richard Wagner which becomes Adorno's archetypal crux:

> That works of art transcend themselves in the process whereby they are concretely realized does not in itself guarantee their truth. Many works of very great quality are true as the expression of what is in itself false conscious-ness. This is something that can be grasped only from the standpoint of a transcendent critique, such as that of Nietzsche on Wagner. The limitations of Nietzsche's critique lie not merely in the fact that he judges the work from above rather than engaging its claims on their own merits. He has in fact a too limited conception of the very nature of truth-content itself: a kind of culture-philosophical conception, which takes no account of the historical moment which is immanent in aesthetic truth. The distinction between what is true in itself and something that is merely an adequate expres-sion of false consciousness is untenable, if only because there has not yet to the present day ever existed anything like true consciousness, from which such a distinction might be observed somehow from above. The full represen-tation of false consciousness properly names something which can also be named truth-content. The understanding of works of art, therefore, besides their exegesis through interpretation and critique, must also be pursued from the standpoint of redemption, which very precisely searches out the truth of false consciousness in aesthetic appearance. Great works cannot in that sense lie. Even where their content is mere appearance [*Schein*], in so far as it was historically necessary it includes a truth to which they testify; only the unsuccessful works are untrue. (AT 196/188)

Rightly or wrongly, Adorno felt that his Wagner book had made the most fundamental analytical contribution to this problem, which neces-sarily confronts anyone obliged to come to terms – whether intellectually, culturally or pedagogically – with classics of a conservative, if not indeed sometimes outright reactionary, stamp. His solution – the most difficult of all, since it requires one simultaneously to insist on what is false and ideological and also on what is utopian in the work – seems to me prefer-able to the alternatives, in which one either transforms a reactionary writer into a progressive one by fiat, or else smashes the canon altogether.

It has already become clear that the philosophical 'truth-content' of the work somehow – at least in 'great bourgeois' music and art – partici-pates in its technical innovations. But these are themselves 'contradictions' in some very fundamental sense: thus the remarkable chromatic color-ation of Wagner's music is deeply at one with the disintegration in it of the classical musical material (and even with his own technical inept-ness). Yet the very splendor of that technical breakdown, whose tenden-

tially atomistic logic releases all kinds of new 'productive forces', is itself
a figure for the relationship between his 'moment of truth' and the regressive position of the subject in a bourgeois society that has already begun
to anticipate its own limits. It should, however, be noted that this particular dialectic of ideology and truth excludes cheating and liberal whitewash-
ing and wishful thinking: Wagner's character ('a sentimental Marat') has
of course always offered a rich minefield of defects and imperfections,
from egotism and cowardice all the way to the shame of the turncoat
and the unreliability of the social toady. But nowhere have the crystalliza-
tions of these unlovely traits within the form and detail of the music
drama been so implacably pursued as here by Adorno. This harshness,
the remorselessness of the ideological judgement, is, however, the price
that must be paid for the dialectical acknowledgement of the truth it
also contains:

> Tristan's 'How could that vision leave me?', which refers to the presentiment
> of nothingness as something, seizes hold of the moment in which a complete
> negativity perfects the chimera of Utopia. It is the moment of awakening.
> The passage in Act III of *Tristan*, where the horn in the orchestra soars above
> the boundary separating nothingness from something to catch the echo of
> the shepherd's melancholy song as Tristan stirs – that passage will survive
> as long as the fundamental experiences of the bourgeois era can still be felt
> by human beings. Together with that other passage, the scene of Brünnhilde's
> awakening, it is evidence of that glimmering awareness without which the
> concept of nothingness, or so Wagner's music would have us believe, could
> not be conceived of. If compassion is reserved for animals, then it is logical
> for them to accompany such a moment: Brünnhilde's horse indeed seems
> to survive archaic times over into this now of consciousness (archaic time
> being, according to Schopenhauer, that of nothingness itself). (W 192/151)

(It does not seem superfluous to add that the motto of Adorno's book
reads 'Horses are the survivors of an age of heroes'). The 'case' of Wagner,
however, finally suggests that even formally, the doctrine of 'truth-content' cannot be generalized or transformed into an interpretive method:
everything in Adorno's view of Wagner indeed returns us to the unique
moment of this work, in which something of a German bourgeoisie
that has not come to 'maturity' already lives its own decline, and where
its very untimeliness generates a regressiveness that is at one and the
same time formally innovative and productive. But it would be sheer
critical mannerism to transfer this characteristic analysis to other figures
of the modern, as though it alone embodied Adorno's 'method'. The
method, however at least in principle, implies that every historical situ-

ation will be distinct, even though all are also frozen under the magic spell of the total system.

Adorno's aesthetics is therefore inseparable from ideological analysis, the necessity of whose historical 'moment' it repeatedly stresses: something which then brings us back in conclusion to what has already been characterized as the anti-political character of this same aesthetic. Adorno is very clear about the specific historical situation from which this position springs:

> The relationship between social praxis and art, always variable in any case, seems to have changed profoundly in the last forty or fifty years. During the First World War, and before Stalin, the artistic and political vanguards were always linked in spirit; whoever came of age in that time was inclined to feel that art was a priori what it had in fact rarely been historically, namely politically left by definition. (AT 373-7/359-60)

This is a useful reminder, since in the Anglo-American cultural field the constitutive affinity between modernism in art and revolutionary politics has rarely been stressed – indeed, most often reversed and denied for ideological purposes. Meanwhile, to stress the historical situation from which such opinions spring and to which they react is also to imply their historical variability and the possibility of the emergence of a different situation in which such antagonisms no longer hold or in which their very polar terms are perhaps transformed beyond recognition.

What must be principally stressed here, however, is that while Adorno seems to exclude the possibility of political works of art, often with some vehemence, what he in reality opposes may better be identified as a political aesthetic, one which stresses and valorizes the function of works of art within situations of immediacy, and in the realm of the day-to-day struggle and the Event, rather than their deeper expression of social struggle or historical contradiction (something, on the contrary, always implicit in *Aesthetic Theory*, as we have shown). What this means is that the individual works may wander out of one category into another: everything changes when something normally called 'political art' turns out to have been that seemingly different and incompatible thing called 'great art', as witness Adorno's subtle appreciation of his great adversary, Brecht:

> Brecht's efforts to smash subjective nuances and quarter tones with a tough objectivity which included conceptual toughness are very precisely aesthetic means, and in his finest works a principle of stylization rather than preaching; hard to tell exactly what the author 'meant' in *Galileo* or *The Good Person of Sezuan*, except to stress the distance and non-coincidence between the objec-

tivity of the representation and its subjective intention. Brecht's allergy to expressive values, his preference for a quality that may have led him to misunderstand what the positivistic conception of a 'protocol sentence' was all about – all of this is itself the figure for a certain kind of expression that can come to language only through the latter's determinate negation. (AT 55/47)

(And later on, the song of the cranes from *Mahagonny* will be instanced as a supreme realization of this peculiar and unique Brechtian aesthetic.)

It would seem, indeed, that what is for Adorno intolerable about any specifically political aesthetic has less to do with its politics than with its stress on art as such, rather than the individual works of art – the monads – which Adorno wishes radically to distinguish from art as a process or an institution. A peculiarly Hobbesian expression indeed recurs in *Aesthetic Theory* from time to time to characterize the relationship of the various individual works to each other: a *bellum omnium contra omnes* (AT 47/60). And see elsewhere: 'they refuse to be compared. They want to annihilate one another' (MM No. 47, 92/75). Sometimes the Hegelian version is also offered (a permutation so significant, in a different order of things, for French existentialism): 'each work of art seeks the death of the other' (AT 60/52; 313–14/301). Yet such language, which seeks to characterize the nominalism of 'truth-content' and the irreducibility of the unique historical conjunctures in which the great works are embedded, does not always seem appropriate to describe this enormous historical sky in which the aesthetic monads hang gleaming like so many planetary bodies; it might be better to say that they somehow repel each other instinctively. Each one demands to exist as an absolute in terms of which the existence of others can scarcely be acknowledged. So Beethoven is not at war with Wagner, exactly, or with Greek tragedy; but each can reveal its absolute truth only by means of the eclipse of all the others. In much the same way the historical situation of each one is an absolute present – a present of struggle, praxis, suffering – whose claims on reality are sapped by any chronological historicism or relativism of the archive. A political aesthetic also wishes to affirm this primacy of the present and the event; but it is clear that for Adorno it also means lining the monads up on sides and in teams, and substituting general demands of style and discussions about art in general for engagement with the works themselves. The hostility to 'political art' this seems to suggest might just as adequately be characterized as a hostility to avantgardes and to programmatic slogans.

It is self-defeating, however, to conclude an exploration of Adorno's work within the aesthetic itself, a zone from which many readers will wish to be heliported out and which will confirm their impressions of the ultimately useless character of this philosophy, still evidently seeking to stage a *Zweckhaftigkeit ohne Zweck*. (Significantly, in Germany today, as we shall see in conclusion, the relegation of Adorno to mere aesthetics is now the canonical method for dealing with this particular survival of the dialectic.) And it is certain that aesthetic experience as such leads nowhere, virtually by definition, save in the sense in which it stands as a figure for a utopian existence that would not be dominated by instrumental motives and would above all be free of the ultimate 'end', which is that of self-preservation. On the other hand, every reader of Adorno will also remember that aesthetic experience is necessarily particular or concrete, and not merely 'by definition': indeed, we have seen Adorno argue that the guilt of art in general – the unjustifiable privilege and luxury of 'aesthetic experience' in general – is unresolvable as such, and qualifiable only in the individual work itself. But this then means that aesthetic experience also always leads us back to history – to the history of capitalism from which the work emerged, and to the constellation of classes and instrumental rationality which is its semantic content and makes its utopian dimension possible. It would then be equally justifiable to say that aesthetics always leads back to history itself, and that for art the 'non-identical' is society.

Meanwhile, the vital relationship of Adorno to political thinking lies in the form rather than the content of his thoughts, which, conceptualizing aesthetic form or philosophical content rather than politics as such, is capable of detecting within them – with a starker, more luminous articulation than can normally be achieved within political analysis or social history – the complex mobilities of the historical dialectic.

CONCLUSIONS

Adorno in the

Postmodern

One

One sometimes has the feeling that objections to Adorno's work and positions fall into two groups that ought under normal circumstances to cancel each other out. For one group, Adorno's work remains too Marxist; for the other (a much smaller group, it must be admitted) he is not Marxist enough, and maybe not even Marxist at all. The plot thickens if you introduce rumors of latent (or overt) Hegelianism, a reproach that could conceivably be anathema to both parties: for the anti-Marxists confirming the ineradicable Hegelian roots of Marxism itself, for the Marxists on the other hand signifying an idealism inconsistent in any number of ways with materialism, politics, Marxist aesthetics, or whatever.

Nor are these battle lines clarified by a second set of objections that seems obscurely related to the first, but across all their borderlines in a seemingly random manner: this view taxes Adorno with a 'modernism' whose sense, after the postmodern, now largely transcends any merely aesthetic commitment to modern art and has come to characterize a whole range of old-fashioned philosophical habits and procedures (by contrast with the way in which 'postmodern' philosophy, sociology, political science, history, aesthetic theory, is done today). It does not seem to me terribly promising to try to combine in advance the thematics of these two kinds of critique, the one turning on Marxism, the other turning on modernism: an effort that would probably take the form of wondering whether Marxism is a modernism, not necessarily a rewarding experiment. I will, however, try to introduce a certain symmetry into them by arguing, if not for a 'postmodern' Adorno, then at least for one consistent with and appropriate for the current postmodern age.

As far as the first set of objections is concerned I would, of course be only too willing to agree with the denunciation of Adorno as a Marxist, since that has been one of the arguments of this book; but even here, the fact that the indictment arises from two such distinct philosophical and ideological positions as those of Jean-François Lyotard[1] and of Jürgen Habermas[2] must give us pause. Let me therefore first (in answer to the 'not-Marxist-enough' position) summarize my own findings, and the reasons for which I feel able to reassert the essential Marxism of this thinker.

The basic exhibits here are clearly enough the fundamental Marxian law of value and also the omnipresent conceptual instrument called 'totality'. Both of these have already been addressed; I will therefore here restate them with some concision. The law of value – or at least some general Marxian sense of the dynamic of capitalism and of the tendential laws of its development and history – is always presupposed by Adorno's interpretations; I have also tried to show that the historical paradigm of *Dialectic of Enlightenment*, in which the law of value seems to be 'only one principle among many principles of social integration by means of instrumental reason',[3] is in fact an alternate rewriting of social history in terms of natural history which leaves the Marxian paradigm intact.

I have observed in passing, indeed, that Adorno's philosophical presuppositions are not merely Marxist, they sometimes reflect a rather old-fashioned Marxism: this is so particularly in the areas of culture and of ideology. The title of the 'Culture Industry' chapter itself should have alerted us to the discovery that Adorno has no conception of culture as such, in the way in which more recent theorists like the late Raymond Williams have developed the idea; in the notorious chapter in question, Adorno's concern is with the entertainment business and not with a theory of the cultural sphere he would never have accepted in the first place. (Art or the aesthetic constitutes such a sphere, but its evaluation is in Adorno irredeemably negative, as we have seen; the position of the aesthete as such is absolutely refused; individual works of art, however, negotiate another kind of vulnerable and provisional status on an *ad hoc* basis.)

By the same token, the peculiar footwork that juxtaposes a slashing and very often class-conscious ideological analysis of a text with some evocation of its 'truth-content' strikes me as finding its explanation in the relatively conventional and old-fashioned conception of ideology as mere 'false consciousness' which Adorno shared with most of his generation (excepting Lukács, who was older, and Sartre, who reflected other preoccupations; Adorno seems not to have known much about Gramsci). This distinction, which of course once again makes a place for philosophy as such, may no longer be necessary after the Althusserian rewriting of 'ideology' in terms of subject-positions. But the problem to which it corresponds – how reactionary works can have value and even (Heidegger!) how reactionary ideas can have their 'truth-content' – is still very much with us. We lose it if we abandon the concept of ideology as such (to do so is, however, a fundamental proposition of the postmodern).

Meanwhile, it is also clear that if you reproach Marxism with its temporal dimension, which allows it to consign solutions to philosophical problems to a future order of things (Laclau–Mouffe[4]), then Adorno is, if anything, more Marxist than conventional Marxists, since his entire philosophy turns on just such a vision of postponement and lag, deferral and future reconciliation. But it may be admitted that this future-oriented philosophy – which prophesies catastrophe and proclaims salvation – is scarcely consistent with that perpetual present which is daily life under postmodernism and late capitalism.

I have reserved the matter of 'totality' for the final topic in this set of objections. When it is finally understood that this term signifies something like society or economic system, it slowly becomes clear that the only way to evade its use is resolutely to stigmatize the very concept of 'society', as Laclau and Mouffe have done, and to try to limit one's remarks and analyses to something more modest called 'the social' (they do not always succeed in doing this). I have already referred, on the matter of whether this is a transindividual or indeed transcendent concept in Adorno, to his short Encylopaedia entry on 'Society', in which the quintessence of his sociological thought is made succinctly available.[5]

On totality, however, the reader is also directed to his extraordinary 'Introduction' to the so-called 'Positivist Dispute in German Sociology', where the bull's horns are seized a little more directly than in *Negative Dialectics*:

> It is almost tautological to say that one cannot point to the concept of totality in the same manner as one can point to the facts, from which totality distances itself as a concept.[6]

The misconception seems to be based on the idea that if you talk about something repeatedly, you must like it; to point something out insistently turns into the advocacy of the thing, very much on the principle of messengers who bring bad news (and suffer the consequences). But totality is not celebrated in Adorno, even though the critical use of its concept is: the much-quoted dictum that, as against Hegel, 'the whole is the untrue' does not imply that we ought to stop talking about it – quite the contrary:

Totality is not an affirmative but rather a critical category. Dialectical critique seeks to salvage or help to establish what does not obey totality, what opposes it or what first forms itself as the potential of a not yet existent individuation. The interpretation of facts is directed towards totality, without the interpretation itself being a fact. There is nothing socially factual which would not have its place in that totality. It is pre-established for all individual subjects since they obey its 'contrainte' even in themselves and even in their monadological constitution and here, in particular, conceptualize totality. To this extent, totality is what is most real. Since it is the sum of individuals' social relations which screen themselves off from individuals, it is also illusion – ideology. A liberated mankind would by no means be a totality. Their being-in-themselves is just as much their subjugation as it deceives them about itself as the true societal substratum. This certainly does not fulfill the desideratum of a logical analysis of the concept of totality, as the analysis of something free from contradiction, which Albert uses against Habermas, for the analysis terminates in the objective contradiction of totality.[7]

Ultimately, indeed, as I hope to have shown in the course of the preceding work, the critical instrument of contradiction is inseparable from a conception of totality; my impression is also, however, that these conceptual instruments survive today only in Marxism as such, so that on the whole, in my opinion, the refutation of Adorno's non-Marxism is sustained. I will have more to say about the imputation of Hegelianism below.

Two

The accusation of Marxism, however, is more complicated; it seems to me to include several distinct kinds of anxieties that can, I think, best be disentangled by examining the position on Adorno held by progressive (or Habermasian) currents in the Federal Republic today, here expertly summarized by Herbert Schnädelbach:

> What henceforth makes immediate commerce with Adorno's texts impossible for us today are in my opinion three developments in the history of theory. First of all, there has been a fundamental scene change on the philosophical stage in the last twenty years, and other fronts have come into being, quite different from those on which Critical Theory once sought to make its stand. Our problem is no longer logical positivism along with various kinds of idealistic system-building; but rather the undifferentiated celebration of the multiple, along with irrationalism [various kinds of French poststructuralism are evidently meant here], which however also still yokes its chariot to the [Frankfurt-School-type] 'critique of instrumental reason'.
>
> Then too, we must respect the new kinds of precise discrimination that the reception of analytic philosophy in [West] Germany has taught us, sometimes against our own will; this philosophy has not solved many problems, perhaps, but it has certainly allowed us to formulate them better.
>
> Thirdly, the problems of mentalism as a form of language impelled the reflections of Wittgenstein, Ryle and many others; and have also forced German academic 'consciousness philosophy' to rethink its traditional paradigms.[8]

As if all that were not enough, Schnädelbach later on adds that, in any case, 'negative dialectics as the well-known "ontology of the false condition" [*Ontologie des falschen Zustandes*, ND 22/11] is a concept that cannot be recuperated'.

There is, to be sure, no little irony in this West German expression of satisfaction at having adopted the more advanced Anglo-American philosophical fashions and at having liquidated, as a token of one's own achievement of a higher stage, the final traces of the national heritage in philosophy. It leads one to conjecture that Schnädelbach's first point was not altogether accurate after all, and that some of the old enemies – most notably positivism, in its broader sense – are still very much alive! So that this particular 'analysis' strikes one as being little more than the declaration that you have changed sides. The irony is of course compounded by the general exhaustion of analytic philosophy in the Anglo-American realm itself in recent years, and the search for a renewal by way of the very continental philosophies here renounced (in the true spirit of the dialectic of enlightenment) as archaic and old-fashioned.

A second paradox of Schnädelbach's interesting assessment lies in the wilful separation between his first and third points, as though he were somehow not aware that it was primarily by way of the very post-structuralism initially indicted for irrationality and obscurantism that the critique of philosophies of the subject and of consciousness (centering on, but certainly not limited to, phenomenology) was primarily staged. What is under the first heading denounced as a renunciation of Reason turns out, under the third heading, to be celebrated as a welcome critique of philosophies of consciousness.

Leaving the polemic thrust of the passage aside, however, and without wishing to undertake the reevaluation of poststructuralism which would evidently be required (and would demand at least a full-length book in its own right),[9] a few observations about the relationship of Adorno to these trends may be offered. With respect to the relationship between thinking and language, it is certain that Adorno is a traditional, that is to say a prestructuralist, philosopher – or, if you prefer a different kind of terminology, that he remains a philosopher rather than undergoing the sea-change into that new and postmodern thing, a *theorist*. Poststructuralism's triumph and its linguistic obscurity, along with its idiosyncratic forms of cultural politics, derived fundamentally from the conviction that there could be no thinking separate from language, and that everything identified or designated as 'thought' was rather already in some more profound way a proto-linguistic event. What this 'discovery' does is to dispel the illusion that the philosophical 'system' could be anything more than a book or a *Darstellung* (and not a form of Truth, however you used that word); it also makes for great discomfort with the category of consciousness, most particularly with the notion of self-consciousness as such, but also, in a secondary way, with the older notions of sensation and perception (and thereby with the body in any immediate fashion).

Whatever Adorno says about philosophy's modern relationship to language itself, to rhetoric and to problems of material and linguistic *Darstellung* (these are primarily to be found at the end of the 'Introduction' to *Negative Dialectics*), it can be asserted with some confidence that he never 'goes as far' as the poststructuralists, and that some notion of thinking is preserved beyond a material embodiment in language which would probably have seemed positivistic to him in the way in which it also, effectively enough, squeezes out the last vestiges of transcendence, consciousness, and truth. However tortured the Archimedean problems of the negative dialectic as such, they are only analogous to and not at all identical with the even more elaborate Archimedean dilemmas of deconstruction; both need something outside the system in order to criticize it, but in Adorno's case this something would remain an idea, while in Derrida's it ought ideally to be a linguistic possibility: the similarity comes from the fact that in neither case can this urgent need be met, except by an elaborate formal subterfuge.

On the other hand, what needs to be added here is that the 'concept' functions in Adorno as a constricting and reifying system almost as ironclad as language itself for poststructuralism. The concept – with its inner properties of system and identity – is something we can scarcely think our way out of or around; it stands between us and some utopian reinvention of thought just as impenetrably as does the 'language of Western metaphysics' for the French critiques of philosophy – both then sharing the premiss that a new kind of thinking (or a new kind of language) will not be possible until the social system, to which the older one was integral, has been transformed beyond recognition.

As for Reason,[10] I cannot feel that it offers the most vital standard today under which to do battle, even though Habermas's notion of communication has rehabilitated it in ingenious ways. But those ways still involve a leap and a metaphorical reidentification of the findings of contemporary language philosophy with philosophical ideals of the bourgeois past that smack uncomfortably of the history manuals or the revolutionary museums. The staging of such an identification is a political and cultural decision, and I have not seen any public discussion of the strategic decision in question. One would be willing to accept Habermas's judgement on the utopian content of those great bourgeois revolutionary ideals, but only provided that the reason he used to give is still attached – namely, that their ongoing vitality results from their never having been realized in the first place (an idea distantly reminiscent of Adorno himself). Still, at a time when those ideals of parliamentary democracy and market freedom are everywhere being celebrated as more advanced values than the conceptions of economic equality that were in fact their historical sequel – in such a period, which we now call postmodern, the revival of the Enlightenment conception of Reason seems open to ambiguity, nor is it clear that it can be recuperated from the enemy so easily.

The principal tactical weakness of the defense of reason lies, however, in the very success of the critique of instrumental reason itself, which in a time of universal cynicism can no longer be rolled back. But we must also mention the remarkable achievements of some of the currents of thought associated with poststructuralism which, following Freud, set out to show in a variety of ways that what we used to call the 'irrational' was by no means so unreasonable as all that, and amounted to a practice of intentionality by other means. These demonstrations then went a long way towards fulfilling Freud's own profoundly Enlightenment program: 'wo Es war, soll Ich werden' – 'the id shall be transformed into consciousness'; what used to be unconscious shall be reclaimed from the sea. So everything from the emotions to fascism, and from advertising to religion and mysticism, looks far more transparent to us than it did to the earliest respectable burghers (who needed a stronger concept of the irrational to domesticate their own unconscious drives); and this increasing sense of the deeper intentionality of everything we used to think of as irrational – this widening of the terrain of a more supple conception of meaning, if not reason – also accounts, incidentally, for the transformations in the classical Marxian notion of ideology as false consciousness which were mentioned above. From that perspective also, Reason does not seem a great deal more contemporary than the older Marxian notion of 'science' (which used to accompany 'ideology' as its good sibling).

It is with any newer concept of reason as with Saussure's communicational loop: it makes a difference whether we are talking about the sender or the receiver. In this case, reason does not mean the sender's point of view, that is to say, always doing what is reasonable or rational; it means the receiver's point of view – always *understanding* what the actor's reasons were, why the thing was done in the first place (or why this or that position or value is defended). But after Freud (indeed, after Marx), after Nietzsche, after Foucault on madness, after a whole enormous enlargement in our *sympathy* with what people do (this word, however, meant in Rousseau's sense as *Verstehen*, and not in any way approval or endorsement) – our very notion of reason may be expected to have expanded well beyond its former boundaries and to include much that for strait-laced respectable burghers used to count as 'irrational'. (As for exposing the 'reasons' in language, for the purpose of Kantian universality tests, I fear that in the era of 'cynical reason' even the most 'irrational' will be willing to tell you in great detail why they feel like doing what they propose to do.)

Indeed, it seems possible to accommodate these newer modes of interpretation by way of the conceptuality of a somewhat different tradition than the one in which the only opposite number to Reason is the Irrational itself in all its demonic forms. Indeed, this other tradition was also that of the Frankfurt School, which is surely why Habermas's reproach – the apparently devastating demonstration that the critique incorporated in *Dialectic of Enlightenment* provides no place of truth from which it can be launched or sustained in the first place – falls oddly flat. For in Hegel's restoration of the dialectic as a superior mode of truth (rather than as the sophistical instrument of superstition for which Kant reserved the term) the Kantian faculties become reordered; *Vernunft*, or dialectical reason, now emerging above and subsuming the understanding or *Verstand*, the term for which the expression analytical reason (or, as the Frankfurt School rebaptized it, instrumental reason) should be reserved. Dialectical reason, which corresponds to a social organization that does not yet exist, has not yet come into being in any hegemonic form. The poststructuralists, individually as well as collectively, have themselves been as hostile to the ideal of the dialectic as Habermas himself. On the other hand, their various hermeneutics of the cultural and the 'irrational' must surely be thought of as contributions to some future enlargement of the power of dialectical thinking.

The problem with the concept of Reason is therefore not reason itself but its opposite number, the private term of the irrational, or irrationalism, which is now enlarged to become the dumping ground for anything one wishes to exclude. This leads us to the second objection to Adorno current in the Federal Republic today, and at least implicit in Schnädelbach's remarks, but certainly explicit in Habermas himself – namely, the conclusion that the critique of instrumental reason is dangerous, since among other things it makes any concept of Reason – that is, of *philosophy* itself – impossible. Adorno's 'philosophy' comes thus finally be seen as a matter of aesthetics.[11] But it does not take a philosophically very alert eye – indeed, any non-philosophical humanist will have instantly grasped the further implication – to understand that in that case 'what is living' is really the same as 'what is dead' in Adorno's philosophy. For it is clear that the aesthetic – the third realm in Habermas's conception of modernity: he follows Kant fairly closely on this point – is a kind of sandbox to which one consigns all those vague things we have enumerated above under the heading of the irrational: but this is the proper place for them, because here they can be monitored and, in case of need, controlled (the aesthetic is in any case conceived as a kind of safety-valve for irrational impulses). But if the reproach is not a trivial one – something that would be the case if one argued for the aestheticality of Adorno's thought simply by denying validity to everything else he ever touched on – then it draws its force from a separation between abstract thinking and 'mere' aesthetic representation which must be argued as such (and is, for example, superseded in poststructuralism). The evocation of Schelling in this regard is suggestive, but hardly conclusive; indeed, it might slowly come to prove the opposite when one reviews Adorno's hostility to the Romantics and his commitment to Hegel as well as to Kant.

Habermas has opened a more interesting line of argument with his suggestion[12] that *mimesis* is the source of this tendential aestheticalization of Adorno's philosophy, in so far as it is both an indispensable and an indefinable concept. Mimesis is 'the placeholder for this primordial reason that was diverted from the intention of truth', but in order for the concept to occupy this now central position, 'Horkheimer and Adorno would have to put forward a *theory* of mimesis, which, according to their own ideas, is impossible'. But as we have tried to show above, they see mimesis as an impulse at work in thought and philosophy fully as much as in art, which is to say that it entertains no particularly privileged relationship to art itself.

To put all this the other way round (since in my opinion the misunderstanding develops fully as much in that direction): the presence, within Adorno's aesthetics, of a conception of the truth-content of the work of art is surely not at all the same thing as the assertion that the work of art affords the only means to truth and thereby replaces philosophy or, as Bubner outrageously puts it, 'reverses the relationship in which art and philosophy stand with respect to each other in Hegel'[13] – a characterization that might better apply to Lukács, for whom 'philosophy' as such has already been realized, but not to Adorno, for whom it notoriously 'lived on'. (Bubner goes on to deplore the philosophical demands with which Adorno overloaded denatured art proper, but this is another matter altogether and has more to do with his modernism than with the alleged 'aesthetic' character of his philosophy). A non-philosopher and 'culture-worker' may be forgiven the suspicion that these worries reflect the perplexities of social scientists and philosophers who have never taken culture or daily life seriously (let alone aesthetics) when confronted with a philosopher in whose texts the rate of aesthetic reference seems abnormally and incomprehensibly high.

But in fact Adorno, unlike Kant and unlike Lukács, has very little to say about the 'specificity' of aesthetic experience, which he takes for granted but is not concerned to ground or defend. The problems raised by Adorno's aesthetics – the problems his aesthetics wishes to raise

raise, those most urgent and interesting for it – are on the contrary always historical ones: the nature of the modern, the crisis of nominalism, the destiny of form. If everything in Adorno leads into the aesthetic, everything in Adorno's aesthetics leads out again in the direction of history. I have argued that his contribution to philosophy lay in the demonstration that all abstract philosophical questions are fundamentally historical ones, questions that 'participate' (in the sense of Platonic *methexis*) in the social and the economic. It is very precisely this same lesson that we confront repeatedly in all his aesthetic writings as well; these, as we have seen, are a veritable organon of the rewriting or transcoding of formal questions into substantive socioeconomic ones. In that case, it may by no means be so reassuring in the long run to have successfully demonstrated that Adorno's philosophy is 'merely' aesthetic.

The third objection current even in progressive thought in the Federal Republic today is in many ways the most interesting, but it is precisely because it points ahead to new kinds of explorations that it cannot be fully dealt with here. This is what stirs behind the seemingly perfunctory repudiation of the famous slogan *'Ontologie des falschen Zustandes'* [ND 22/11] and in some larger sense it stakes out Adorno's claim to 'have' a philosophy in any more basic (non-aesthetic) fashion. What is implicit in the slogan is in fact what later became known by the term Capital-logic – that is to say, the attempt of younger philosophers, very much inspired by Adorno himself, to develop a critique of traditional logic by way of the derivation of logical categories from commerce and from capital. One powerful 'chapter' of Capital-logic is already developed (and reviewed above) in the identification posited by Adorno between the 'identity' of the concept and the structure of exchange; but any fully fledged development of this new philosophical approach would involve a great deal more than that, and would clearly have to stipulate the two distinct stages in Marx already referred to: the logic of the commodity, first of all, and the rather different and far more complex and dialectical logic of capital or of value that develops on top of it.

Indeed, if the derivation from the moment of exchange is generally called 'identity', and summons in its train the group of themes and analyses we have already developed, that based on the more complex emergence of capital as such must be distinguished from it. Exchange (of a local variety) is presumably age-old, and notions of identity and logical comparison have been with us since the first hominids. Capital, however, is a later original historical construction on that, which brings with it its own original logical derivations, most of which center around the paradoxical movement of capital as a single general force which is also at one and the same time a multiplicity of individual forces. This move-

ment, which constitutes the very architecture of the three volumes of
Marx's *Capital*, has been identified and elaborated on by Rosdolsky in
his commentary to the *Grundrisse*.[14] It may, then, be expected to generate
logical forms rather distinct from those of simple identity; and in fact
we will identify them in terms of Adorno's other great thematic motif,
the tension between the universal and the particular. For this complex
of themes there is, however, not quite the ready slogan that lay to hand
for 'identity' (along with the ubiquitous 'non-identity'); but it will be
convenient to see its operations clustering around the more historical
crisis term, 'nominalism'. The working out of a more systematic capital-
logic must then carefully disentangle these two motifs of identity and
nominalism, which are themselves derivations of exchange and capital,
respectively.

But Habermas's relatively perfunctory dismissal of this line of inquiry
in fact conflates these two distinct moments:

> Marx analyzes the double form of the commodity as a use value and an
> exchange value, as well as the transformation of its natural form into the
> value form; for this purpose he draws upon Hegel's concept of abstraction
> and treats the relation between use value and exchange value like that between
> essence and appearance. Today this presents us with difficulties; we cannot
> employ unreconstructed basic concepts from Hegel's logic just like that. The
> extended discussion on the relation of Marx's *Capital* to Hegel's *Logic* has
> illuminated these difficulties rather than resolved them. I shall therefore not
> go any deeper into the analysis of the commodity form. Lukács doesn't either.
> He is interested only in the reification effects that come about to the degree
> that the labor power of producers becomes a commodity . . .[15]

This statement is an important parting of the ways, this time from so-
called reification theory, and it is if anything more significant than Habermas's critique of production in Marx (which, since Marx is not nearly
so productionist as he argues, left Marx and Marxism relatively intact).
The observations on Lukács himself are pertinent but irrelevant, since
Capital-logic springs rather from Adorno, and necessarily goes well
beyond the problem of the logical category that corresponds to the simple
commodity form (Adorno's own impatience with simple 'reification
theory' testifies to his sense of the complexity of the logical problems
involved).

In the postmodern period it is generally not effective to seek to argue
on the basis of acquired momentum; for example, to assert that this
or that having been effectively disproven once and for all, we can now
go on to something else. Kant was wiser; he understood that his own
'disproof' of the ontological proof of God (definitive if anything ever

was) would have 'no practical consequences' whatsoever. But where – in various post-Marxisms, for example – it is asserted by a Habermas, or a Derrida, or even a more banal Hindess and Hirst, that this or that mode of looking at things is now definitively outmoded, we may confidently expect the putatively extinct specimens to reappear in the lists in the near future. (And much the same can be said of the way in which analytic philosophy has been supposed to liberate us from various 'pseudo-problems' or 'metaphysical survivals'.) The point is, however, that since the postmodern eschews tradition and a canon, nothing of this kind can in it *ever* be taken for granted; no one will admit that anything has been proven or disproven once and for all; and as the movement of theory has to be recreated at every moment, it cannot in this traditional way 'acquire momentum'.

At any rate, I also happen to think that Habermas's prognosis of the *Zeitgeist* (or the 'spiritual situation of our time') is simply incorrect: any number of straws in the wind point to an impending Hegel revival, of a new kind, likely to draw a revival of Capital-logic along with it, and not only in those fields (essentially political theory of the so-called state-derivation type[16]) where it still flourishes. But the Hegel who emerges from this rereading will be an unfamiliar materialist-mathematical Hegel, one who comes *after* the *Grundrisse*; quite unlike the idealist-conservative Hegel who *preceded* the writing of Marx's first great work, the unpublished commentary on the *Philosophy of Right*. Meanwhile, an exploration of the influence of the abstract or logical forms of capital in the whole newly developing field of the study of everyday life and of 'culture' (in a wider sense than Adorno was willing to use the term) may be expected to correct some of the implications of the notorious, but seminal, 'Culture Industry' chapter.

Three

Another constellation of objections can now be formulated, as has already been suggested, in terms of some putative essential 'modernism' in Adorno's thinking – a theme which will lead us on to a few final reflections on his relevance for our own, 'postmodern' period. But this is now a somewhat different issue from Adorno's relationship to aesthetic modernism as such and turns on his own modernity as a writer – that is to say, essentially as a philosopher; one can indeed, without much difficulty, imagine 'modern' philosophical projects utterly unsullied by any cultural or aesthetic sympathies whatsoever.

It does not seem particularly effective to begin such an exploration with a check list, although we have already seen a number of traits in Adorno's work that would be candidates for such a list of the most characteristic signs and symptoms of the 'modern' – I have already mentioned the breath of auto-referentiality that hovers over his work, particularly when it assigns itself a unique function to preserve values and a language elsewhere in the process of dissolution and disappearance. The question of the standpoint then powerfully emerges – not yet the more desperate Archimedean point of the 1960s speculation (students or underclasses as the 'subject of history'?): and it is most often forthrightly answered in terms of class privilege, as in the opening paragraph of *Minima Moralia*, thrown down like a gauntlet, or the scarcely more evasive discussion in *Negative Dialectics* (51/41): 'Only those not completely molded [by the administered world] can resist it.' This goes further in the dialectic of intellectuals of a certain independent means than Horkheimer was ever willing to, but clearly makes for problems in the 1960s when the species has virtually become extinct. It is not clear that the charismatic artists of the modern period – who enthusiastically outfitted themselves with the trappings of seers and prophets – had any more clear-sighted grasp of the nature of the limbs they themselves sat on; but a comparable auto-referentiality is to be found in them whenever the question of the poet (which replaces this one of the philosopher) rears its head.

The immediate historicity of the theme in Adorno's hands then suggests an obvious next step, and everyone's principal candidate for the fundamental modernist characteristic *par excellence* – namely, time and temporality, and a certain kind of philosophical history, or perhaps we should rather more closely specify this motif as an attention to temporality as a mode of grasping history, the use of existential time protensions and retensions as an instrument for grasping the dynamics of an external collective history otherwise available only in the 'facts' and the *faits divers*. Neither perspective by itself would then be 'modern' – the historicist passion as such, or the 'inner sense' dear to diarists and autobiographers; on the other hand, the enormous technical – one wants to say, technological – expansion in subjectivity in the modern, which includes a remarkable new and enlarged laboratory for temporal registrations and inscriptions, does seem to develop hand in hand with a distracted alertness to those distant sounds from the street that betoken unimaginable historical convulsions in the making, and the ends and beginnings of whole worlds.

If this second, historical and social dimension of the modern has been lost on North Americans, whose modernist pantheon is mainly collected under the rubrics of 'time' and 'the self', this is – as Adorno is there to instruct us – because subjects of the American constitution prefer to think of crisis and catastrophe, revolution, *Weltuntergang* – even the passing of the old aristocracy and any number of 'ends of eras' as such – as profoundly European in some bad and reprehensible sense ('history' would then be what the Europeans have to be ashamed of, as opposed to the forthright monetary indecency Adorno attributes to North Americans in 'Olet' [MM 259–61/195–6]).

What qualifies for this specifically modern function of temporality in Adorno we have already begun to identify: most notably in the coordination between a personal and idiosyncratic sense of missed occasions and unseasonable survivals and a now more than merely non-synchronous historical paradigm, in which the 'stages' of social and productive development pile up, fall out, keep us waiting, or turn out to have happened already and already been forgotten.

But in my opinion no isolated theme of this kind, even one so fundamental as temporality itself, is sufficient to account for the modernist cast of a certain kind of thought (or formal expression); the reason has already been given in advance in Benjamin's and Adorno's (profoundly modernist) fascination with the 'constellation' as such – a mobile and shifting set of elements in which it is sheer relationship rather than substantive content that marks their structure as a whole. This means that in a constellation there can be no 'fundamental' features, no centers, no 'ultimately determining instances' or bottom lines, except for the relationship of all these contents to each other. The notion is virtually Althusserian *avant la lettre*; it also still retains something like a nostalgia for centeredness and for unified (if not necessarily organic) form, as Derrida has shown in an influential essay on Lévi-Strauss's not unrelated concept of structure.[17] In this essay, which has sometimes been taken as the opening move in what we now call poststructuralism, it seems appropriate to suggest that Derrida's unmasking of the secret *modernism* of Lévi-Strauss constitutes a first step in the inauguration of a *post*modernism based on play and randomness (in short, on the 'aesthetic' itself, when you stop to think about it).

This is, then, in my opinion, the place from which to set out in an account of Adorno's modernism, particularly since it demands a return to all those problematical conceptions of totality and of the universal and the particular which are 'central' to Adorno on the present reading. But Derrida's analysis is of course couched in the language of the nascent postmodern and staged from its future or emergent perspective; from the perspective of the modern, things look rather different and it will be more appropriate to rewrite the description in terms of a simultaneous crisis of and commitment to *representation* itself. For what Adorno teaches us – but also the return, under the postmodern, to the now sealed books of the classics of the modern pantheon, – is that questions of representation become interesting and agonizing, all-important, only when a concept of totality is maintained in place as something more than a mere 'regulative idea'.

The representation of individual items is at best a matter of aesthetic appreciation or belletristic interest; nor does representation really emerge as an issue and a dilemma in its own right when the possibility of some realistic access to the social totality is taken for granted and given in advance. It is only with the second or monopoly stage of capitalism, and the emergence of a classical imperialist system beyond the confines of the various national experiences, that a radical aesthetic and epistemological doubt about the possibility of grasping society as a whole begins to be felt: and it is precisely this radical doubt that inaugurates modernism as such and constitutes the representational drama specific to it. On the other hand, when, in the postmodern and the multinational era, 'totality' no longer seems to be a relevant issue, becoming either something you are resigned to missing or do not wish to achieve for moral and political reasons, then the most urgent representational problems (of a philosophical as well as of a formal nature) fall away.

The central tension in Adorno's work was, however, precisely that of a relationship between universal and particular which is at one with the objective tension between the social totality and its subjects. This specifically modernist tension is then inscribed in the individual sentences just as it determines the *ad hoc* architectonic solutions of the negative dialectic itself as a mode of philosophical *Darstellung*; it must also, as I have argued, be recaptured in the apologetics of the 'essay' as form, whose values are more easily mistaken for the now more familiar postmodern ones. Finally, Adorno's rehearsal of the modernist problematic of representation is belated enough to include a matter of crucial interest for us today, which we must ourselves generally bring from the outside of our own present to the modern classics, and this is a reflection on and a thematization of the passing of the modern itself, the reasons for its obliteration, and some dawning apprehension of an intellectual landscape in which the negative, or 'critical theory', will have definitively become a thing of the past.

Four

It is now time to assess the value of Adorno for us in full postmodernism as this last develops in uneven transnational zones, within which the national inequalities are also preserved. (Perhaps this should be qualified: for us, as intellectuals in the advanced capitalist countries; perhaps even only for 'us', as North American intellectuals.)

We must begin by acknowledging the possibility of a case for Adorno's postmodernism as well, or at least for a certain postmodern Adorno. But this case would have to be based on other musical writings than the canonical ones, the bleak retrospective monuments to the high moderns, such as the dolmens *Philosophy of Modern Music* erects to Schoenberg and Stravinsky. But less familiar texts – above all the essay 'Vers une musique informelle'[18] – abundantly document his sympathy with and support for the new postwar musical production organized around the Cologne radio station and the experimental music concerts in Kranichstein and Darmstadt associated with now famous names like Boulez and Stockhausen. Such sympathy, along with the books on Mahler and Berg, make it clear that we were wrong to confuse Adorno's historical assessment of the central significance of Schoenberg with any particular personal taste or inclination for the Viennese composer and theoretician, whose dead end he repeatedly characterized as such.

Meanwhile, we were also wrong to take the rhetoric of the analysis literally, and to assume that a powerful articulation of what looked like terminal contradictions in the musical system – but similar judgements were issued on the other arts, whose analogous contradictions betokened a blockage in the very nature of historical time – in any way implied that you should stop composing; nor did he do so himself. The concept of a *'musique informelle'* is thus already exceedingly postmodern, in the way it includes a revolt against the irreversible necessities of modernist aesthetic time, change, and progress, along with its more predictable reaction against systems of Schoenberg's type in the form of the occasional or the aleatory; rules made up to be used only once, along with the effort to drop out of (musical) history. (There is even a kind word for John Cage, and the whole thing makes one think a little of Italian *pensiero debole* translated into the musical realm.) This relaxation of the logic of history is of course very different from the new aesthetics Benjamin tried to invent and to project, in a similarly contradictory situation.

But it is very consistent with one particular strand in Adorno's thinking, which he sometimes staged as the very program of his own work: namely the stress, particularly in the essay on 'The Essay as Form',[19] on the repudiation of system and the commitment to the fragmentary and the occasional, to a freedom in the instant that eschewed the traditional Germanic longing for the *Hauptwerk* and the architectonic truth. This particular rhetoric, which has reminded some of Jena Romanticism,[20] does not strike me as particularly convincing in Adorno – or in Lukács, who started it,[21] and who may also, like Adorno, be seen to be arguing inconclusively against his own powerful *esprit de système*, rather than (like Nietzsche) expressing some blithe and irresponsible temperamental freedom from the temptation altogether.

It is true that Adorno wrote a great many short pieces, dabbled in the 'fragment' (above all in *Minima Moralia*), and produced aphorisms of a particularly deadly and unerring variety. But the crux of the matter lies in his conception of philosophizing itself, after the end of the great systems: do the 'models' of *Negative Dialectics* imply a practice of *philosophie informelle* of the type proposed by Richard Rorty and sometimes also described as 'postmodern'? This would imply philosophizing of a an occasional kind, an *ad hoc* problem-solving and a kind of 'open thinking', as he put it himself, 'unprotected against the risk of decline into randomness; nothing assures it of any ultimate saturation with the topic at hand that would rule out such a risk' (ND 45/35). The rhetoric of the open and the closed, which ought by now instantly to awaken the gravest suspicions and set the alarm bells ringing, is ominous enough; I have not, however, read the models of *Negative Dialectics* in this random or aleatory fashion, and it should be clear that I do not find characterizations of Adorno as postmodern any more convincing than those that see him as a 'late Romantic'. That he included a place for the possible emergence of postmodernism is, however, beyond any doubt.

But the relevance of Adorno for postmodernism, in its strong sense as a cultural dominant, is to be sought elsewhere, in the philosophical and sociological polemics. In fact, what Adorno called positivism is very precisely what we now call postmodernism, only at a more primitive stage. The shift in terminology is to be sure momentous: a stuffy petty-bourgeois republican nineteenth-century philosophy of science emerging from the cocoon of its time capsule as the iridescent sheen of consumerist daily life in the Indian summer of the superstate and multinational capitalism. From truth to state-of-the-art merchandise, from bourgeois respectability and 'distinction' to the superhighways and the beaches, from the old-fashioned authoritarian families and bearded professors to permissiveness and loss of respect for authority (which, however, still governs). The question about poetry after Auschwitz has been replaced with that of whether you could bear to read Adorno and Horkheimer next to the pool.

This, then, is indeed some first service they might do for us: to restore the sense of something grim and impending within the polluted sunshine of the shopping mall – some older classical European-style sense of doom and crisis, which even the Common Market countries have cast off in their own chrysalid transmogrification, but which the USA can now use better than they can, being an older and a now ramshackle society by contrast (a little like finally being older than your own father, as Sartre once put it). It is, however, a representational problem – pictures of decaying rails and abandoned factories we already had in the thirties; critiques of consumer society and its images (bright teeth and smiles) we had in the fifties. These are now old stuff, even in their unexpected structural combination with each other; the real problem perhaps being, as has been said above, the very matter of representation itself, of the representation of this totality, about which all of postmodernism concurs that even if it exists it would be unrepresentable and unknowable. The dialectic – even that frustrating and infuriating thing, the *negative* dialectic – is perhaps a way of squaring this circle that we haven't yet tried: starting at least from way back inside the head and its stereotypes without believing for one minute that any of them are personal or subjective. If such thought could finally manage to climb up, and look out of one of the sockets (like the character in *Endgame*), it might glimpse something real for a moment before the ladder collapsed.

Positivism becomes postmodernism when it has, like philosophy on the older paradigm, fulfilled and thereby abolished itself. Adorno insists on one side of its mission, thereby giving us one useful description: it wants to abolish the subjective, as that takes the form of thoughts, interpretations and opinions (perhaps it also wants to abolish the language that corresponds to those things: poetic, emotive, rhetorical). This is to say that it is a nominalism, and as such wants to reduce us to the empirical present (or to use the empirical present as the sole pattern for imagining other situations and other temporal moments). It wishes to abolish value as such, and any thinking that raises the issue of ends (the formulation of the so-called 'critique of instrumental reason'), not excluding the dialectic itself, but very much including all the other visionary ideologies of which it equally also promises the 'end'.

The postmodern is in that sense the fulfillment and abolition of liberalism as well, which, no longer tenable as an ideology and a value any more than traditional conservatism, can function more effectively after its own death as an ideology, realizing itself in its most traditional form as a commitment to the market system that has become sheer common sense and no longer a political program. All the critiques of such positivism are true and useless at the same time, because they can mobilize only antiquated representations and dated ideologies. At that point even talking about the not-being of thinking ceases to be effective, which was what was desired in the first place. What no longer is is as absent as what never was, or what is not yet or is not to be; only being is left, only we don't call it that any more since the word itself is meaningless without its opposite, nothingness, which has been withdrawn from circulation.

Adorno was a doubtful ally when there were still powerful and oppositional political currents from which his temperamental and cantankerous quietism could distract the uncommitted reader. Now that for the moment those currents are themselves quiescent, his bile is a joyous counter-poison and a corrosive solvent to apply to the surface of 'what is'. Even his archaic economics now seems apt and timely; very much in the spirit of his own construction of time, the utterly outmoded doctrine of monopoly capital may be just the image we need, in the absence of our own images, since it incited him to track the system into its most minute recesses and crannies, without paranoia, and with an effectiveness that can still set an example to those demoralized by the decentralization of the current one, which offers rows of identical products (or their modular transformations) instead of the grim and windowless headquarters we thought we were looking for.

In an earlier situation of uneven development, Adorno's dialectic (and so-called Western Marxism generally) could be grasped as a specific and restricted First World Marxism, the property of intellectuals, a specialized intellectual instrument very different from the ones demanded by underdevelopment or socialist construction (but no less valid, in its proper use and situation, than they were). Equally unevenly, an abrupt new expansion of the world system has annulled those inequalities and replaced them by others we as yet understand less well. Liberation movements across a neocolonial Third World have dried up overnight; while the institutions of actually existing socialism have seemed to melt away like the snow on a sunny day. The socialist transformation of human beings and social relations envisaged by Marx, however, had its condition of possibility in a regime of high productivity and advanced technology, which wishful thinking cannot conjure into being. Stalinism is disappearing not because it failed, but because it succeeded, and fulfilled its historical mission to force the rapid industrialization of an underdeveloped country (whence its adaptation as a model for many of the countries of the Third World). As Gorz has observed, in that sense communism is the 'first stage' towards socialism! (It is sufficient to remember how in Poland industrialization under a single global management – the state – was the precondition for the emergence of a national labor movement.) The problem, as yet nowhere resolved, is how to ensure the arrival of a *second* step.

In effect, what follows the abdication by the Party of its ideological responsibilities to reinvent and project a vision of the socialist model is a vacuum in the state which is at once, but only provisionally, filled by the spectacle of intellectuals, or the intelligentsia itself, in power: some future Marx may outdo the analogous pages of *The Eighteenth Brumaire* in satirizing the euphoria with which this caste celebrates and seals the acquisition of its own professional guild-values ('freedom' of speech and 'free' elections) and then aimlessly confronts its production crisis and begins to bicker, reuniting only to hold out a hand for money to the great ally and defender of 'freedom', a United States which, having benevolently neutralized the Soviet Union, goes on to reconquer Panama and to gear up for more such local 'defensive' operations around the world.

Into the void of this interregnum only big business can flow, buying up nationalized industries on the cheap and reaping the benefits of the cheap labor thrown open to the multinationals by the utter collapse of autonomous national states. The rapid deterioration of the former Second World into a Third World status *tout court* is then the *telos* of this current history, and the functional goal towards which it moves; the shedding of the old snake skin of a worn-out stage, and the emergence of a new and more genuinely global capitalism, determine the ruthless unmasking of the structural weakness of socialism in the East (as well as spelling the end and sounding the knell of autonomous development in the Third World), where an idealistic and revolutionary posture seems displaced into the popular opponents of the state for as long as it takes until the latter are fully transformed into consumers or 'immiserated' laborers for foreign capital.

None of which 'disproves' Marxism, which remains on the contrary the only current mode of thought intent on directing our attention to the economic consequences of the new 'Great Transformation', at the risk of throwing cold water on its superstructural illusions. Capital and labor (and their opposition) will not go away under the new dispensation; nor can there possibly exist in the future, any more than in the past, any viable 'third way' between capitalism and socialism, however tainted the rhetoric and conceptuality of this last may have become for people to whom bureaucrats fed it by rote. No future is conceivable, however, from which the deeper ideological commitment to politics – that is to say, left politics – is absent. Obviously, the sources of such commitment are unconscious and overdetermined by family and childhood, as well as by class, experience; and even a fully postmodernized First World society will not lack young people whose temperament and values are genuinely left ones and embrace visions of radical social change repressed by the norms of a business society. The dynamics of such commitment are derived not from the reading of the 'Marxist classics', but rather from the objective experience of social reality and the way in which one isolated cause or issue, one specific form of injustice, cannot be fulfilled or corrected without eventually drawing the entire web of interrelated social levels together into a totality, which then demands the invention of a politics of social transformation. The privilege of the Marxian texts – and the reason why his name, perhaps abusively, remains related to such a politics in contradistinction to other social thinkers – is that Marx made this totalizing experience at the very beginning of his career, as the trajectory of the very first published and unpublished articles demonstrates. Whether the word Marxism disappears or not, therefore, in the erasure of the tapes in some new Dark Ages, the thing itself will inevitably reappear.

As for the current situation, however, Korsch long ago showed us, within the Marxian corpus itself, how the very mood and methodology of the analyses varied across the great internal polarity of voluntarism and fatalism (or determinism) according to the changes in the objective social situation, and its great cyclical rhythms that alternate from situations of promise and change (so-called 'pre-revolutionary' ones) to those of a locked social geology so massive that no visions of modification seem possible (at least to those ephemeral biological subjects that we are). Ours seems for the moment closer to this last than to the former, and the thoughts we find useful must vary accordingly.

This is the spirit in which I have proposed Adorno as a dialectical model for the 1990s. His introspective or reflexive dialectic befits a situation in which – on account of the dimensions and unevenness of the

new global world order – the relationship between the individual and
the system seems ill-defined, if not fluid, or even dissolved. The over-
emphasis in Adorno on what he calls theory – defined as the detection
of the absent presence of totality within the aporias of consciousness
or of its products – is not a bad lesson for intellectuals today, when
the older notion of critical theory as permanent negativity and implacable
social critique seems better to characterize the practice of a Sartre than
the ideals of postmodern thinkers. The 'current situation' to be sure
has any number of urgent demands besides dialectical theory; still, 'not
only theory, but also its absence, becomes a material force when it seizes
the masses'.

Notes

NOTES ON TRANSLATION

1. Quoted by Walter Benjamin in 'The Task of the Translator', in *Illuminations*, transl. Harry Zohn, New York, 1969, p. 81.

2. In *Telos*, no. 65, Fall 1985, pp. 147–52.

INTRODUCTION

1. As on a book jacket: Born 11 September 1903 in Frankurt-am-Main, died 6 August 1969 in Switzerland. Dissertation in Philosophy (on Husserl), 1924, University of Frankfurt; 1925, studied musical composition in Vienna with Alban Berg; 1927 on, frequent visits in Berlin to Benjamin, Brecht, Bloch, Weill, and others; inaugural lecture as Assistant Professor of Philosophy at Frankfurt, 1931, not yet in close association with Horkheimer's Institute for Social Research; definitive emigration to the United States in 1938, after failure to establish himself at Oxford; participation in the Princeton Radio Research Project; closer collaboration with Horkheimer and a move to Southern California; definitive return to West Germany in 1953 as Professor of Philosophy and Sociology at the University of Frankfurt; succeeds Horkheimer as Director of the Institute in 1964. See, for more bibliographical and historical detail, Rolf Wiggershaus, *Die Frankfurter Schule*, Munich 1987. This book, which draws richly on unpublished material and letters and has obviously had the benefit of Habermas's participation, offers the most substantial historical picture of the Frankfurt School from its beginnings to its most recent mutations. Unlike Martin Jay's pioneering work (*The Dialectical Imagination*, Boston, MA 1973), which told the story (only up to the return to Germany) from Horkheimer's point of view, Wiggershaus presents a decidedly critical perspective on the Institute's central figure.

2. Susan Buck-Morss has in particular insisted on the way in which virtually the whole program of *Negative Dialectics* is already present in the so-called inaugural lecture of 1931, entitled 'The Actuality of Philosophy' and reprinted in *Gesammelte Schriften*, vol. 1, Frankfurt 1983, pp. 325–44; transl. in *Telos*, no. 31, Spring 1977, pp. 120–33. See her *Origins of Negative Dialectics*, New York 1977, pp. 24–5, 63–5.

3. Wiggershaus, pp. 688–9.

4. Wiggershaus, pp. 503-8; the volume also includes detailed accounts of the various 'empirical' projects, before and after (and during) the Emigration.

5. See Axel Honneth, 'Communication and Reconciliation: Habermas's Critique of Adorno', in *Telos*, no. 39, Spring 1979, pp. 45-61; and see of course Habermas himself, especially *Theorie des kommunikativen Handelns*, vol. 1, (Frankfurt 1981, ch. 4, esp. pp. 489-534; and *The Philosophical Discourse of Modernity*, transl. Frederick Lawrence, Cambridge, MA 1987, ch. 5, pp. 106-30.

6. See, for example, the assessment of Kant: 'His timid bourgeois detestation of anarchy matches his proud bourgeois antipathy for tutelage' (ND 248/250). The analysis of Wagner's 'social character' is also rich in such judgements, e.g.: 'It is the fawning stance of the momma's boy who talks himself and others into believing that his kind parents can deny him nothing, for the very purpose of making sure they don't' (W 15/16).

7. See, for example, H. Mörchen, *Macht und Herrschaft im Denken von Heidegger und Adorno*, Stuttgart 1980; or R. Bubner, 'Kann Theorie aesthetisch werden?' in *Materialien zur Aesthetischen Theorie*, ed. Lindner and Ludke, Frankfurt 1979, esp. p. 111.

8. *Gesammelte Schriften*, vol. 6, Frankfurt 1976, pp. 637/8.

9. See his interview with Gérard Raulet entitled 'Structuralism and Poststructuralism', *Telos*, no. 55, Spring 1983, pp. 195-211 (in Wiggershaus, p. 12).

10. See 'Immanence and Nominalism in Postmodern Theory', in *Postmodernism, Or The Cultural Logic of Late Capitalism*, Durham, NC 1990. The most stimulating and judicious comparison of French poststructuralism with the various Germanic traditions is to be found in Peter Dews, *Logics of Disintegration*, London 1987; on Derrida and Adorno, see also Rainer Nägele, 'The Scene of the Other', in *Literature*, vol. 11, nos 1-2, Fall-Winter 1982-3, pp. 59-79. Perry Anderson draws a very interesting parallel between Adorno and Althusser in *Considerations on Western Marxism*, London 1976, pp. 72-3.

PART I

1. Sabine Wilke astutely points out the fundamental structural ambiguity at work in parataxis as such, in 'Kritische und Ideologische Momente der Parataxis: Eine Lekture von Adorno, Heidegger und Hölderlin', *Modern Language Notes* 102 (3), April 1982, pp. 627-47, esp. p. 646. And note Empson's cognate discussion of classical parataxis - 'the Homeric *but* where one expects "and"' - in *Some Versions of Pastoral*, New York 1960, p. 136.

2. *Marxism and Form*, Princeton, NJ 1971, p. 307.

3. Lévi-Strauss, *Structural Anthropology*, vol. 1, New York 1963, pp. 341-78.

4. We have all problably overstressed the 'Freudo-Marxism' of the Frankfurt School, which is finally realized only in Marcuse. The attacks on Freud in *Minima Moralia* are ferocious (see, for example, No. 136), although it is true that he is there seen as a profoundly *American* thinker whose 'therapy' goes along with obligatory good health, clean teeth and a permanent smile on your face. This assessment of Freud should be juxtaposed with the remarkable appreciation in 'Sociology and Psychology', Part II, *New Left Review*, no. 47, 1968 (or *Gesammelte Werke*, vol. 8, Part I, Frankfurt 1972, pp. 42-85).

5. It should be noted that his valorization of the essay as form has very different consequences in the social sciences, where it undermines the belief in the exhaustiveness of empirical detail (their version of a belief in representation) and substitutes for that the provisional model or the local hypothesis. The essay here opens a wedge between full history and abstract sociology, and as it were allows each of these tendencies to correct or defamiliarize the other. But see notes 19 and 20 to Conclusions, below.

6. Le Président de Brosses, *Du Culte des dieux fétiches*, Paris 1760. But see also Part II, note 12.

7. Thus Hegel's 'logic deals only with particularity, which is already conceptual' (ND 322/328).

8. Pollock's work is often discussed – by Martin Jay (*The Dialectical Imagination*, ch. 5), Helmut Dubiel (*Theory and Politics*, transl. B. Gregg, Cambridge, MA 1985) and others; to my knowledge only Giacomo Marramao discusses the relationship to Grossman, in 'Political Economy and Critical Theory', *Telos*, no. 24, Summer 1974. I make a few suggestions of my own below, but in my opinion the definitive study of the Frankfurt School's economic dimension remains to be written. It should be added that what Pollock calls 'late capitalism' has nothing to do with the current or postmodern stage of the world system, for which some of us also use this term.

9. See Gilles Deleuze, *Cinéma I: L'Image-mouvement*, Paris 1983, chs 2 and 3.

10. Quoted in Karl-Heinz Bohrer, *Plötzlichkeit*, Frankfurt 1981, p. 14.

11. Dolf Oehler, 'Charisma des Nicht-identischen', in T.W. Adorno, special issue, ed. H.L. Arnold, text + kritik (1977), p. 155. Indeed, if one likes to put it that way, he scarcely says anything else in his great essay on Beckett either, but I defy any intelligent reader to come away with a similar impression! (NL, 281–321; or 'Trying to Understand *Endgame*', *New German Critique*, no. 26 [Spring-Summer 1982]).

12. A next step which will be called 'Capital-logic' (see Conclusions).

13. 'Gesellschaft', in *Gesammelte Schriften*, vol. 8, Frankfurt 1972 or 'Society', *Salmagundi*, nos 10–11, Fall 1969/Winter 1970, pp. 144–53. This volume of the *Collected Works* contains the most extensive collection of Adorno's sociological interventions (but for an English translation of some of these, see note 23 below). And see also, in English, the useful collaborative volume *Aspects of Sociology*, Boston, MA 1972.

14. 'Society', p. 145.

15. 'Society', p. 146.

16. 'Sociology and Psychology', *New Left Review*, no. 46, November–December 1967, pp. 67–80; no. 47, January–February 1968, pp. 79–97; no. 46, p. 69.

17. Ibid., p. 69.

18. Ibid., p. 70.

19. Ibid., p. 73.

20. Ibid., p. 74.

21. Ibid., pp. 77–8.

22. Ibid., p. 78.

23. *The Positivist Debate in German Sociology*, ed. G. Adey and D. Frisby, New York 1976, p. 84.

24. See the volume referred to in the preceding note for the protocols of its most dramatic confrontation.

25. 'Society', p. 148.

26. 'History does not merely touch on language, but takes place in it' (MM 293/219); yet 'Lyric and Society' also reminds us that it can there 'take place' negatively (see below).

27. T.W. Adorno, *Prismen*, Frankfurt 1955; transl. S. and S. Weber: *Prisms* London 1967, p. 50/49.

28. Manfredo Tafuri, *Architecture and Utopia*, Cambridge, MA., 1979.

29. Pierre Bourdieu renews this position in our own time, with the powerful anti-cultural and anti-intellectual demystifications of books like *Distinction* (London 1985).

30. *Prisms*, p. 82/75.

31. Ibid., 18/26.

32. *Origin of German Tragic Drama*, Walter Benjamin, *Ursprung des deutschen Trauerspiels*,

Gesammelte Schriften, Frankfurt 1980, vol. 1, Part I; transl. J. Osborne, London, 1977): 'Epistemo-Critical Prologue', p. 207/27. All further refs in text as OGT.

33. See below, Conclusions, note 20.

34. See Introduction, note 2 and, on the *Passagenwerk*, Susan Buck-Morss, *Dialectics of Seeing: Walter Benjamin and the Arcades Project*, Cambridge, MA 1990.

35. *In These Great Times: A Karl Kraus Reader*, ed. Harry Zohn, Montreal 1976, p. 70.

36. Benjamin, *Gesammelte Schriften*, vol. 4, p. 142.

37. 'Aura' seems to have been derived from the 'irrationalist' philosopher Ludwig Kages (see Wiggershaus, pp. 224 ff). The source of mimesis is more obscure, particularly since Adorno's use of the concept has very little in common with Benjamin's. See, however, Michael Cahn, 'Subversive Mimesis; T.W. Adorno and the Modern Impasse of Critique', in *Mimesis in Contemporary Theory*, vol. 1, ed. M. Spariosu, Philadelphia 1984. Habermas interprets the centrality of the concept as a compensation for the lack of any positive conception of Reason:

> As the placeholder for this primordial reason that was diverted from the intention of truth, Horkheimer and Adorno nominate a capacity, *mimesis*, about which they can only speak as they would about a piece of uncomprehended nature. They characterized the mimetic capacity, in which an instrumentalized nature makes its speechless accusation, as an 'impulse'. The paradox in which the critique of instrumental reason is entangled, and which stubbornly resists even the most supple dialectic, consists then in this: Horkheimer and Adorno would have to put forward a *theory* of mimesis, which, according to their own ideas, is impossible. (*The Theory of Communicative Action*, vol. 1, transl. Thomas McCarthy, Boston, MA 1984, p. 382).

Dialectic of Enlightenment will be discussed below; in my opinion, however, mimesis is rather the substitute for the traditional subject–object relationship.

38. In his *Figuren des Scheins*, Bonn 1984, Rainer Hoffman makes a beginning on the stylistic-syntactic analysis of Adorno. Friedemann Grenz's valuable *Adornos Philosophie in Grundbergriffen*, Frankfurt 1974, posits the practice of two fundamental types of sentences in Adorno (both of them '*geschichtsphilosophisch*' – p. 12): these are 'physiognomic negations' on the one hand, and the more familiar Hegelian 'determinate' negation on the other (pp. 180, 202, 203). Gillian Rose, meanwhile, suggests that in Adorno arguments

> taken from traditional philosophy ... are transformed into principles of social criticism by use of the figure of chiasmus: arguments which expose illegitimate abstraction in philosophy reveal principles of abstraction in society; arguments which expose the illegitimate dominance of the subject in philosophy reveal modes of social domination. (*The Melancholy Science*, New York 1978).

This is all the more pertinent, since chiasmus is in general the fundamental deep figure of the Marxian or materialist dialectic (I believe that it occurs seldom in Hegel).

39. See David Bordwell, Janet Staiger and Kristin Thompson, *The Classical Hollywood Cinema*, New York 1985, ch. 31, 'Alternative modes of film practice'.

40. That of F. Pollock; see above, note 8.

41. R. Bubner, 'Adornos Negative Dialektik', in *Adorno-Konferenz 1983*, ed. Friedeburg and Habermas, Frankfurt 1983, p. 36.

42. I. Kant, *Critique of Pure Reason*, transl. J.M.D. Meiklejohn, Chicago 1952, p. 43.

43. J.P. Sartre, *Search for a Method*, transl. H. Barnes, New York 1963, pp. 8 ff.

44. Georg Lukács, *History and Class Consciousness*, transl. R. Livingstone, Cambridge, MA. 1971, esp. 'Reification and the Consciousness of the Proletariat'.

45. See, for example, *The Differentiation of Society*, New York 1982.

46. See, for a near-contemporaneous period piece, Richard M. Weaver's *Ideas Have Consequences*, Chicago 1948, which uses the diagnosis of nominalism for a classic Cold

War jeremiad on the decadence of the modern age. I am grateful to Richard Rorty and Gayatri Spivak for this reference. In general, superstructural (or 'spiritual') diagnoses of the breakdown of the social order will be right-wing (see also, and above all, Heidegger himself); while infrastructural ones will be left-wing.

47. See above, Introduction, note 2.

48. 'The words that are not means appear senseless; the others seem to be fiction, untrue' (DA 132/147).

49. Significantly, this is the only passage lifted without modification into the later text (see *Gesammelte Schriften*, vol. 1, pp. 354-5).

50. The following reflection, from 'Sociology and Psychology', seems to me enormously revealing:

Fear constitutes a more crucial subjective motive of objective rationality. It is mediated. Today anyone who fails to comply with the economic rules will seldom go under straight away. But the fate of the *déclassé* looms on the horizon. Ahead lies the road to an asocial, criminal existence: the refusal to play the game arouses suspicions and exposes offenders to the vengeance of society even though they may not yet be reduced to going hungry and sleeping under bridges. But the fear of being cast out, the social sanctions behind economic behaviour, have long been internalized along with other taboos, and have left their mark on the individual. In the course of history this fear has become second nature; it is not for nothing that the word 'existence' in usage uncontaminated by philosophy means equally the fact of being alive and the possibility of self-preservation in the economic process. (*New Left Review*, no. 46, 1967, p. 71.)

51. Marshall Sahlins, 'The First Affluent Society', in *Stone Age Economics*, Chicago 1972, ch. 1.

52. 'No differently will the world one day appear, almost unchanged, in its constant feast-day light, when it stands no longer under the law of labor, and when for homecomers duty has the lightness of holiday play' (MM 144/112).

53. See, on Weber, my 'Vanishing Mediator', in *The Ideologies of Theory*, vol. 1, Minnesota 1988.

54. See, on Greek concepts of labor, J.P. Vernant, 'Travail et nature dans la Grèce ancienne', in *Mythe et pensée chez les Grecs*, Paris 1965; also the Cahn reference in note 24 above.

55. This is the way in which a focus on the media reinflects and displaces Pollock's theory of state capitalism, a kind of left version of the James Burnham managerial-society thesis current during this period. The convergence features of the two theories save them from lapsing into the simpler idea of 'totalitarianism' that came to dominate Cold War apologetics shortly thereafter; but the stress here on emergent technology, shared across the advanced countries, and in particular between Roosevelt's USA and Hitler's Germany, anticipates contemporary trends in media theory (see my forthcoming *Signatures of the Visible*).

56. Thus I cannot agree with Martin Jay's notion of a gradual disillusionment of the Frankfurt School with Marxism (but see his valuable *The Dialectical Imagination* and *Marxism and Totality*): one must distinguish between personal opinion (or cowardice) and the deeper principles that inform an intellectual work. As for Helmut Dubiel, he takes the following line (in *Theory and Politics*):

The fact that so many readers of the Circle's writings of the 1940s do not recognize the conscious abandonment of the Marxist theoretical tradition can be explained by the fact that their basic positions are not developed as criticisms of Marx. Their philological distance from his writings, maintained throughout the various development periods of the Circle's theory, of course do not aid the reader in recognizing the break with Marxist theory once it had been made. A critique of Marx from the perspective of *Eclipse of Reason* was developed for the first time by pupils of Horkheimer and Adorno. But the break remained unrecognizable in subsequent years because Horkheimer and, especially, Adorno maintained a Marxian form of argumentation ... (p. 93).

When is a break not a break? A clever defense attorney would tear this equivocal analysis to shreds; not least because the 'pupils' mentioned turn out to be Habermas and Wellmer, who may have developed 'a critique' of Marx, but certainly developed an even more devastating one of Horkheimer and Adorno themselves!

57. *Minima Moralia* is even more explicit; speaking of buildings, space and dwelling (in 18); it says: 'The possibility of residence is annihilated by that of socialist society, which, once missed, saps the foundations of bourgeois life' (41/39).

58. But the not always disinterested defense of contemplation and disengagement is certainly everywhere in Adorno (see, for instance, MM No. 82, 'Keeping one's distance', where the figure and the strategy of 'distance' are strongly and internally related to the 'bad immediacy' of the various positivisms).

59. But see also MM 143/111, 157/121, 224/170.

PART II

1. See below, Part III, chapter 7.

2. See, most famously, Adorno on the *intérieur*: Kierkegaard, *Gesammelte Schriften*, vol. 2 (1979), pp. 38–69; and MM No. 106.

3. T.S. Eliot, 'Tradition and the Individual Talent', *Selected Essays*, New York 1950, pp. 10–11.

4. 'Just as, in the nature and finite areas of its life, art has its *before*, so also does it have an *after*, that is to say, a circle that passes beyond art's mode of apprehending and representing the Absolute ...' G.W.F. Hegel, *Aesthetik*, vol. 1, 1955, p. 110.

5. See also AT 465/433.

6. See Joseph Horowitz, *Understanding Toscanini*, Minnesota 1987; also Adorno's own essay on Toscanini, called 'Die Meisterschaft des Maestro', in *Gesammelte Schriften*, vol. 16, Frankfurt 1978, pp. 52–67.

7. Raymond Williams, *Marxism and Literature*, Oxford 1977, p. 110.

8. See my 'On Negt and Kluge', *October* 46, Fall 1988, pp. 151–77.

9. Terry Eagleton's complaint in *Against the Grain*, London 1986; see also MM 280/210: 'He who has laughter on his side has no need of proof.'

10. The Culture Industry 'builds the need for happiness in and exploits it. It thus has its moment of truth in the way in which it satisfies a substantial need developing out of the tendentially increasing renunciation demanded by society; but becomes the absolutely untrue in the way in which it offers that satisfaction.' (AT 461/430)

11. Actually, we owe this brilliant formula to the translator!

12. See above, Introduction, note 5.

13. Andreas Huyssens has pointed out (in *After the Great Divide*, Bloomington, IN 1986) the intimate relationship between the Wagner book and Adorno's theory of the Culture Industry. Indeed, the emergence of this last now proves to be endogamous, something that art does to itself in its disintegration during the imperialist period (Adorno suggests, in the light of the *Gesamtkunstwerk*, that Nietzsche should have called *his* Wagner book 'The Birth of Film out of the Spirit of Music'). In Benjamin's thought the stage of the 'reproducible work of art' follows that of the emergence of high modernism in

the language and form of Baudelaire; in Adorno, both are simultaneous with Wagner. In addition, a rich discussion of 'phantasmagoria' (ch. 6) lays claim to prolong and continue Marx's notion of commodity fetishism in the aesthetic realm.

PART III

1. Adorno did allow himself to say things like this: 'Music down to this very day has existed only as a product of the bourgeois class, a product which, both in the success and failure of its attempts at formulation, embodies this society and gives aesthetic documentation of it. ... Within the existing order it must be doubted whether any music other than bourgeois music exists' (*Philosophy of Modern Music*, Frankfurt 1958; New York 1973).

2. As in *War and Peace*, Book VIII, chapter 9:
In the second act there was scenery representing tombstones, and there was a round hole in the canvas to represent the moon, shades were raised over the footlights, and from horns and contrabass came deep notes while many people appeared from right and left wearing black cloaks and holding things like daggers in their hands. They began waving their arms. Then some other people ran in and began dragging away the maiden who had been in white and was now in light blue. They did not drag her away at once, but sang with her for a long time and then at last dragged her off, and behind the scenes something metallic was struck three times and everyone knelt down and sang a prayer. All these things were repeatedly interrupted by the enthusiastic shouts of the audience. (transl. Louise and Aylmer Maude, New York 1942, p. 622)

3. 'Great architecture finds its transfunctional voice there where it is able to express its own instrumental purposes mimetically from the inside as its content. Scharoun's Philharmonic [in Berlin] is beautiful because – in order to establish spatially ideal conditions for orchestral music – it becomes *like* orchestral music, without borrowing allusions programmatically from it' (AT 72/66).

4. *Mahler*, Frankfurt 1960, p. 127.

5. In his *Theory of the Avant-garde*, Minnesota 1984.

6. See also the beautiful meditation on the meaning and origin of the 'disinterested' in art, in MM No. 144.

7. See on this above, pp. 21–2; and also 182–3.

8. In *What is Literature?* and vol. 3 of *L'Idiot de la famille*.

9. See, however, the very balanced and reasonable discussion of hearing in ch. 1 of the *Introduction to the Sociology of Music*, where, after passing in review a typology of musical listeners – the expert, the good listener, the cultural consumer, the emotional listener, the listener out of *ressentiment*, the jazz expert and the jazz fan, and the consumer of music as entertainment, concluding with anti-listeners such as the indifferent, the unmusical and the anti-musical – Adorno wisely suggests that the problem of musical education must pass through the mediation of the social totality:
The antagonistic condition of the whole is expressed in the fact that even musically correct forms of behavior can realize aspects of the whole that are relatively negative by way of their structural position within it. ... The expert listener requires a specialization of a type hitherto inconceivable, the proportional regression of the type of the merely good listener – is probably a function of that specialization. ... The failure in the face of culture, however, ought to lead to some further conclusions as to the failure of culture before human beings, and as to what the world has made of them in the first place. (*Einleitung in die Musiksoziologie*, in *Gesammelte Schriften*, vol. 14, Frankfurt 1973, pp. 197–8.

10. 'Vers une musique informelle', *Gesammelte Schriften*, vol. 16, p. 523.

11. See my 'Marxism and Historicism', in *The Ideologies of Theory*, vol. 2.

12. Gertrude Stein, *Four in America*, intro. Thornton Wilder, New Haven, CT 1947, p.vii.

13. See Part II, note 2.

14. Translated in *Telos*, no. 20 (Summer 1974), pp. 56–66.

15. But see Part I, note 4.

16. Introduction to M. Jay, *The Dialectical Imagination*, Boston, MA 1973, p. xii.

CONCLUSIONS

1. Jean-François Lyotard, 'Adorno como diavolo', in *Des dispositifs pulsionnels*, Paris 1973, pp. 115–33.

2. See above, Introduction, note 5.

3. Dubiel, *Theory and Politics*, p. 93.

4. Ernesto Laclau and Chantal Mouffe, *Hegemony and Socialist Strategy*, London 1985.

5. See above, Part I, note 13.

6. *The Positivist Dispute in German Sociology*, p. 10.

7. Ibid., p. 12.

8. 'Dialektik als Vernunftdkritik', in *Adorno-Konferenz 1983*, ed. Friedeburg and Habermas, Frankfurt 1983, pl.69.

9. But see Peter Dews, *Logics of Disintegration*.

10. See the Habermas references in Introduction, note 5, above.

11. See above all Bubner, 'Kann Theorie aesthetisch werden?' in *Materialien zur Aesthetischen Theorie*, ed. Lindner and Ludke, Frankfurt 1976. Adorno repudiates a 'literary' or 'aesthetic' conception of philosophy in *Negative Dialectics* (26–7/24–5).

12. *Theory of Communicative Action*, vol. 1, Boston, MA 1984), transl. T. McCarthy, pp. 382–3.

13. *Materialien*, p. 132.

14. Roman Rosdolsky, *The Making of Marx's Capital*, London 1977. See also the pathbreaking commentaries on the *Grundrisse* and the manuscripts of the 1860s by Enrique Dussel: *la Producción teórica de Marx*, Mexico City 1985; and *Hacia un Marx desconcido*, Mexico City 1988.

15. Habermas, *Theory of Communicative Action*, vol. 1, p. 357.

16. See, for an expert and thorough summary of this tradition, Bob Jessop, *The Capitalist State*, New York 1982, ch. 3. See also *Value, Social Form and the State*, ed. Michael Williams, New York 1988, whose editor begins:

> The chapters which follow have all been sparked by opposition to the widespread reversion of contemporary Marxism to the methodological preoccupations of orthodox social science: positivism, analysis, individualism and naturalism. This reversion, manifested most recently in self-styled 'analytical Marxism' . . ., is based upon the tacit (and sometimes explicit) rejection of the crucial place of the Hegelian dialectic in Marxist theory, the role of forms of consciousness in regulating bourgeois society and of the insights of Marx's early writings on the state, civil society and critique of right. (p. 1)

17. J. Derrida, 'La Structure, le signe et le jeu dans le discours des sciences humaines', *L'Ecriture et la différence*, Paris 1967, pp. 409–28.

18. *Gesammelte Schriften*, vol. 16, Frankfurt 1978, pp. 493–540.

19. *Noten zur Literatur*, pp. 9–33. He also considered the 'Introduction' to his Husserl

book something of a manifesto in this same respect (see *Against Epistemology*, transl. Willis Domingo, Cambridge, MA 1983, pp. 3-40). What one misses in the 'Essay as Form' is any consideration of the generic and institutional infrastructure of the 'essay' in cultural journalism, the feuilleton, etc., determinants which considerably reduce and demystify the putative 'freedom' of the genre.

20. Any reading of the 'Fragment' chapter in the now canonical account by P. Lacoue-Labarthe and J.L. Nancy of the Jena Romantics, called *The Literary Absolute*, will bring considerable differences to mind; even if one does not consider the Jena Romantics to be charlatans, their self-defeating insistence on the necessarily incomplete nature of all expression is very distant in spirit from Adorno's way of confronting what for him also was a *necessary* dilemma of the representation of 'totality'.

21. See 'On the Nature and Form of the Essay', in *Soul and Form*, transl. Anna Bostock, London 1974.

INDEX

Printed in the United States
By Bookmasters